Advanced
Turbo
Prolog™:
Version 1.1

Advanced Turbo Prolog™: *Version 1.1*

Herbert Schildt

BORLAND·OSBORNE/McGRAW·HILL
PROGRAMMING   SERIES

Osborne **McGraw-Hill**
2600 Tenth Street
Berkeley, California 94710
U.S.A.

For information on translations and book distributors outside of the
U.S.A., please write to Osborne **McGraw-Hill** at the above address.
A complete list of trademarks begins on page 311.

Advanced Turbo Prolog™: Version 1.1

Originally appeared under the title *Advanced Turbo Prolog™*, published
by Osborne/McGraw-Hill, 1987.

234567890 DODO 8987

ISBN 0-07-881285-2

Contents

Foreword

The emergence of the Turbo Prolog programming language marks a significant advance in application development for microcomputers. The ideal tool for the design of programs with problem-solving and logic capabilities, Turbo Prolog heralds the new generation of applications that go beyond interaction between humans and machines. Turbo Prolog is based on Prolog, one of the leading languages for artificial intelligence research and applications, and its potential to develop powerful, intuitive programs is almost limitless.

Advanced Turbo Prolog, first published by Osborne/McGraw-Hill in early 1987, accomplishes two objectives. First, readers receive an overview of the artificial intelligence field. Second, with the help of many sample programs, they learn to implement the techniques of artificial intelligence in Turbo Prolog. In short, this book is a clear and practical introduction to fifth generation language tools and how to use them.

This revision of *Advanced Turbo Prolog* includes Turbo Prolog version 1.1. Also, Appendix B has been added to present the Turbo Prolog Toolbox, a collection of frequently used routines for developing and using applications. Many examples are included. This new appendix is an extremely useful introduction and complement to the Turbo Prolog Toolbox.

Advanced Turbo Prolog has been written by Herb Schildt, the well-known author of numerous books on programming languages. His previous books include *C Made Easy*, *Advanced C*, *Modula-2 Made Easy*, and *Advanced Turbo Pascal*.

The potential of new applications with problem-solving capabilities — and the exciting positive impact these will have on the general population as well as on program developers — become more evident each day. *Advanced Turbo Prolog: Version 1.1* will help make those applications a reality.

Philippe Kahn
President
Borland International, Inc.

Preface

This book uses a problem-solving approach to help you sharpen your Turbo Prolog programming skills. Because Turbo Prolog is designed primarily as a fifth-generation artificial intelligence language, the applications in this book show you how to implement machine intelligence. In addition to improving your Turbo Prolog programming ability, you will gain an overview of the entire field of artificial intelligence, including

- expert systems

- problem solving

- logic and uncertainty

- natural-language processing

- robotics

- machine learning, and

- vision and pattern recognition.

Chapter 1 begins with a brief history of AI and then discusses exactly what artificial intelligence means and implies. Chapter 2 deals with problem solving and Chapter 3 with expert systems. Chapter 4 moves on to natural-language processing. Next come vision, robotics, and machine learning in Chapters 5, 6, and 7, respectively. The final three chapters deal with comparing logic and uncertainty, making the computer appear human, and linking Turbo Prolog with existing programs. Appendix A concerns interfacing Turbo Prolog with other programming languages. Appendix B covers the Turbo Prolog Toolbox.

In addition to illustrating various concepts, one of the most important features of this book is that all of the applications can serve as starting points from which you can evolve complete systems. For example, you can easily expand and enhance the expert system that is developed in Chapter 3 or the natural-language parsers of Chapter 4.

Frankly, I enjoyed writing this book. (Oh, to be honest, I have enjoyed writing all of my books, but this one was special.) Ever since I was an undergraduate student, I have been fascinated with the prospect of creating machine intelligence. As a graduate student, I had the opportunity to study the field in some depth — mostly by using LISP. However, it was difficult to earn money by programming AI applications at that time, so my interest in the field stayed primarily as a hobby. Also, I have always found LISP a bit too cumbersome and disliked the large number of parentheses that its syntax requires.

I first became acquainted with Prolog in 1982. I was completely enchanted by its clean syntax, its elegance, and its power. Prolog immediately became my AI language of choice. For this reason, I was very excited to get one of the first copies of Turbo Prolog.

What makes Turbo Prolog so exciting is that it has put back the fun in programming. It also opens the door for thousands of programmers to develop intelligent programs. There is no doubt in my mind that, as programmers, you and I stand at the beginning of the microcomputer revolution's second wave. It is my sincere hope that you will enjoy reading this book as much as I have enjoyed writing it. However, more important, I hope that you will create some wonderfully "smart" programs.

As you probably know, keying in listings from a book can be a problem. You can easily make mistakes or accidentally omit a line. The process can be time-consuming and frustrating. For these reasons, I have decided to offer an IBM-PC compatible diskette containing all of the listings in this book. The cost of the diskette is $24.95. You can obtain it by completing the order form that follows this preface and mailing it along with your payment. If you are in a hurry, you may call (217) 586-4021 (the number of my consulting company, Universal Computing Laboratories, Inc.) to place your order.

—HS

Disk Order Form

Please send me _____ copies, at $24.95 each, of the listings in *Advanced Turbo Prolog: Version 1.1.* Foreign orders: add $5.00 for shipping and handling.

_____

Name

_____

Address

_____

City   State   ZIP

_____

Telephone

Method of payment: Check __ VISA __ MC __

Credit card number: _____

Expiration date: _____

Signature: _____

Send to: Herbert Schildt
          RR 1, Box 130
          Mahomet, IL 61853

This is solely the offer of Herbert Schildt. Osborne/McGraw-Hill takes no responsibility for the fulfillment of this offer.

Artificial Intelligence: A Quick Overview

Until recently, many people viewed the field of artificial intelligence, or AI, as the darker side of computer science: it was believed that, like Shelley's Dr. Frankenstein attempting to create life, the AI programmers worked to create thought. Artificial intelligence researchers were, at times, paradoxically regarded as both computer science's elite and its "lunatic fringe." When forced to give a view on the feasibility or practicality of machine intelligence, mainstream, wage-earning programmers, usually careful to avoid references to AI, would always say that "much research was still to be done," and that "sometime in the distant future, there will be important discoveries, but so far the field has produced precious little." Views on artificial intelligence have definitely changed!

In less than five years, artificial intelligence has gone from a small backwater of computer science to being the hottest thing to happen to computers since perhaps the transistor. This rapid change is based on four main factors: the success of expert systems, which were the first truly financially successful AI products; the well-publicized commitment of the Japanese to AI; the creation of a good AI language, Prolog; and, finally, the fact that AI's time has come.

With the creation of Turbo Prolog, AI programming has become accessible to all programmers. For so long, full-featured AI languages were available only on large mainframe computers. Turbo Prolog made it possible to write real AI applications on a microcomputer. Because of the excellent support of commonly available hardware features, such as color, graphics, and sound, Turbo Prolog makes it easy to develop professional-looking programs.

In the course of this book, you will explore the various types of tasks that Turbo Prolog is well suited to performing. By developing actual applications that illustrate the various areas of AI, you will be sharpening your Turbo Prolog skills. There are several aspects and topics that compose the general subject of artificial intelligence. The most important and most common of these are the subjects of the remaining chapters. However, before you move on to these applications, this chapter first reviews the history of AI to help give you a general background. Then it will try to show you just exactly what an "intelligent" program is. Finally, the chapter reviews the main topics of AI, which form the remainder of the book.

A Short History of AI

It is difficult to pinpoint an exact starting date for what is commonly called AI. Perhaps credit for the birth of AI should be given to A. M. Turing for his invention of the stored program computer. Remember: first computers were actually dedicated machines that literally had to be rewired to solve different problems. Turing's recognition that a program could be stored as data in the computer's memory and executed later formed the basis for all modern computers. The storing of programs allowed the computer's function to be changed quickly and easily by simply running a new program. This capability implies that a computer *might* be able to change its *own* function — that is, to learn or think!

However, what is commonly thought of as AI began around 1960 when, at MIT, John McCarthy created LISP — the first artificial intelligence language. LISP has certain similarities to Prolog: for example, it can easily process lists and it uses recursion as the primary form of program control. However, LISP lacks many of Prolog's advanced features and easy syntax.

The term *artificial intelligence* is generally credited to Marvin Minsky, also of MIT, who in 1961 wrote a paper entitled "Steps towards Artificial Intelligence (*The Institute of Radio Engineers Proceedings* 49 [January 1961])." The 1960s were a period of intense optimism over the possibility of making a computer think. After all, it was the decade that saw the first chess-playing computer, the first computerized mathematical proofs, and the famous — and highly publicized — ELIZA program, written in 1964 by Joseph Weizenbaum of MIT. ELIZA was a program that acted like a Rogerian psychoanalyst. In this style of analysis, the psychiatrist takes a passive role, generally simply echoing the patient's own remarks rather than leading the conversation — just the type of task that a computer can easily do. At the time, the program caused quite a stir. People asked, "Should computers be used in this way? Is it possible that the computerized psychiatrist can actually be better than a human one? Should this be allowed?" Even Weizenbaum, ELIZA's creator, wrote the book *Computer Power and Human Reason* (San Francisco: W. H. Freeman & Co., 1976) to essentially discredit his own program! (Remember: the 1960s were also a period of intense *fear* of automation. It is sometimes hard to understand the emotions that existed just over 20 years ago.)

Because of the apparent successes of AI, it seemed that the goal of producing a program that has humanlike intelligence was just around the corner. However, this was not to be so.

What was not clearly understood in the 1960s was the difficulty of generalizing these specific successes into a flexible, intelligent program. (This book will look at some of the reasons for this.) A common problem is that as programmers attempted to increase the generality of certain programs, these attempts required greater computing resources than were currently available. For example, either memory was quickly exhausted or execution time became too slow.

By the mid 1970s, computers with large memories were common and computing speeds had increased dramatically. However, even with these improvements, many of the older approaches to AI continued to fail because there was inherent inefficiency. To understand this, consider a task as simple as sorting an array of numbers. If you use a bubble sort, the sort time will be proportional to N^2, where N is the number of elements. This means that if sorting a 10-element array takes 1 second, then sorting a 100-element array will take 100 seconds, and so on. You can see that, at some point, there is an array that will take longer to sort than the average person lives! No matter how fast the computer becomes, an algorithm whose time is proportional to N^2 will quickly become too slow. A better approach is to change the sorting algorithm so that it is more efficient. For example, the time of the QuickSort algorithm is proportional to $N^{1.2}$—a very significant improvement. The difference between these two curves is shown in Figure 1-1. Just as new sorting algorithms were needed to improve sorting times, it took the advent of improved routines, which enable programs to execute faster or to make better use of memory, to allow many AI problems to be solved. In fact, the creation of Prolog is one of these breakthroughs, as Chapter 2 shows.

By the end of the 1970s, several successes —such as natural-language processing, knowledge representation, and problem solving — had been achieved in specific areas of AI. Thus, the stage was set for the introduction of the first commercial product, the expert system. An expert system is a program that contains knowledge about a certain field and, when interrogated, responds much like a human expert. One of the first expert systems was MYCIN, which was developed at Stanford

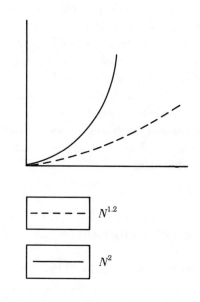

Figure 1-1.   A comparison of an N^2 curve and an $N^{1.2}$ curve

University and which was created to help physicians diagnose illnesses. This book will cover expert systems in considerable depth later.

One of the most important AI events that occurred in the 1970s was virtually overlooked in the United States until the 1980s. This event was the creation of Prolog in 1972 by Alain Colmerauer in Marseilles, France. Like LISP, Prolog was a language that was designed to help solve AI-related problems; but unlike LISP, it had several special features, such as a built-in database, and it had a rather simple syntax. Essentially, by 1980, LISP was the AI language of choice in the United States, while Prolog had the same status in Europe. The situation changed in 1981 with the announcement by the Japanese that they would be using Prolog as the basis for their much-touted "fifth-generation" computers. American programmers were caught off guard.

Although Prolog has been gaining popularity in the United States since 1981, it was mostly used at universities because few complete Prolog implementations existed for microcomputers. Among those few complete implementations, there was a lack of standardization. This is the reason that the release of Turbo Prolog must also rank as an important event in AI history. Turbo Prolog offers to a wide range of programmers the chance to develop AI programs on their own personal computers. It also provides a standard Prolog that programmers can use on a very large variety of machines. It can be safely said that these events and changes are only the beginning of the practical application of AI, and that its pace will increase.

What Is an Intelligent Program?

Before you can explore the realm of AI by using Turbo Prolog, you must understand what it means for a program to be intelligent and how an intelligent program differs from "nonintelligent" programs. This is not an easy matter because there is much debate on the subject. As you will see, there are powerful arguments to support both the side that claims that all programs are intelligent and the side that claims that none are. It will be the job of this section to determine a reasonable definition for an intelligent program.

To determine what an intelligent program is implies that you know what intelligence means. One dictionary defines *intelligence* as "the capacity to apprehend facts and propositions and their relations and to reason about them." This definition leads to the question, "What does *reason* mean?" Essentially, in this context, it means to *think* —which is where the trouble lies. It was suggested long ago that no one can explain *how* a person thinks, but everyone can tell *what* they think. The fact is that no one really understands how a person thinks. (If one did, it might not be such a big job to make a computer do it.)

If you stay with a strict interpretation of the definition of intelligence, then you could make a good case that *all* programs are intelligent. Consider this: The first part of the definition of intelligence is the ability to apprehend facts, propositions, and relations. Actually, computers are amazingly well suited to performing these types of tasks. For example, a relational database can store (apprehend) information, accept queries (propositions), and, as its name implies, represent relations. Certainly, some types of information, such as visual images, are much harder for a computer to apprehend than others, but the definition of intelligence does not demand that the apprehension take a specific form —it only demands that the apprehension does take place. Thus, what computers normally do —gather, store, and access information — satisfies the first requirement for intelligence.

However, can the database *reason* about these facts, which is the second requirement for intelligence? Perhaps. The answer depends upon what you will accept as the definition of *reason*. If you accept the database's manipulation of information —the act of searching, sorting, query processing, filing, and the like —as reasoning, then you must say that the database is an intelligent program. This implies that most computer programs are intelligent. Remember that most computer programs manipulate information in reasonable, logical ways. Therefore, this form of reasoning must qualify as intelligence.

Somehow, this conclusion is difficult to accept. It implies that virtually all programs belong in the field of artificial intelligence, an implication that is not true. Your intuition and experience with specific examples of intelligent programs tell you that there is a difference. But what is it? If you try to justify your inability to accept that a relational database is a thinking program, you might say that it cannot be a thinking program because what the database program does is not akin to thinking in the way that *people* think. But then you are faced with the fact that the *exact same task* when done by a file clerk obviously demands intelligence on the part of that clerk. Hence, a paradox: if the database program performs the task, then it is not thinking; yet if a person does the same task, then that person is thinking. This problem stems, in part, from pride. As a human being, you probably like to think that it is your brain that separates you from animals, that people have a monopoly on cognitive thought. You may allow that higher mammals can think simple thoughts and even reason on a primitive level, while humans go far beyond that. But that a mere machine can think, on any level, is an uncomfortable idea. Therefore, whenever some bright programmer creates a smart program, the tendency is to say, "Well, it's not *really* smart. It just 'acts' smart." Not saying this would be an admission that the monopoly on thought had been lost.

Look at this problem a different way. One could say that a well-trained dog is smart if it retrieves its master's newspaper from the front porch. One could even say a one-year-old child is quite intelligent if he or she can do the same task. Yet it is relatively simple to construct a computer-controlled robot to do precisely the same task. However, most people would not be inclined to say that the robot was intelligent simply because it could bring in the morning paper. The reason for this is that most people would say that a robot that brings in the paper is simply a machine that runs a program created by a programmer somewhere, and that the robot is not *thinking* about the task, but simply *doing* it. (Some people would actually suggest that the programmer of the robot is doing the thinking — at a distance of both time and space.)

The example of the robot and the newspaper also brings up a different problem that goes back to the fact that people do not know how they think. Because the program to retrieve the paper from the front porch is easy to develop, the tendency is to say that the program cannot be intelligent *because* it is understandable. This is sometimes called the magic principle: On an emotional level, most people consider thinking to be akin to magic. Because they do not understand the thought process, they tend to make the erroneous assumption that any device that is made and understood by humans cannot be intelligent because humans *do understand* it. In essence, most people believe that the creation is always less than the creator.

There is also that troubling question of free will. Throughout history, thought has always been connected with the concept of free will: that is, that thinking can only be done by an entity with the *will to think*. In fact, Descartes, the seventeenth-century philosopher, proclaimed that it was thinking that proved his very existence when he wrote what became the famous philosophical quote, "I think, therefore I am." What makes this concept troubling is that in the example of the robot and the newspaper, it appears that both the baby and the dog choose to bring in the newspaper (as opposed to doing something else), but the robot *is programmed to* do this. Indeed, it must do it because its program tells it that it cannot do something else. However, can a computer, which is a seemingly deterministic device, ever *choose* to do anything? There is no doubt that this question will become one of the major philosophical and legal issues of the twenty-first century. This question can quickly polarize a roomful of programmers. There are those programmers who firmly believe that a "machine is a machine": It cannot have free will because it does not have a mind, only circuits. Therefore, it is impossible for a computer to choose to do anything, especially think. This is a compelling argument. However, the argument of the other programmers may be more persuasive. To understand this argument, imagine that a computer is monitoring a truck scale in a brick yard. When the weight reaches a certain point, the computer shuts off the brick-loading conveyor. Did the computer decide to shut off the scale? Yes! It clearly was in control of the situation and *chose* to stop the conveyor when the weight reached a particular level. If the computer did not make the decision, then who did? The proponents of this argument state that the computer's ability to perform a conditional branch constitutes the ability to make decisions.

At this point, many people are convinced that it is impossible to make a program intelligent. First, the computer is a deterministic device. Second, there are questions of autonomy. Third, since few people know about the thought process, how can anyone make a computer think? And so the argument continues. Just as the conclusion that all programs are intelligent was unsettling, this conclusion also fails to satisfy.

The difficulties that are illustrated by the discussion just given actually relate to a failing of the definition of intelligence. What the dictionary definition missed was the fact that the term *intelligence* implies human intelligence. This implied association makes it difficult to admit the possibility that a machine can think or that a program running on a computer can be intelligent because most programs do not do the same task in the same way as a person. On the other hand, when this implication is removed, it is easy to say that all programs are intelligent. If you understand this difference, the definition of an intelligent program becomes straightforward. For a program to be intelligent requires that it *act* intelligent —that is, like a human. Its thought processes do not have to be exactly or always the same as a human's. So here is the definition of an intelligent program:

> An intelligent program exhibits behavior similar to that of a human when confronted with a similar problem. It is not necessary that the program actually solve, or attempt to solve, the problem in the same way as a human.

Notice that the program need not think like a human, but that it must act like one. (After all, even people do not always think the same way.)

Hence, intelligent programs, in some way, exhibit humanlike intelligent behavior, whereas nonintelligent programs do not.

AI's Major Areas

The field of artificial intelligence is composed of several areas of study. Here are the most common and important of these areas:

- Searching (for solutions)
- Expert systems
- Natural-language processing
- Pattern matching and recognition
- Robotics
- Learning
- Logic
- Uncertainty and "fuzzy logic."

Some of the areas represent final applications, such as expert systems; others, such as natural-language processing and solution searching, are AI building blocks that are added to other programs to enhance their performance. Each category is the subject of a later chapter; however, this section briefly describes what they are about.

The term *searching* as applied to AI refers to the search for solutions to a problem. (It does not mean finding a specific piece of information in a database.) For example, you may use AI-based searching in a program that attempts to find the shortest route between two cities or that tries to prove a mathematical theorem.

Expert systems are AI's first commercially viable product. An expert system has two primary attributes. First, it allows you to enter information about a subject into the computer. This information is sometimes called the knowledge base. Second, it allows you to interrogate this knowledge base and it acts as though it were an expert on the subject, which is the reason for its name.

To many AI researchers, natural-language processing (sometimes referred to as NLP) is the most crucial of all AI goals to achieve because it enables the computer to understand human language directly. As you will see later, the worst obstacle to reaching this goal is the size and complexity of human languages. Another obstacle is the problem of trying to make the computer aware of the contextual information that is present in all but the simplest situations.

Pattern matching and recognition are important to several applications, including robotics and image processing. For example, when given a digitized television picture, how can the computer know where one object ends and another begins, or that one object can be on top of another? Like natural-language processing, pattern matching and recognition are needed to allow the computer to interface directly to the human world.

As applied to robotics, AI is the study of how to control motion, which is called spatial reasoning. For such industrial robots as the ones that assemble automobiles, the problems of AI are mostly concerned with providing smooth, natural motions from a set of discrete locations. For autonomous robots, there is the more difficult problem of interfacing to a human world, with its obstacles, unexpected events, and changing environment. It is this type of robot that you will be most concerned about in this book.

One of the more interesting areas of AI is learning. This area deals with making programs learn from their mistakes, from observations, or by request. Learning simply means making the computer capable of benefitting from experience.

One of the few products of AI that have some current practical importance are those programs that you can use to study the logical correctness of an argument by applying the standard rules of logic. In this context, *argument* refers to any logically connected statements that yield a goal. This includes mathematical proofs, formal logic, and syllogistic (philosophical) logic.

Most decisions that you make are made with incomplete knowledge. For example, when you buy a house, you do not know that all of the plumbing is sound, or that the roof does not leak, and so forth. Your decision to buy is based upon several assumptions that have a certain probability, or likelihood, of being true. For a computer to be able to think by using incomplete knowledge implies the use of fuzzy logic — that is, decision making that is based on incomplete or probabilistic information.

With the foundation provided by this chapter, you are ready to sharpen your Turbo Prolog skills by exploring the fascinating world of AI.

Problem Solving: The Search For Solutions

Fundamental to most AI applications is problem solving. There are basically two types of problems. The first type can be solved by using some type of deterministic procedure that is *guaranteed* success. This procedure is called a computation. Solving problems by computation only works on those types of problems for which computational procedures exist, as in mathematics. You can easily translate the methods used to solve these types of problems into an algorithm that a computer can execute. Since few real-world problems lend themselves to computational solutions, they must be placed in the second type. This type consists of problems that are solved by searching for a solution. This is the method of problem solving that AI is concerned with.

One of the most difficult obstacles to overcome when you try to apply AI techniques to real-world problems is the sheer magnitude and complexity of most situations. In the early days of artificial intelligence research, developing good search methods was a primary goal out of necessity and desire. It was necessary that programmers devise good search techniques to solve these problems because of the limitations of the computers used at that time. In addition, programmers desired good search techniques because it was, and is still, believed that searching is central to problem solving, which is a crucial ingredient of intelligence.

Representation and Terminology

Imagine that you have lost your car keys. You know that they are somewhere in your house, which looks like this:

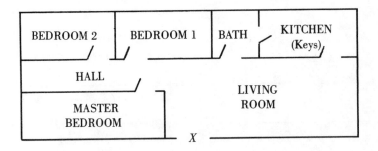

The *X* indicates that you are standing at the front door. As you begin your search, you first check the living room. Then you go down the hall to the first bedroom, then back to the hall to go to the second bedroom, and then back to the hall again to go to the master bedroom. Not having found your keys yet, you backtrack further by going back through the living room and finding your keys in the kitchen. Figure 2-1 shows a graph of the path that you followed to find your keys.

The fact that you can represent a problem as a graph is important because it gives you a simple way to visualize the way that the different search techniques work. (Also, being able to represent problems as graphs allows the AI researcher to apply various theorems from graph theory. However, this is beyond the scope of this book.) Thus, with this in mind, study the following definitions:

Node. A discrete point and possible goal.
Terminal node. A node that ends a path.
Search space. The set of all such nodes.
Goal. The node that is the object of the search.
Heuristic. Describing information about the likelihood that any specific node is a better choice to try next, rather than another node.
Solution path. A directed graph of the nodes visited that lead to the solution.

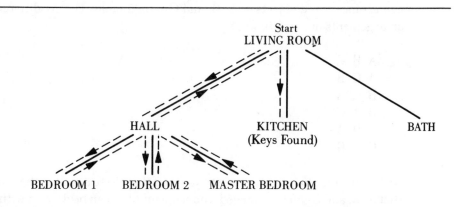

Figure 2-1.   A graph of the solution path to find the missing keys

In the missing keys example, imagine that each room in the house is a node; the entire house is the search space; the goal, as it turns out, is the kitchen; and the solution path is as was shown in Figure 2-1. The bedrooms and the bath are terminal nodes because they do not lead anywhere. This example did not use heuristics, but you will see some later in this chapter.

Combinatorial Explosions

At this point, you may think that searching for a solution is as simple as starting at the beginning and working your way to the conclusion. In the extremely simple case of the missing keys, this search method is not a bad way to do it. However, in most problems that you would want to use a computer to solve, the situation is very different. Generally, you will use the computer to solve problems in which the number of nodes in the search space is very large, and as the search space grows, so does the number of different possible paths to the goal. The trouble is that each node added to the search space will add more than one path: that is, the number of paths to the goal will increase faster with each new node.

To understand this increase, consider the number of ways that you can arrange three objects — A, B, and C — on a table. The six different arrangements are as follows:

```
A B C
A C B
B C A
B A C
C B A
C A B
```

Although you can quickly prove to yourself that these are all of the ways that A, B, and C can be arranged, the same number can be derived with a theorem from the branch of mathematics called combinatorics, which is the study of the way that things can be combined. The theorem states that the number of ways that N objects can be combined (or arranged) is equal to $N!$ (N factorial). The factorial of a number is the product of all

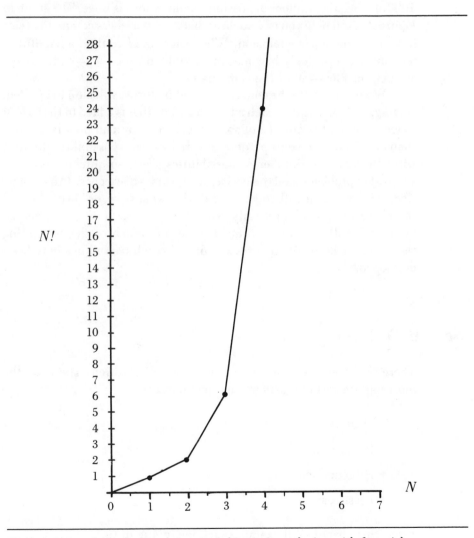

Figure 2-2.   A graph that shows a combinatoric explosion with factorials

whole numbers equal to or less than itself down to 1. Therefore, 3! is $3\times2\times1$, or 6. Given this information, you can see that, if you had 4 objects to arrange, then there would be 4!, or 24, combinations. With 5 objects, the number is 120; with 6 objects, it is 720. However, with, say, 1000 objects, the number of possible combinations is huge. The graph in Figure 2-2 will help you to visualize what AI researchers commonly refer to as a combinatoric explosion. When there is more than a handful of possibilities, it quickly becomes impossible to examine — and, indeed, even enumerate — all of the combinations.

When you relate the concept of combinatoric explosion to problem solving, you can see that each additional node that is added to the search space increases the number of possible solutions by a number far greater than one. Hence, at some point, there are too many possibilities to work with. Because the number of possibilities grows so quickly, only the simplest of problems lend themselves to exhaustive searches. (An exhaustive search examines all nodes.) While the exhaustive, or "brute force," search technique theoretically will always work, it is not practical because it will consume too much time, too much of the computing resources, or both. For this reason, other search techniques have been developed.

Search Techniques

There are several ways to search for a possible solution. These are the most important and most common techniques:

- Depth-first
- Breadth-first
- Hill-climbing
- Least-cost.

Later, this chapter will examine each technique in turn.

Evaluating a Search

Evaluating the performance of a search technique can be very complicated. In fact, the evaluation of searches forms a large part of AI. However, for the purposes of this discussion, there are two basic measurements that are important:

1. How quickly the search finds a solution.

2. How quickly the search finds a good solution.

There are several types of problems for which all that matters is that you find a solution —any solution —with the minimum effort. For these the first measurement is important. However, in other situations, what is important is that the solution be somewhat close to the optimal solution.

Both the length of the solution path and the actual number of nodes traversed determine the quickness of a search. Remember that backtracking from dead ends is essentially wasted effort, so what is desired is a search that backtracks little.

It is important to understand that there is a difference between finding an optimal solution and finding a good solution. The difference lies in the fact that finding an optimal solution often entails a nearly exhaustive search, while finding a good solution means finding a solution that is within a set of constraints —it doesn't matter if a better solution exists.

As you will see, all of the search techniques that are described in this chapter will work better in certain specific situations than others, so, to an extent, it is difficult to say whether one search method will *always* be superior to another. But some search techniques will have a greater probability of being better for the average case. Also, keep in mind that the way that a problem is defined will sometimes help you choose an appropriate searching method.

Before you examine the various search techniques, here is a problem that you will use various searches to solve. Imagine that you are a travel agent and a rather bothersome customer wants you to book a flight from New York to Los Angeles with XYZ Airlines. Even though you tell the customer that XYZ does not have a direct flight from New York to Los Angeles, the customer insists on flying only on XYZ. Looking at XYZ's scheduled flights, you find the following:

New York to Chicago	1000 miles
Chicago to Denver	1000 miles
New York to Toronto	800 miles
New York to Denver	1900 miles
Toronto to Calgary	1500 miles
Toronto to Los Angeles	1800 miles
Toronto to Chicago	500 miles
Denver to Urbana	1000 miles
Denver to Houston	1500 miles
Houston to Los Angeles	1500 miles
Denver to Los Angeles	1000 miles

You quickly see that there is a way to fly from New York to Los Angeles on XYZ if you use connecting flights. So, you book the customer on a flight.

However, your task is to write Turbo Prolog programs that do the same thing — and in an even better way.

A Graphic Representation

The flight information given in XYZ's schedule book can be translated into the directed graph shown in Figure 2-3.

A directed graph is simply a graph in which the lines that connect each node have arrows attached to them to indicate the direction of motion. In a directed graph, it is impossible to travel in the opposite direction from the arrow.

However, the flight schedule may be a little easier to understand if you redraw this graph as a tree, as shown in Figure 2-4. The rest of this chapter will refer to this version. Various cities appear more than once in the tree to simplify its construction.

Now you are ready to develop the various search programs that will find paths from New York to Los Angeles.

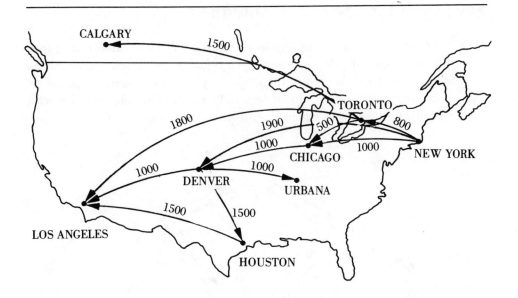

Figure 2-3. A directed graph of XYZ's flight schedule

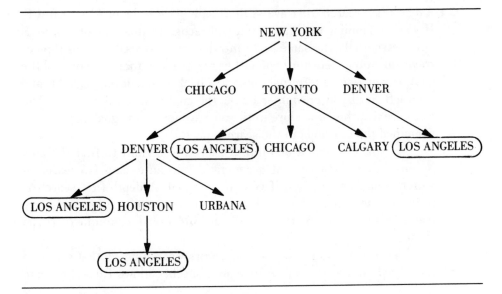

Figure 2-4. A tree version of XYZ's flight schedule

The Depth-First Search Technique

You may remember reading in the Turbo Prolog manual that Turbo Prolog uses a depth-first search technique. A depth-first search means that each possible path to the goal is explored to its conclusion before another path is tried. To understand exactly how this search works, consider this tree in which F represents the goal:

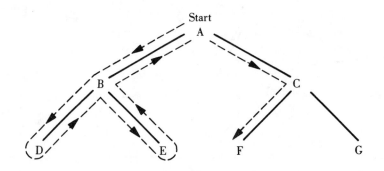

A depth-first search will traverse this graph in the order of ABDBEBACF. If you are familiar with trees, you will recognize this type of search as being essentially the same as an inorder tree traversal. In this type of traversal, you go left until you either reach a terminal node or find the goal. If you reach a terminal node, you back up one level, go right, and then left until you encounter either the goal or a terminal node. You would repeat this procedure until you have found the goal or you have examined the last node in the search space.

As you can see, a depth-first search is certain to find the goal because, as a worst case, it degenerates into an exhaustive search — which would be the case if G were the goal. A depth-first search is probably the best method that you can follow when no heuristics are used. This is the reason that it is the default search technique of Turbo Prolog.

Because Turbo Prolog uses depth-first searching, all that you need do to see how it works is to write a program that allows Turbo Prolog to find a solution to the problem. You first need a knowledge base of XYZ's flight schedule. This section will use Turbo Prolog's built-in database capability for this. The program will need two knowledge bases. The first one is defined as

```
flight(symbol, symbol, integer)
```

which is used to define a flight with its distance from one city to the next. The second database, called **visited**, provides a simple way to keep track of the cities visited as the program computes the flight path. This second database not only gives you insight into the way that each search mechanism operates by showing what cities were tried for each solution, but also serves as a way to see each route. Hence, the **visited** database will occasionally contain cities not on the final flight path because they represent the dead ends of each search, which are those cities that were tried and rejected. This will show you how efficient each search technique is in relation to the problem. (You may find it an interesting exercise to rework the code so that only the cities actually on the route are displayed.) The second database is

```
visited(symbol)
```

Therefore, the first part of the program is

```
database
  flight(symbol, symbol, integer)
  visited(symbol)
```

The key routine in finding a route between New York and Los Angeles is called **isflight** and is shown here:

```
/* see if there is a connection between the
   two cities */
isflight(T,T2,D):-
  flight(T,T2,D),
  add_to_route(T).
isflight(T,T2,D):-
  flight(T,X,D2),
```

```
    X<>T2,
    add_to_route(T),
    isflight(X,T2,D3),
    D=D2+D3.
isflight(T,_,D):-
    /* report dead ends to illustrate
       how the search is progressing */
    write("dead end at ",T),
    nl, D=0, fail.
```

The routine works as follows. The first clause will succeed if there is a flight between **T** and **T2**. If this flight exists, then the routine binds **D**, the distance between the two cities, to the distance that is specified in the knowledge base, and places **T** in the **visited** database. Therefore, if you called this routine with

```
isflight(denver, houston, X)
```

then the first clause would succeed and bind the value 1500 to **X**.

However, imagine that you called **isflight** with

```
isflight(chicago, houston, X)
```

In this case, the first clause would fail because there is no direct flight that connects these two cities, so the second clause is tried. The second clause attempts to find a connection between the origin city and any other city. If it finds a connection then it calls **isflight** recursively to see if this other city connects to the destination. If it does, as in this case, the first clause succeeds and execution resumes back in the second clause where the proper distances are added together. Notice that the second clause adds cities to the **visited** database. Therefore, in this case, the program finds that there is a path from Chicago to Houston via Denver. Verify for yourself that, as presented here, **isflight** will perform a depth-first search of the knowledge base.

The program will use an internal goal both to initialize the flight knowledge base and begin execution of the program. Here is the goal portion.

```
goal
  assert(flight(newyork, chicago,1000)),
  assert(flight(chicago, denver,1000)),
  assert(flight(newyork, toronto, 800)),
  assert(flight(newyork, denver, 1900)),
  assert(flight(toronto, calgary, 1500)),
  assert(flight(toronto, los_angeles, 1800)),
  assert(flight(toronto, chicago, 500)),
  assert(flight(denver, urbana, 1000)),
  assert(flight(denver, houston,1500)),
  assert(flight(houston, los_angeles, 1500)),
  assert(flight(denver, los_angeles,1000)),
  findroute,nl,
  write("more? "),
  readln(Q),
  Q=n.
```

Because you may want to see the effects of forcing the program to search for multiple (or all) solutions, the prompt for **more?** has been added. If it is answered with anything other than **n**, then the goal fails, forcing backtracking.

The entire depth-first search program is shown here. You should enter this program into your computer at this time.

```
/* Depth-first search */
database
  flight(symbol, symbol, integer)
  visited(symbol)
predicates
  route(symbol, symbol, integer)
  isflight(symbol, symbol, integer)
  displayroute
  purge
  findroute
  add_to_route(symbol)
goal
  assert(flight(newyork, chicago,1000)),
  assert(flight(chicago, denver,1000)),
  assert(flight(newyork, toronto, 800)),
  assert(flight(newyork, denver, 1900)),
  assert(flight(toronto, calgary, 1500)),
  assert(flight(toronto, los_angeles, 1800)),
  assert(flight(toronto, chicago, 500)),
  assert(flight(denver, urbana, 1000)),
  assert(flight(denver, houston,1500)),
  assert(flight(houston, los_angeles, 1500)),
  assert(flight(denver, los_angeles,1000)),
```

```
    findroute,nl,
    write("more? "),
    readln(Q),
    Q=n.

clauses
  /* ask for the origin and destination */
  findroute:- /* no min distance */
    write("from: "),
    readln(A),
    write("to: "),readln(B),
    route(A,B,D),
    write("distance is ",D),nl,
    not(displayroute).

  /* set up to either find the route */
  route(A,B,C):-
    isflight(A,B,C).

  /* or report failure */
  route(_,_,D):-
    write("no route or not"),
    nl,
    write("within specified distance"),nl,
    D=0, purge.

  /* see if there is a connection between the
     two cities */
  isflight(T,T2,D):-
    flight(T,T2,D),
    add_to_route(T).
  isflight(T,T2,D):-
    flight(T,X,D2),
    X<>T2,
    add_to_route(T),
    isflight(X,T2,D3),
    D=D2+D3.
  isflight(T,_,D):-
    write("dead end at ",T),
    nl, D=0, fail.

  /* add to the list of cities visited */
  add_to_route(T):-
    not(visited(T)),
    assert(visited(T)),!.
  add_to_route(_).

  /* get ready for another run */
  purge:-
    retract(visited(_)),
    fail,!.
```

```
/* display those cities on the route */
displayroute:-
  write("route is: "), nl,
  visited(A),
  write(A),nl,
  fail,!.
```

Notice that the **findroute** predicate prompts you for both the city of origin and the destination. This means that you can use the program to find routes between any two cities. However, for the rest of this chapter, it is assumed that New York is the origin and Los Angeles is the destination. Also, for simplicity, the program stores the names of the cities as symbols, which requires that the names be in lowercase.

When run, the first solution displayed

```
Distance is 3000
newyork
chicago
denver
```

If you refer back to Figure 2-4, you will see that this is indeed the first solution that would be found by using a depth-first search. (In this case, the destination city, Los Angeles, is implied to be at the end of the list.) By typing y when prompted for more, you will see the second solution as

```
Distance 5000
newyork
chicago
denver
houston
```

If you again refer to Figure 2-4, you can see that this is the second depth-first search solution. Turbo Prolog's backtracking caused it to go back to Denver in order to try to find another path. In this case, it found Houston to Los Angeles.

It is not until the third try that Turbo Prolog finds the optimal solution, which is New York to Toronto to Los Angeles with a distance of 2600 miles. Figure 2-5 shows the paths that were traveled to find these solutions.

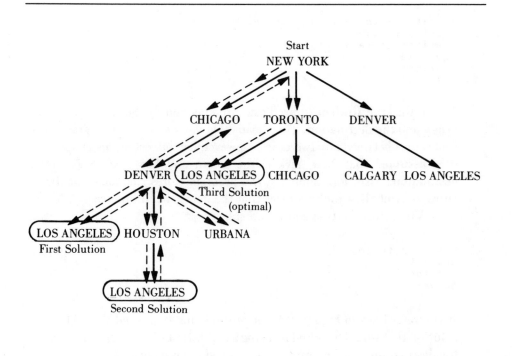

Figure 2-5. Depth-first's path to an optimal solution

Evaluating the Depth-First Search

In this example, the depth-first search found a fairly good solution on its first try, a poor one on its second try, and the optimal one on the third try. Also, for this specific example, depth-first searching succeeded in finding a solution on its first try with no backtracking —which is very good. But it traversed nearly all of the nodes to arrive at the optimal solution —which is not so good.

However, you should note that depth-first can be quite poor in those situations where you must explore a particularly long branch only to find that there is no solution at its end. In this case, depth-first will waste considerable time, not only in its exploration of this chain, but also in its backtracking to the goal. It is situations like this that lead you to breadth-first searching.

The Breadth-First Search Technique

Breadth-first searching is the opposite of depth-first searching. In this method, you check each node on the same level before you proceed to the next deeper level. Here is this traversal method with C as the goal:

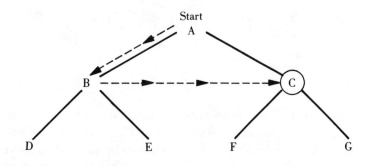

This illustration shows that the nodes ABC are visited. Like depth-first searching, breadth-first searching guarantees that it will find a solution, if one exists, because it will eventually degenerate into an exhaustive search.

In order to transform the route-seeking program given in the previous section to perform a breadth-first search, you must circumvent Turbo Prolog's default depth-first search mechanism. To do this requires only an alteration to the **isflight** procedure, as shown here:

```
isflight(T,T2,D):-
  flight(T,T2,D),
  add_to_route(T).
```

```
isflight(T,T2,D):-/* make breadth first */
  flight(T,X,D2),
  flight(X,T2,D3),
  add_to_route(T),
  add_to_route(X),
  D=D2+D3.
isflight(T,T2,D):-
  flight(T,X,D2),
  X<>T2,
  add_to_route(T),
  isflight(X,T2,D3),
  D=D2+D3.
isflight(T,_,D):-
  write("dead end at ",T),
  nl, D=0, fail.
```

As you can see, the clause

```
isflight(T,T2,D):-/* make breadth first */
  flight(T,X,D2),
  flight(X,T2,D3),
  add_to_route(T),
  add_to_route(X),
  D=D2+D3.
```

has been added. The clause works as follows. When the first clause fails, upon entry to the second, it is known that **T** does not have a route to **T2**, whatever **T2** may be, so the second clause checks to see if there is any other city that **T** connects with. If there is, then the clause checks that city to see if it is the destination. If it is not, Turbo Prolog's normal backtracking will check for any other connecting flights leaving from **T** until either it encounters the destination or there are no more flights. If none of these efforts lead to the goal, only then does the third clause take over, progressing another layer deeper.

You should now substitute this version of **isflight** in the program. When you run this program, the first solution is

```
Distance is 2600
newyork
toronto
```

and the second is

```
Distance is 2900
newyork
denver
```

with the first one being optimal. The third solution will find the 3000-mile route newyork, chicago, denver. Figure 2-6 shows the breadth-first path to the first solution.

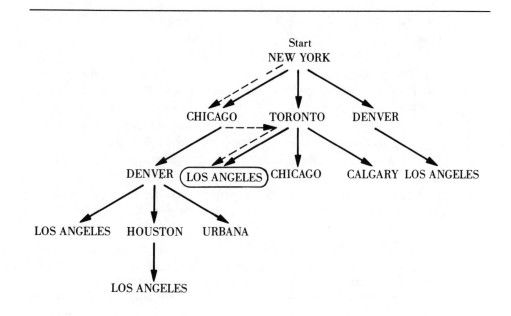

Figure 2-6.   Breadth-first's path to the first solution

Evaluating the Breadth-First Search

In this specific example, breadth-first has performed well by finding the first solution without backtracking. As it turns out, this solution is also the optimal solution. In fact, the first three solutions are the best three routes there are. However, remember that you cannot generalize this result to other situations because it depends upon the physical organization of the information as it is stored in the computer. However, it does show how radically different depth-first and breadth-first searches are.

Adding Heuristics

You have probably guessed by now that both the depth-first and breadth-first search routines are blind. They look for a solution by relying solely upon moving from one goal to the other without the use of "educated guesses." While this may be fine for certain controlled situations where you as the programmer have information that tells you to use one method over the other, what a generalized AI program needs is a search procedure that is, on the average, superior to either of these two techniques. The only way to achieve such a search is to add heuristic capabilities.

As you recall, heuristics are simply rules that qualify the possibility that a search is proceeding in the correct direction. To understand this, imagine that you are lost in the woods and need water. The woods are so thick that you cannot see far ahead and the trees are too big to climb to get a look around. However, you have four pieces of knowledge: first, that rivers, streams, and ponds will most likely be in valleys; second, that animals frequently make paths to their watering places; third, that when you are near water, it is possible to "smell" it; and, fourth, that you can hear running water. So, to find your way to water, you begin by moving downhill because water is unlikely to be uphill. Next, when you come across a deer trail that also runs downhill, you follow it because you know that this may lead to water. You then hear a slight rush off to your left. Knowing that this may be water you cautiously move in that direction. As you progress, you begin to detect the increased humidity in the air —you can "smell" the water. Finally, you find a stream and have your drink of water. As this shows, heuristic information, although imprecise and not guaranteed, increases the chances that a search method will find a goal quickly, or optimally, or both. In short, it increases the odds in favor of a quick success.

You may think that it is easy to include heuristic information in programs that were designed for specific applications, but that it would be impossible to create generalized heuristic searches. However, this is not the case, as you will see.

Most often, heuristic search methods are based on maximizing or minimizing some aspect of the problem. In fact, the two heuristic approaches that you will examine use opposite heuristics and will yield different results.

The Hill-Climbing Search Technique

In the problem given earlier of scheduling a flight from New York to Los Angeles, there are two possible constraints that a passenger may want minimized. The first is the number of connections that have to be made. The second is the length of the route. Remember that the shortest route does not necessarily imply the fewest connections. A search algorithm that attempts to find as a first solution one that minimizes the number of connections will use the heuristic information that states that the longer the distance covered, the greater likelihood that you will be placed closer to the destination —thereby reducing the number of connections. In AI, the search method that uses this heuristic information is called hill-climbing.

Formally, the hill-climbing algorithm chooses as its next step the node that appears to place it closest to the goal. It derives its name from the analogy of a hiker being lost in the dark, halfway up a mountain. If you assume that the hiker's camp is at the top of the mountain, then, even in the dark, the hiker knows that each step that goes up is in the right direction.

For the flight-scheduling problem, working only with the information that is contained in the knowledge base, you can incorporate the following hill-climbing heuristic into the routing program: choose the connecting flight that takes you the farthest away from your present location in the hopes that that choice will take you closer to the destination. To do this, you must again modify the routine **isflight** and add the support clause **findlargest**, as shown here:

```
isflight(T,T2,D):-
  flight(T,T2,D),
  add_to_route(T).
isflight(T,T2,D):-/* climb hill */
  findlargest(T,X),
  add_to_route(T),
  flight(T,X,D2), /* bind the distance */
  isflight(X,T2,D3),
  D=D2+D3.
isflight(T,T2,D):-
  flight(T,X,D2),
  X<>T2,
  add_to_route(T),
  isflight(X,T2,D3),
  D=D2+D3.

findlargest(A,B):-
  flight(A,X,D),
  flight(A,Y,D2),
  X<>Y, /* if not largest, then
  D2>D,     backtrack */
  B=Y.
```

The specific change is the addition of the following clause:

```
isflight(T,T2,D):-/* climb hill */
  findlargest(T,X),
  add_to_route(T),
  flight(T,X,D2), /* bind the distance */
  isflight(X,T2,D3),
  D=D2+D3.
```

The modification to the program works as follows: First, **findlargest** attempts to bind the city that is the farthest away from **T** to **X**. If **findlargest** succeeds, then it adds **T** to the route and uses the assertion

```
flight(T,X,D2)
```

to bind the distance to **D2**. Finally, **isflight** is called recursively. Notice that **findlargest** employs Turbo Prolog's standard backtracking routines to find the city that is the farthest from the current location.

The entire hill-climbing program is shown here. You should enter this program at this time:

```
/* hill climbing */
database
  flight(symbol, symbol, integer)
  visited(symbol)
predicates
  route(symbol, symbol, integer)
  isflight(symbol, symbol, integer)
  displayroute
  purge
  findroute
  add_to_route(symbol)
  findlargest(symbol,symbol)
goal
  assert(flight(newyork,chicago,1000)),
  assert(flight(chicago,denver,1000)),
  assert(flight(newyork, toronto, 800)),
  assert(flight(newyork, denver, 1900)),
  assert(flight(toronto, calgary, 1500)),
  assert(flight(toronto, los_angeles, 1800)),
  assert(flight(toronto, chicago, 500)),
  assert(flight(denver, urbana, 1000)),
  assert(flight(denver, houston,1500)),
  assert(flight(houston, los_angeles, 1500)),
  assert(flight(denver,los_angeles,1000)),
  findroute,nl,
  write("more? "), not(purge),
  readln(Q),
  Q=n.

  clauses
    /* ask for the origin and destination */
    findroute:-
      write("from: "),
      readln(A),
      write("to: "),readln(B),
      route(A,B,D),
      write("distance is ",D),nl,
      not(displayroute).
```

```
/* set up to either find the route */
route(A,B,C):-
  isflight(A,B,C).
/* or report failure */
route(_,_,D):-
  write("no route or not"),
  nl,
  write("within specified distance"),nl,
  D=0, purge.

/* see if there is a connection between
   the two cities */
isflight(T,T2,D):-
  flight(T,T2,D),
  add_to_route(T).
isflight(T,T2,D):-/* climb hill */
  findlargest(T,X),
  add_to_route(T),
  flight(T,X,D2),
  isflight(X,T2,D3),
  D=D2+D3.
isflight(T,T2,D):-
  flight(T,X,D2),
  X<>T2,
  add_to_route(T),
  isflight(X,T2,D3),
  D=D2+D3.

findlargest(A,B):-
  flight(A,X,D),
  flight(A,Y,D2),
  X<>Y,
  D2>D,
  B=Y.

/* add to the list of the cities visited */
add_to_route(T):-
  not(visited(T)),
  assert(visited(T)),!.
add_to_route(_).

/* get ready for another run */
purge:-
  retract(visited(_)),
  fail,!.

/* display cities on the route */
displayroute:-
  write("route is: "), nl,
  visited(A),
  write(A),nl,
  fail,!.
```

When the program is run, the first solution found is

```
Distance is 2900
newyork
denver
```

This result is quite good. It has the minimal number of stops on the way —only one —and is quite close to the shortest route. Furthermore, it does this without wasting time or effort through extensive backtracking. However, the second solution is not quite so good:

```
Distance is 4900
newyork
denver
houston
```

This solution climbs a false hill: As you can easily see, the route to

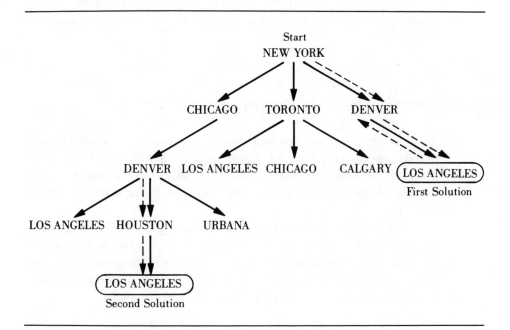

Figure 2- 7.   Hill-climbing's path to the first two solutions

Houston does not take you closer to the goal of Los Angeles. Figure 2-7 shows the first two solution paths that use the hill-climbing search.

Evaluating the Hill-Climbing Search

The hill-climbing search is fairly good in many circumstances because it tends to reduce the number of nodes that need to be visited before it reaches a solution. However, it can suffer from three possible maladies. First is the problem of false hills, as seen in the second solution of the example. This case must use extensive backtracking to find the solution. Second is the problem of "plateaus," in which all next steps look equally good (or bad). In this case, hill-climbing is no better than depth-first searching. Third is the problem of a "ridge." Hill-climbing falls down in this case because the algorithm will cause the ridge to be crossed several times during backtracking.

In spite of these potential troubles, the hill-climbing search will generally lead to an optimal solution quicker than any of the nonheuristic methods.

The Least-Cost Search Technique

The opposite of the hill-climbing search is the least-cost search. Think of this strategy as being similar to standing in the middle of a street on a big hill while wearing roller skates: you have the definite feeling that it is a lot easier to go down, rather than up! Thus, least-cost takes the path of least effort.

Applying the least-cost search to the flight-scheduling problem implies that the shortest connecting flight will be taken in all cases, so that the route found will have a good chance of having the shortest distance. Unlike hill-climbing, which minimized the number of connections, least-cost minimizes the number of miles traveled.

To use least-cost, you must again alter **isflight** as shown here:

```
isflight(T,T2,D):-
  flight(T,T2,D),
  add_to_route(T).
isflight(T,T2,D):-/* find shortest */
  findsmallest(T,X),
  add_to_route(T),
  flight(T,X,D2),
  isflight(X,T2,D3),
  D=D2+D3.
isflight(T,T2,D):-
  flight(T,X,D2),
  X<>T2,
  add_to_route(T),
  isflight(X,T2,D3),
  D=D2+D3.

findsmallest(A,B):-
  flight(A,X,D),
  flight(A,Y,D2),
  Y<>X,
  D>D2,   /* find the shortest */
  B=Y.
```

As you can see, the only change between least-cost and hill-climbing is that least-cost finds the shortest connecting flight each time.

The first solution that this routine finds is

```
Distance is 2600
newyork
toronto
```

The second solution is

```
Distance is 3300
newyork
toronto
chicago
denver
```

As you can see, the routine did actually find the shortest route during its first attempt, and its second solution was not nearly as bad as that of hill-climbing. In Figure 2-8 you can see least-cost's path to the first two solutions.

Evaluating the Least-Cost Search

The least-cost search has the same advantages and disadvantages of hill-climbing, except in reverse: there can be false valleys, lowlands, and gorges; but, overall, least-cost tends to work fairly well. However, do not assume that least-cost is generally better just because it performed better than hill-climbing on this particular problem. You can only say that, on the average, it will outperform a blind search.

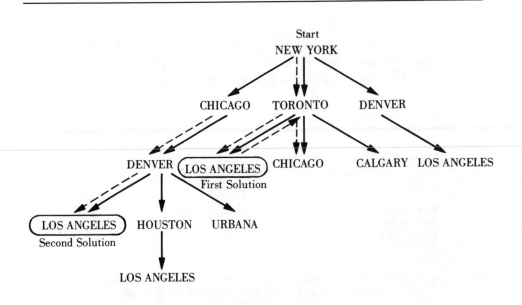

Figure 2-8.   Least-cost's path to the first two solutions

Choosing a Search Technique

As you have seen, the heuristic techniques will tend to work better than blind searching. However, it is not always possible to use a heuristic search because there is sometimes not enough information available to allow you to qualify the likelihood of the next node being on a path to the goal. Therefore, you can separate the rules for choosing a search method into two categories: the first for problems that can utilize a heuristic search, and the second for those that cannot.

If you cannot apply heuristics to a problem, then, given the fact that Turbo Prolog already uses depth-first searching, you should generally use it as well. The only exception to this rule is the situation in which you have knowledge that indicates that a breadth-first search will be better, such as when the database is organized in such a way that it is apparent that a breadth-first search will work better.

The choice between hill-climbing and least-cost depends on what constraint you are trying to minimize or maximize. Generally, hill-climbing will produce a solution with the least number of nodes visited, while least-cost will find a path that requires the least effort.

Finding the Optimal Solution

All of the search techniques described so far are concerned with finding a solution. As shown by the heuristic searches, there are efforts to improve the likelihood of finding a good, and preferably optimal, solution. However, sometimes only the optimal solution is desired. So, before you leave the scheduling example, let's develop a program that will find the optimal schedule, with the assumption that you want to minimize distance. This section will use Turbo Prolog's default search method of depth-first since it is the one that you will most commonly use.

The key to finding the shortest schedule is to force Turbo Prolog to generate multiple solutions, keeping only those solutions whose distance is less than the previous. Hence, when there are no more solutions for Turbo Prolog to generate, only the optimal one will be left.

In order to accomplish this, you must develop a new clause called **findoptimal**, as shown here:

```
findoptimal(A,B,Max):-
   route(A,B,D), D<Max,
   write("distance is ",D),nl,
   findoptimal(A,B,D).
findoptimal(_,_,_).
```

This routine forces Turbo Prolog to backtrack as long as it can find a solution that has a shorter distance than the previous one. As you may guess, this clause assumes that it will first be called with a distance that is greater than or equal to the shortest distance. For the scheduling example, use a distance of 10,000 because no route is greater than 10,000 miles between New York and Los Angeles.

The entire program is shown here:

```
/* find shortest */
database
   flight(symbol, symbol, integer)
   visited(symbol)
predicates
   route(symbol, symbol, integer)
   findoptimal(symbol, symbol, integer)
   isflight(symbol, symbol, integer)
   findroute
goal
   assert(flight(newyork, chicago,1000)),
   assert(flight(chicago, denver,1000)),
   assert(flight(newyork, toronto, 800)),
   assert(flight(newyork, denver, 1900)),
   assert(flight(toronto, calgary, 1500)),
   assert(flight(toronto, los_angeles, 1800)),
   assert(flight(toronto, chicago, 500)),
   assert(flight(denver, urbana, 1000)),
   assert(flight(denver, houston,1500)),
   assert(flight(houston, los_angeles, 1500)),
   assert(flight(denver, los_angeles,1000)),
   findroute,nl.

clauses
   findroute:-
     write("from: "),
     readln(A),
     write("to: "),readln(B),
     findoptimal(A,B,10000).
   findroute.
```

```
findoptimal(A,B,Max):-
  route(A,B,D), D<Max,
  write("distance is ",D),nl,
  findoptimal(A,B,D).
findoptimal(_,_,_).
route(A,B,C):-
  isflight(A,B,C).

route(_,_,D):-!,
  write("no (more) route"),
  nl,
  D=0, fail, !.

isflight(T,T2,D):-
  flight(T,T2,D).
isflight(T,T2,D):-
  flight(T,X,D2),
  X<>T2,
  isflight(X,T2,D3),
  D=D2+D3.
```

The output from the program is

```
Distance is 3300
Distance is 2600
```

Keep in mind that this approach to finding the optimal solution performs an exhaustive search that will not work with larger problems. An improved version would stop following a path as soon as the length equaled or exceeded the current minimum. You might find it interesting to modify this program to accommodate such an enhancement.

The Farmer, the Fox, the Chicken, And the Grain

You are now ready to leave the flight-scheduling problem to look at a different example of computerized problem solving. In this section, you will create a Turbo Prolog program that can solve the classic "farmer, fox, chicken, and grain" brainteaser. The problem is as follows. A farmer is going to market to sell a fox, a chicken, and a sack of grain. All is fine until the farmer comes to a river that has as its only means of crossing a small boat that is big enough for only the farmer and one other item. The problem is that if the farmer leaves the fox and chicken together unattended, then the fox will eat the chicken. But if the farmer leaves the chicken and the grain together, then the chicken will eat the grain. What is the sequence of moves the farmer must make to transport everything from one side of the river to the other successfully?

Because a Turbo Prolog program must *solve* this problem, you are allowed to give the program only two characteristics: first, it must have knowledge of what constitutes legal combinations of objects; and, second, it must know both the initial and goal states.

The main challenge is deciding how to represent this problem in a program. Although there are many ways to do this, a good one is to create two knowledge bases, each of which will hold the items that are on a particular side of the river. These knowledge bases will be called **rightbank** and **leftbank**. Assume that the farmer is moving from the right bank to the left bank. Therefore, initially, **rightbank** will contain three assertions —fox, chicken, and grain —and the **leftbank** will be empty. As you think about the problem, it becomes clear that it is unnecessary to worry about where the farmer is. Since only the combination of the three other items is critical, you do not need to factor the farmer into the search space. Given this approach, the goal of the program is

```
goal
    assert(rightbank(chicken)),
    assert(rightbank(grain)),
    assert(rightbank(fox)),
    crossed_river.  /* find the solution */
```

where **crossed _ river** is the clause that recognizes when everything is across the river.

The **crossed _ river** clause defines the goal of having everything on the left side of the river, as shown here:

```
/* get everything to left bank */
crossed_river:-
   setup,          /* setup graphics display */
   rightbank(X),  /* get something to move */
```

```
move(X),         /* try to move it */
leftbank(chicken),  /* see if */
leftbank(fox),      /* everything */
leftbank(grain),    /* is on leftbank */
cursor(20,8),       /* otherwise backtrack */
write("everything on left bank"),
nl,nl.
```

This clause uses Turbo Prolog's normal depth-first searching and back-tracking to find a solution. It will continue to try moves until all three of the **leftbank** statements are true.

The **move** clause, given here, actually performs the work:

```
/*  try a move */
move(X):-
   checkfarmer,     /* animate the farmer */
   assert(leftbank(X)),
   retract(rightbank(X)),
   sail(X,left),
   legal,!.   /* see if allowed combination*/

move(X):-
   /* If this clause executes then the preceding
      move created an unacceptable situation
      so the farmer must move something back. */
   leftbank(Y),Y<>X,
   retract(leftbank(Y)),
   sail(Y,right),
   assert(rightbank(Y)),!.
move(X):-
   retract(leftbank(X)),
   sail(X,right),
   assert(rightbank(X)).
```

Whenever there is an illegal situation created, it forces the farmer to correct it. You can tell the program what the legal moves are by using the **legal** clause, which is

```
/* see if move is a legal combination */
legal:-
   leftbank(fox),
   leftbank(grain).

legal:-
   rightbank(grain),
   rightbank(fox).
```

This clause is quite short because you do not have to keep track of the farmer explicitly.

Before you put all of the pieces together, here are some graphics and animation to add so that you can watch the way that the problem is solved. These make use of Turbo Prolog's rich set of graphics predicates, as shown here:

```
/**************************************/
/* Graphics routines                 */
/**************************************/

  river:-    /* draw river */
    line(5000,12000,25000,12000,2),
    line(5000,18000,25000,18000,2).

  /* setup for the crossings */
  sail(fox,left):-
    transportleft(fox,9,25,5).
  sail(chicken,left):-
    transportleft(chicken,12,25,5).
  sail(grain,left):-
    transportleft(grain,15,25,5).
  sail(fox,right):-
    transportright(fox,9,5,25).
  sail(chicken,right):-
    transportright(chicken,12,5,25).
  sail(grain,right):-
    transportright(grain,15,5,25).

  /* animate the crossing going left*/
  transportleft(T,X1,Y1,Y2):-
    Y1=Y2,
    cursor(X1,Y1),
    write("          "),
    cursor(X1,Y1),
    write(T),
    cursor(6,Y1),
    write("          "),
    cursor(6,Y1),
    write("farmer"),
    assert(fposition(left)),!.
  transportleft(T,X1,Y1,Y2):-
    cursor(X1,Y1),
    write("          "),
    cursor(X1,Y1),
    write(T),
    cursor(6,Y1),
    write("          "),
```

```
    cursor(6,Y1),
    write("farmer"),
    Z=Y1-1,river,
    transportleft(T,X1,Z,Y2).

/* animate the crossing going right */
transportright(T,X1,Y1,Y2):-
    Y1=Y2,
    Temp=Y1-1,
    cursor(X1,Temp),
    write("          "),
    cursor(X1,Y1),
    write(T),
    cursor(6,Temp),
    write("          "),
    cursor(6,Y1),
    write("farmer"),
    retract(fposition(left)),!.
transportright(T,X1,Y1,Y2):-
    Temp=Y1-1,
    cursor(X1,Temp),
    write("          "),
    cursor(X1,Y1),
    write(T),
    cursor(6,Temp),
    write("          "),
    cursor(6,Y1),
    write("farmer"),
    Z=Y1+1,river,
    transportright(T,X1,Z,Y2).

/* initial state
setup:-
    graphics(1,1,0),
    river,
    cursor(6,25), write("farmer"),
    cursor(9,25), write("fox"),
    cursor(12,25), write("chicken"),
    cursor(15,25), write("grain"),
    cursor(0,4),
    write("Farmer, Fox, Chicken, And Grain").

/* does the farmer need to be moved? */
checkfarmer:-
    not(fposition(left)).
checkfarmer:-
    movefarmer(5).

/* actually move the farmer by himself */
movefarmer(Y):-
    Y=25,
    cursor(6,24),
```

```
      write("          "),
      cursor(6,25),
      write("farmer"),
      retract(fposition(left)),river,!.
   movefarmer(Y):-
      Temp=Y-1,
      cursor(6,Temp),
      write("          "),
      cursor(6,Y),
      write("farmer"),
      Z=Y+1,river,
      movefarmer(Z).
```

Through the use of these predicates, the program will actually move the farmer and the farmer's entourage across the river. The animation is accomplished by repeatedly writing and erasing the object that is being moved. As written, these routines require a color graphics adapter. If you do not have one, then you may have to make small modifications to the program.

Here is the entire program:

```
/* Farmer, Chicken, Fox, and Grain */
database
   leftbank(symbol)
   rightbank(symbol)
   fposition(symbol)
predicates
   move(symbol)
   legal
   crossed_river
   river
   sail(symbol,symbol)
   setup
   transportleft(symbol, integer, integer, integer)
   transportright(symbol, integer, integer, integer)
   checkfarmer
   movefarmer(integer)
goal
     assert(rightbank(chicken)),
     assert(rightbank(grain)),
     assert(rightbank(fox)),
     crossed_river.
clauses
   /* get everything to left bank */
   crossed_river:-
     setup,
     rightbank(X),
```

```
    move(X),
    leftbank(chicken),
    leftbank(fox),
    leftbank(grain),
    cursor(20,8),
    write("everything on left bank"),
    nl,nl.

/*   try a move */
move(X):-
    checkfarmer,
    assert(leftbank(X)),
    retract(rightbank(X)),
    sail(X,left),
    legal,!.   /* see if allowed combination*/

move(X):-
    /* If this clause executes then the preceding
       move created an unacceptable situation
       so the farmer must move something back. */
    leftbank(Y),Y<>X,
    retract(leftbank(Y)),
    sail(Y,right),
    assert(rightbank(Y)),!.
move(X):-
    retract(leftbank(X)),
    sail(X,right),
    assert(rightbank(X)).

/* see if move is a legal combination */
legal:-
    leftbank(fox),
    leftbank(grain).

legal:-
    rightbank(grain),
    rightbank(fox).


/***********************************/
/* Graphics routines             */
/***********************************/

  river:-  /* draw river */
    line(5000,12000,25000,12000,2),
    line(5000,18000,25000,18000,2).

  /* setup for the crossings */
  sail(fox,left):-
    transportleft(fox,9,25,5).
  sail(chicken,left):-
    transportleft(chicken,12,25,5).
```

```
sail(grain,left):-
  transportleft(grain,15,25,5).
sail(fox,right):-
  transportright(fox,9,5,25).
sail(chicken,right):-
  transportright(chicken,12,5,25).
sail(grain,right):-
  transportright(grain,15,5,25).

/* animate the crossing going left*/
transportleft(T,X1,Y1,Y2):-
  Y1=Y2,
  cursor(X1,Y1),
  write("           "),
  cursor(X1,Y1),
  write(T),
  cursor(6,Y1),
  write("           "),
  cursor(6,Y1),
  write("farmer"),
  assert(fposition(left)),!.
transportleft(T,X1,Y1,Y2):-
  cursor(X1,Y1),
  write("           "),
  cursor(X1,Y1),
  write(T),
  cursor(6,Y1),
  write("           "),
  cursor(6,Y1),
  write("farmer"),
  Z=Y1-1,river,
  transportleft(T,X1,Z,Y2).

/* animate the crossing going right */
transportright(T,X1,Y1,Y2):-
  Y1=Y2,
  Temp=Y1-1,
  cursor(X1,Temp),
  write("           "),
  cursor(X1,Y1),
  write(T),
  cursor(6,Temp),
  write("           "),
  cursor(6,Y1),
  write("farmer"),
  retract(fposition(left)),!.
transportright(T,X1,Y1,Y2):-
  Temp=Y1-1,
  cursor(X1,Temp),
  write("           "),
```

```
   cursor(X1,Y1),
   write(T),
   cursor(6,Temp),
   write("           "),
   cursor(6,Y1),
   write("farmer"),
   Z=Y1+1,river,
   transportright(T,X1,Z,Y2).
/* initial state
setup:-
   graphics(1,1,0),
   river,
   cursor(6,25), write("farmer"),
   cursor(9,25), write("fox"),
   cursor(12,25), write("chicken"),
   cursor(15,25), write("grain"),
   cursor(0,4),
   write("Farmer, Fox, Chicken, And Grain").

/* does the farmer need to be moved? */
checkfarmer:-
   not(fposition(left)).
checkfarmer:-
   movefarmer(5).

/* actually move the farmer by himself */
movefarmer(Y):-
   Y=25,
   cursor(6,24),
   write("           "),
   cursor(6,25),
   write("farmer"),
   retract(fposition(left)),river,!.
movefarmer(Y):-
   Temp=Y-1,
   cursor(6,Temp),
   write("           "),
   cursor(6,Y),
   write("farmer"),
   Z=Y+1,river,
   movefarmer(Z).
```

Figure 2-9 shows the initial state, Figure 2-10 shows an intermediate state, and Figure 2-11 shows the goal state of the program.

Enter this program into your computer and observe its operation. It is quite amazing because there is no doubt that the computer is actually solving the problem. All that you have done is define the initial and goal

---

Farmer, Fox, Chicken, And Grain

farmer

fox

chicken

grain

Figure 2-9.   The initial state of the solution of the farmer, fox, chicken, and grain problem

---

states, and the rules for what states are legal. This program makes an excellent AI problem-solving demonstration. You might want to try modifying it so that the farmer has more items, which creates a more difficult problem.

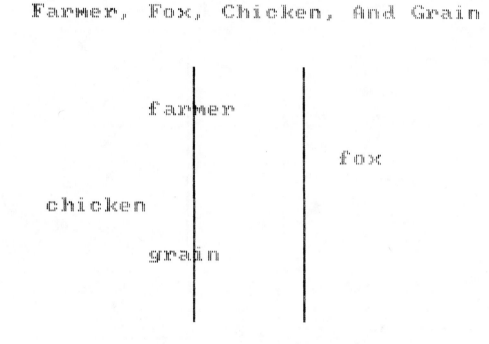

Figure 2-10.   An intermediate state of the solution of the farmer, fox, chicken, and grain problem

Back to the Missing Keys

To conclude this chapter on problem solving, it seems only fitting to provide a Turbo Prolog program that finds the missing car keys that were

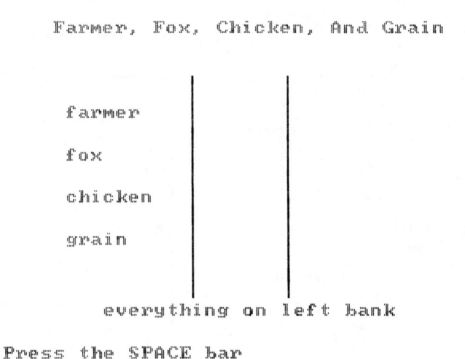

Figure 2-11.   The goal state of the solution of the farmer, fox, chicken, and grain problem

described in the first part of this chapter. By now, you should have a fairly good understanding of how to use Turbo Prolog to solve problems, so the program is presented for your enjoyment without any further explanation.

```
/* find the keys */
database
  connects(symbol, symbol)
predicates
  keys(symbol, symbol, symbol)
  isroom(symbol, symbol, symbol)
  findkeys
goal
  assert(connects(lr, bath)),
  assert(connects(lr, hall)),
  assert(connects(hall, bd1)),
  assert(connects(hall, bd2)),
  assert(connects(hall, mb)),
  assert(connects(lr, kitchen)),
  assert(connects(kitchen, keys)),
  findkeys.

clauses
  findkeys:-
    keys(lr,keys,X),
    write("keys are in ",X),nl.

  keys(A,B,R):-
    isroom(A,B,R).

  keys(_,_,R):-
    write("no keys in house"),
    nl, R=no_found.

  isroom(T,_,R):-
    connects(T,keys),
    R=T.
  isroom(T,T2,R):-
    connects(T,X),
    X<>T2,
    isroom(X,T,R).
  isroom(T,_,_):-
    write("dead end at ",T),
    nl, fail.
```

3

Expert Systems

Expert systems are exciting for primarily two reasons: first, they are generally useful, practical programs that fulfill an actual need; and second, they are achievable. These are the reasons that they constitute most of AI's commercially successful programs. The first part of this chapter will show you what expert systems are and the various ways that they can work. The second part of the chapter will develop a complete, general-purpose expert system.

What Is an Expert System?

As stated in Chapter 1, expert systems are programs that mimic the behavior of a human expert. They use information that the user supplies to render an opinion on a certain subject. Thus, the expert system asks you to answer questions until it can identify an object that matches your answers. To understand what an expert system does, consider the following dialog between a fruit expert and someone who is seeking advice.

Expert	Is it green?
User	No.
Expert	Is it red?
User	Yes.
Expert	Does it grow on a tree?
User	No.
Expert	Does it grow on a cane?
User	Yes.
Expert	Does the cane have thorns?
User	Yes.
Expert	It is a raspberry.

The goal of a computerized fruit expert system is to be able to reproduce this dialog. More generally, an expert system attempts to give advice to the user on its subject of expertise.

What Are the Advantages
Of an Expert System?

The desirability of an expert system is based primarily on availability and convenience. Unlike a human expert who has to sleep, eat, relax, take holidays, and so on, the expert system is available for use 24 hours a day, every day of the year. Also, many expert systems can be created, while there may be a limited number of human experts, making it virtually impossible in many situations to have an expert available when needed. In addition, unlike humans, the computerized expert never dies — taking the knowledge with it. The knowledge in an expert system can be easily copied and stored, making the permanent loss of the expert knowledge quite rare.

Another advantage of an expert system over human experts is that the computerized expert is always at peak performance. When a human expert gets tired, the reliability of the expert advice may suffer. However, the computerized expert will always generate the best opinions possible — within the limitations of its knowledge.

A less important advantage of an expert system is its lack of personality. As you probably realize, not everyone's personalities are compatible. If you do not get along with an expert, then you may be reluctant to utilize the expert's knowledge. The reverse situation is also true: a human expert who does not like you may not be able to provide reliable information. But a computerized expert does not (or at least should not) have a personality, so these problems are eliminated.

A final advantage of an expert system is that after a computerized expert exists, you can acquire a new expert by simply copying the program from one machine to another. A human needs a long time to become an expert in certain fields, which makes it difficult to acquire new human experts.

Some Examples of Commercial
Expert Systems

If it were not for an expert system called MYCIN, expert systems might have stayed in the AI research laboratory and not progressed into the outside world. One of AI's greatest image problems has been that many people, including other programmers, felt that AI techniques only worked on simple problems (sometimes called toy problems) that required a strict set of rules and assumptions. These people believed that AI could never be used to solve hard problems. MYCIN changed all that.

MYCIN was the world's first successful expert system. Developed at Stanford University in the mid 1970s, MYCIN was designed to help physicians diagnose certain bacterial diseases. Diagnosing illnesses essentially means comparing symptoms that are exhibited by the patient with the symptoms of a disease until a match is found. The trouble is that it is difficult for a physician to diagnose all of the many different diseases that exist quickly and confidently. Hence, MYCIN satisfied the need to confirm the diagnoses of the physicians.

Another example of a commercially viable expert system is PROS-PECTOR, which was created in 1978 by Richard Duda, Peter Hard, and Rene Reboh. PROSPECTOR is an expert in geology: it predicts the likelihood that certain mineral deposits may be found in a particular region. There have been several variations on this program, including programs that are experts at predicting the discovery of oil, natural gas, and helium.

The early 1980s saw the introduction of dedicated expert systems that could provide tax consulting, insurance advice, and legal aid. Many programmers believe that by the end of the 1980s, there will be a large market for "personal" expert systems for use around the home and office. These systems will cover many subjects —from gardening and lawn care to auto repair. In fact, expert systems may prove to be the most common type of program run on personal computers.

How Expert Systems Work

Every expert system has two parts: the knowledge base and the inference engine. This section will describe the most common ways that these parts can be implemented.

The Knowledge Base

The knowledge base is a database that holds specific information and rules about a certain subject. Here are two terms that you should know for this discussion:

- *Object.* The conclusion that is defined by its associated rules.

- *Attribute.* A specific quality that, together with its rule, helps define the object.

Therefore, you can think of the knowledge base as a list of objects with their associated rules and attributes.

For most expert system applications, you can define an object by a list of attributes that the object either does or does not possess. Thus, for most purposes, the rule that is applied to an attribute states that the object either "has" or "has not" the attribute. For example, an expert system that identifies various types of fruit might have a knowledge base like this:

Apple

has	been grown on tree
has	round shape
has not	been grown in the Deep South
has	red or yellow color

Grape

has	been grown on vine
has	small size
has	purple color
has not	a vine with thorns
has	ability to make wine

Orange

has	been grown on tree
has	round shape
has not	been grown in the North
has	orange color

If you think about this knowledge base, you can see that you can simplify it: you can use only one rule — "has" — and use a negative form of the attribute if you must establish a "has not" relationship. Thus, the rule simply becomes "possesses," and the simplified knowledge base looks like this:

Apple
- grows on tree
- round
- does not grow in the Deep South
- color is red or yellow

Grape
- grows on vine
- small in size
- color varies
- vine does not have thorns
- can be used to make wine

Orange
- grows on tree
- round
- cannot grow in the North
- color is orange

Although certain sophisticated expert systems may need a more complex rule than simply "possesses," this rule is sufficient for many situations and greatly simplifies the knowledge base. For the rest of this book, assume that the knowledge base consists only of objects and attributes.

The Inference Engine

The inference engine is the part of the expert system that attempts to use the information that you give it to find an object that matches. There are two broad categories of inference engines: deterministic and probabilistic. To understand the difference, imagine that there are two experts, one in chemistry and the other in sociology. The chemist can report with *certainty* that if the atom in question has two electrons then it is a helium atom. There is no question about the atom's identity because the number of electrons determines the type of element. However, if you ask the sociologist what is the best way to prevent high school dropouts, the sociologist will give an answer that is qualified as being only probable or as having a certain success ratio. Therefore, the answer is likely, but *uncertain.*

Most disciplines are not deterministic, but rather are probabilistic to a certain extent. However, for many of these, the uncertainty is not statistically important so you can treat them as deterministic situations. The rest of this chapter will deal only with deterministic expert systems because their logic is clearer. (However, Chapter 8 deals with probabilistic systems and uncertainty.)

Beyond the two broad categories of certainty and uncertainty, there are three basic ways to construct the inference engine: forward-chaining, backward-chaining, and rule-value. The differences of the methods relate to how the engine attempts to reach its goal.

The Forward-Chaining Method   Forward-chaining is sometimes called data-driven because the inference engine uses information that is provided by the user to move through a network of logical ANDs and ORs until it reaches a terminal point, which is the object. If the inference engine cannot find an object by using the existing information, then it requests more. The rules that define the object create the path that leads to it; therefore, the only way to reach the object is to satisfy all of its rules. Thus, a forward-chaining inference engine starts with some information and tries to find an object that fits the information.

To understand how forward-chaining works, imagine that your car is malfunctioning and that you telephone your mechanic, who is the expert in this case, for an opinion on the trouble. The mechanic then asks you to describe what is wrong. You explain that your car has power loss, knocking, and the engine keeps on running after you turn the ignition off and that it has not been tuned-up in several months. Using this information, your mechanic tells you that most likely your car is in severe need of a tune-up.

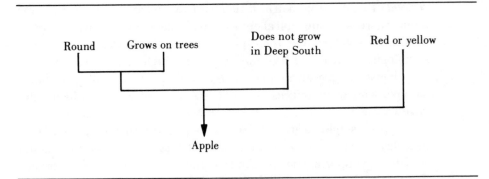

Figure 3-1. Forward-chaining to the object apple

If you think back to the fruit knowledge base described earlier, you can create a diagram that shows how a forward-chaining inference engine would arrive at the object apple, when it is given the proper attributes, as shown in Figure 3-1. As you can see, a forward-chaining system essentially builds a tree from the leaves down to the root.

The Backward-Chaining Method   Backward-chaining is the reverse of forward-chaining: a backward-chaining inference engine starts with a hypothesis (an object) and requests information to confirm or deny it. For example, the simple animal expert system that is included with the Turbo Prolog package uses backward-chaining. Backward-chaining is sometimes called object-driven because the system begins with an object and attempts to verify it.

To understand how backward-chaining works, imagine that your computer suddenly stops working. Your first hypothesis is that it has lost power. To check this, you listen for the fan. Hearing the fan run, you reject this hypothesis and proceed to another. Your second hypothesis is that your computer has crashed because of faulty software. To confirm or reject this possibility, you reset your computer to see if it will reboot successfully. Fortunately, your computer springs to life; your second hypothesis holds true.

If the fruit in question is an apple, applying backward-chaining inferences to the fruit knowledge base produces the diagram in Figure 3-2. As this diagram shows, backward-chaining *prunes* a tree. This is the opposite of forward-chaining, which constructs a tree.

The Rule-Value Method   A rule-value inference engine is theoretically superior to either a forward-chaining or a backward-chaining system because it requests information that has the greatest importance, given the current state of the system. It is commonly an improved backward-chaining engine. The general theory of operation is that the system requests as its next piece of information the one that will *remove the most uncertainty from the system.*

To understand a rule-value approach, imagine that you have called your physician because your child is sick. The doctor first asks if the child has a fever because the answer to this question narrows the greatest

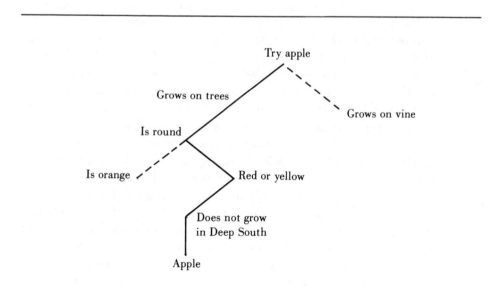

Figure 3-2.   Backward-chaining to the object apple

number of possibilities. If you answer "yes" to the first question, then the doctor asks you if your child is nauseated. As with the first question, the doctor asks this question over other questions because its answer has the greatest impact given the current state. This procedure continues until the doctor can make a diagnosis. In this example, the key point is that the doctor selects each question to make the most rapid progress to a conclusion.

The trouble with rule-value systems is that they are difficult to implement. There are two reasons for this. First, in real-life situations, the knowledge base is often so large that the number of possible combinations exceeds what can be easily grasped. Hence, the system cannot simply determine what information removes the most uncertainty at any given state. Second, rule-value systems require the knowledge base to contain not only the standard object-attribute information, but also a value quantifier that makes constructing the knowledge base more difficult. However, there are certain situations that lend themselves to rule-value inferences more than others. Also, when implemented, rule-value systems generally do a better job than the other two methods.

Choosing a Method   At this point, you might be wondering which of the three types of inference engines is the best to use. The solution is based somewhat on personal preference because all three types will do any task that you want to do. As stated earlier, you may find rule-value systems to be difficult to implement, so, until you are an expert at building expert systems, it is probably best to avoid this method.

The forward-chaining method makes the process of deriving the greatest amount of information from the knowledge base easier because it constructs a tree. Forward-chaining systems commonly find all possible objects that match the attributes. The advantage of the expert system that uses the backward-chaining method is that it requests only enough information to find an object. Thus, because backward-chaining expert systems are goal driven, they only allow relevant information to be input into the system, whereas forward-chaining expert systems may have to discard extraneous information. A backward-chaining system is useful when you want to find only one object —even if other objects also satisfy the attributes. You can make a backward-chaining expert system that finds multiple solutions, but it requires a little more work than constructing a forward-chaining expert system.

In the final analysis, the actual approach that you use is up to you. However, if all things are equal, the backward-chaining approach is a little easier to implement and produces an expert system that looks like what you would expect one to look like. For these reasons, this chapter will develop an expert system that will use backward-chaining.

Creating a General-Purpose Expert System

Now that you have the necessary background on expert systems, it is time to see what an actual expert system looks like. This section will create a general-purpose expert system that uses backward-chaining. It is called general-purpose because it allows the same inference engine to be used with a variety of knowledge bases. It also includes the necessary routines to create the knowledge bases. Before you begin, however, it is important to dispel a few preconceptions that you may have about the way that expert systems should be implemented.

An unfortunate, but understandable, fact is that virtually all introductory books on Prolog (including the Turbo Prolog user manual) use the simple "animal" expert system example. Occasionally, an introductory book may call this system something else, but it is structured approximately in the same way. An exception is the expanded animal expert system provided as a sample program with version 1.1 of Turbo Prolog, which is good implementation of a classification system and is worthy of serious examination. Although this simple expert system illustrates various aspects of Prolog (and certainly stimulates the imagination), it presents an incorrect way to implement an expert system. The inference engine is mixed with the objects and attributes. This means that the knowledge base is "hard-coded" into the program. This is poor programming technique for several reasons. One of the worst reasons is that altering, enhancing, or enlarging the knowledge base implies an alteration to the program code —and a recompilation. This alteration opens the door for all sorts of trouble, ranging from accidental editing errors to mutilation of the actual code by an inexperienced programmer. Another reason that hard-coding the knowledge base into the program is poor programming technique is that in-the-field changes to the knowledge base would require that a user actually make changes to the program — the last thing that any self-respecting programmer would want. Coincidentally, this practice also implies that the user would have access to the source code, something no commercial software developer would allow.

As this discussion shows, the knowledge base must be separate from the inference engine. Only in this way can legitimate software developers create truly workable systems. This also allows the development of general-purpose expert systems, which the user can train in the field without reprogramming. This is the structure that all commercial systems have, and it is the structure that the expert system that this chapter creates will implement.

The Essentials of Operation

Before you see how to write code for an expert system, this section defines, in practical terms, what you need to do to create an inference engine. This section assumes that the knowledge base will consist only of objects and their attributes. To understand what an inference engine must be capable of doing, use the small knowledge base shown here:

Object	Attributes
1	A, B, C
2	A, B, Y
3	B, X
4	A, B, D

On the most primitive level, the inference engine begins by assuming that object 1 is the goal and tries to confirm this by asking if the goal has object 1's attributes. If it does, then the inference engine reports that object 1 is the answer. If not, then the inference engine proceeds to object 2 and inquires about object 2's attributes. This process repeats until either the proper object is found, or there are no more objects. If these are the steps that the inference engine takes, and if object 4 is the goal, the following dialog will take place:

```
expert    does it have A?
  user    yes.
expert    does it have B?
  user    yes.
expert    does it have C?
  user    no.                    /* reject 1 */
expert    does it have A?        /* redundant */
  user    yes.
expert    does it have B?        /* redundant */
  user    yes.
expert    does it have Y?
  user    no.                    /* reject 2 */
expert    does it have B?        /* redundant */
  user    yes.
expert    does it have X?        /* unnecessary */
  user    no.                    /* reject 3 */
expert    does it have A?        /* redundant */
  user    yes.
expert    does it have B?        /* redundant */
  user    yes.
expert    does it have D?        /* found */
  user    yes.
expert    it is 4.
```

An expert system that works like this would not only be tedious to use, but for the most part worthless when there are more than a handful of objects in the system. This type of system exhibits two shortcomings. First, it inquires about the same attribute several times. Second, when it turns to object 3, it asks an unnecessary question. The system should have known from its previous questions that the object in question has attribute B, and it should have rejected object 3 without further trial because object 3 does not have attribute B. Although it is possible that knowing about attribute X *could* have been useful, on the average, the inference engine will be more efficient if it skips over all objects that do not fit the current state. Thus, what is desired is an inference engine that, when given the same knowledge base with object 4 as the goal, produces this dialog:

```
expert   does it have A?
  user   yes.
expert   does it have B?
  user   yes.
expert   does it have C?
  user   no.                    /* reject 1 */
expert   does it have Y?
  user   no.                    /* reject 2 */
                                /* reject 3 */
expert   does it have D?        /* found */
  user   yes.
expert   it is 4.
```

With this type of inference engine as a goal, here are the specifications to which the sample inference engine must conform:

1. The expert system must not inquire about the same attribute twice.

2. The expert system should reject immediately and move past any object that does not have the known necessary attributes.

3. Upon command, the expert system should be able to report why it is following a line of reasoning.

The third specification is added not only as a way of verifying that the expert system is operating correctly, but also as a method of educating the user.

Structuring the Knowledge Base

The first step to creating an expert system is to define the structure of the knowledge base. You will use, as do most commercial expert systems, the

the built-in database facility of Turbo Prolog. The knowledge base is

```
info(symbol, list)·
  /* object, attributes */
```

where **list** will be defined to be a list of symbols.

As you will see, the inference engine must keep track of all attributes that belong to the goal and those that do not. Although you could use lists to do this, it is easier to define two additional databases that store this information temporarily. Hence, the entire database declaration portion of the expert system is

```
database
  info(symbol, list)
    /* object, attributes */
  yes(symbol) /* trail of yes responses */
  no(symbol)  /* trail of no responses */
```

Loading the Knowledge Base

Before you can develop the inference engine, you must create some routines that allow you to place information in the knowledge base. Although you could write a separate program to do this, the same way most commercial expert systems would do it, for simplicity the routines that allow knowledge to be input into the system will be an option built into the expert system developed here. As shown here, **enter** reads the name of an object and calls **attributes**, which inputs the attributes that are associated with that object. This process repeats until the user types **quit**. Then, **enter** prompts for more; if the user types **y** as an answer, then the procedure repeats. Here are these routines.

```
/* enter objects and attributes */
enter:-
  write("What is it?: "),
  readln(Object),
  Object<>"quit",
  attributes(Object,[]),
  write("more? "),!,
  readln(Q),Q="y",
  enter.
```

```
/* actually get the attributes */
attributes(O,List):-
  write(O," is/has/does: "),
  readln(Attribute),
  Attribute<>"quit",
  add(Attribute,List,List2),
  attributes(O,List2).
attributes(Object,List):-
  assert(info(Object,List)),
  writelist(List,1),!,
  nl.
```

Because the user should only have to enter the information once into the knowledge base, at the end of the entry session, another routine will save the information by using Turbo Pascal's **save** command. For simplicity, this expert system will always assume that the knowledge base is contained in the file **x.dat**. (However, it would be easy to allow the user to specify the name of the file. You may wish to make this enhancement yourself.) Under this assumption, the first predicate executed will be **start**, which is shown here:

```
start:-
  consult("x.dat"), /* read in info */
  fail.  /* proceed to next clause */
start:-
  assert(yes(end)),
  assert(no(end)),
  write("Enter information? (y/n): "),
  readln(A),
  A=y,
  not(enter),
  save("x.dat"),!, /* save knowledge base */
  query.
start:-
  query.
```

This is the way that **start** works. The first clause tells the system to read in the knowledge base **x.dat** and then fail. This forces Turbo Prolog to try the second clause. You may think that there is no reason to include the first clause because you could simply place **consult("x.data")** as the first line of the second clause. However, the trouble with this is that, the first time the system is run, there will be no **x.dat** in existence. This means that the **consult** will fail. So, if the **consult** were part of the second clause, the lines of code after the **consult** would never execute.

The two **assert**s that begin the second clause are used to initialize the two support databases. Next, the program will ask if the user wishes to input more, or new, information. If the user answers yes, then the **enter** predicate explained earlier is executed. After the return from **enter**, the routine saves the information to the disk file, and calls the top-level predicate of the inference engine **query**. If the user elects not to enter more information, then the second clause of **start** fails, and the final clause executes a call to **query**.

Constructing the Inference Engine

Now that you can load information into the knowledge base, you are ready to tackle the inference engine. The inference engine is the driving force of the expert system. Although quite simple in an abstract sense, implementing an inference engine can be quite difficult. Although the one that will be developed here is fairly simple, it is actually quite good for many tasks. Remember that commercial expert systems will generally have a greater number of constraints and demands than you are placing on this expert system. Still, the inference engine developed here can serve as a starting point for your more advanced systems.

The top-level predicate of the inference engine is **query** and is shown here:

```
/* request information from user to
   find an object */
query:-
  info(O,A),
  trailyes(A),   /* test old yes responses */
  trailno(A),    /* test old no responses */
  try(O,A),      /* see if it fits */
  purge.
query:-
  purge.
```

Despite its simple appearance, **query** is quite sophisticated because its operation is based upon Turbo Prolog's built-in backtracking capabilities. It works as follows. First, **query** asks the knowledge base to bind an object and its attributes to **O** and **A**. Assuming that there is something in the knowledge base, this step will succeed. Next, the routines **trailyes** and **trailno** screen out objects that do not meet the current state of the system: **trailyes** checks **O**'s attributes list to make sure that it contains all of the attributes that the user has told the system that the object must have; and **trailno** checks to make sure that **O**'s attributes do not contain any that have been rejected. These checks satisfy the first and second specifications, which were given earlier. The predicate **try** asks the user about the attributes. If they all match, then the object has been found and **purge** clears the temporary databases. If they do not match; **try** fails and backtracking occurs with a new object taken from the knowledge base. Finally, if all objects in the knowledge base have been exhausted, then the system simply clears the temporary databases and terminates.

This entire process seems fairly easy. However, you have not yet seen the support routines. First, here are **trailyes** and **trailno**.

```
/* screen out all objects that don't have
    the proper attributes as already
    determined */
trailyes(A):-
  yes(T),!,
  xtrailyes(T,A,[]),!.

xtrailyes(end,_,_):-!.
xtrailyes(T,A,L):-
  member(T,A),!,
  add(T,L,L2),
  yes(X),not(member(X,L2)),
  xtrailyes(X,A,L2).
```

```
/* screen out all objects that have
    attributes already determined as
    not belonging to the object */
trailno(A):-
  no(T),!,
  xtrailno(T,A,[]),!.

xtrailno(end,_,_):-!.
xtrailno(T,A,L):-
  not(member(T,A)),!,
  add(T,L,L2),
  no(X),not(member(X,L2)),!,
  xtrailno(X,A,L2).
```

The predicates **trailyes** and **trailno** are simply used to set up calls to their respective support routines. These predicates help restrict Turbo Prolog's backtracking. Also, the cut (!) is used liberally to prevent backtracking at various points. As you probably know by now, sometimes the hardest part of Turbo Prolog programming is limiting its relentless pursuit of solutions. The support predicate **member** determines whether an element is part of a list. The important point that you should remember about the operation of these routines is that they use the sentinel **end** to terminate their operation: **trailyes** will only return true if **xtrailyes** returns true, and the only way for that to happen is if the clause

```
xtrailyes(end,_,_):-!.
```

succeeds. This can only occur if all attributes that are stored in the temporary database match those of the object under consideration. The same point is true for **trailno**.

The portion of the inference engine that interacts with the user and actually finds the goal object is **try**:

```
/* try a hypothesis */
try(O,[]):-
  write("It is ",O), nl.
try(O,[X|T]):-
  yes(X),!,
  try(O,T).
try(O,[X|T]):-
  write("is/has/does it  ",X," "),
  readln(Q),
  process(O,X,Q),!,
  try(O,T).
```

As shown here, **try** removes one attribute at a time from the object's attribute list and asks the user if this particular attribute is part of the goal object. If the user answers yes to all questions, then a null list is finally produced and the first clause returns true. The second clause is used to prevent redundant questioning. Because the expert system is designed to be general-purpose, the prompting message is as general as possible. However, you could tailor it as you see fit.

The **try** portion uses the support predicate **process**, which takes different actions based on the user's response. **Process** also explains why a certain question is being asked —thus, fulfilling the third specification given earlier. **Process** responds to the command **why** by printing out what object it is currently pursuing and the current list of attributes. **Process** is shown here with its support routine **xwrite**, which is used to display the list of current attributes:

```
/* process various responses */
process(_,X,y):-
  asserta(yes(X)),!.
process(_,X,n):-
  asserta(no(X)),!,fail.
process(O,X,why):-
  write("I think it may be"), nl,
  write(O," because it has: "),nl,
  yes(Z),xwrite(Z),nl,
  Z=end,!,
  write("is/has/does it ",X,"? "),
  readln(Q),
  process(O,X,Q),!.

xwrite(end).
xwrite(X):-
  write(X).
```

Here is the entire expert system program. You should enter this into your computer at this time so that you will be ready for a sample run.

```
/* A simple backward-chaining expert system */
/* that finds only first solution */
domains
        list = symbol*
database
  info(symbol,list)
    /* object,attributes */
  yes(symbol)  /* keep trail of yes responses */
  no(symbol)   /* and no responses */

predicates
  append(list,list,list)
  writelist(list,integer)
  enter
  purge
```

```
    add(symbol,list,list)
    query
    attributes(symbol,list)
    process(symbol, symbol, symbol)
    start
    trailyes(list)
    trailno(list)
    xtrailyes(symbol,list,list)
    xtrailno(symbol, list, list)
    try(symbol,list)
    member(symbol,list)
    xwrite(symbol)
goal
    start.
clauses
    start:-
      consult("x.dat"), /* read in info */
      fail.  /* proceed to next clause */
    start:-
      assert(yes(end)),
      assert(no(end)),
      write("Enter information? (y/n): "),
      readln(A),
      A=y,
      not(enter),
      save("x.dat"),!,query.
    start:-
      query.

    /* enter objects and attributes */
    enter:-
      write("What is it?: "),
      readln(Object),
      Object<>"quit",
      attributes(Object,[]),
      write("more? "),!,
      readln(Q),Q="y",
      enter.

    /* actually get the attributes */
    attributes(O,List):-
      write(O," is/has/does: "),
      readln(Attribute),
      Attribute<>"quit",
      add(Attribute,List,List2),
      attributes(O,List2).
    attributes(Object,List):-
      assert(info(Object,List)),
      writelist(List,1),!,
      nl.

    /* add a symbol to a list */
    add(X,L,[X|L]).
```

```
/* request information from user to
   find an object */
query:-
  info(O,A),
  trailyes(A),   /* test old yes responses*/
  trailno(A),    /* screen for no responses */
  try(O,A),
  purge.
query:-
  purge.

/* screen out all objects that don't have
   the proper attributes as already
   determined */
trailyes(A):-
  yes(T),!,
  xtrailyes(T,A,[]),!.

xtrailyes(end,_,_):-!.
xtrailyes(T,A,L):-
  member(T,A),!,
  add(T,L,L2),
  yes(X),not(member(X,L2)),
  xtrailyes(X,A,L2).


/* screen out all objects that have
   attributes already determined as
   not belonging to the object */
trailno(A):-
  no(T),!,
  xtrailno(T,A,[]),!.

xtrailno(end,_,_):-!.
xtrailno(T,A,L):-
  not(member(T,A)),!,
  add(T,L,L2),
  no(X),not(member(X,L2)),!,
  xtrailno(X,A,L2).


/* try a hypothesis */
try(O,[]):-
  write("It is ",O), nl.
try(O,[X|T]):-
  yes(X),!,
  try(O,T).
try(O,[X|T]):-
  write("is/has/does it  ",X," "),
  readln(Q),
  process(O,X,Q),!,
  try(O,T).
```

```
/* process various responses */
process(_,X,y):-
  asserta(yes(X)),!.
process(_,X,n):-
  asserta(no(X)),!,fail.
process(O,X,why):-
  write("I think it may be"), nl,
  write(O," because it has: "),nl,
  yes(Z),xwrite(Z),nl,
  Z=end,!,
  write("is/has/does it ",X,"? "),
  readln(Q),
  process(O,X,Q),!.

xwrite(end).
xwrite(X):-
  write(X).

purge:-
  retract(yes(X)),
  X=end,fail.
purge:-
  retract(no(X)),
  X=end.

append([],List,List).
append([X|L1], List2, [X|L3]) if
  append(L1,List2,L3).

writelist([],_).
writelist([Head|Tail],3):-
  write(Head),nl,writelist(Tail,1).
writelist([Head|Tail],I):-
  N=I+1,
  write(Head," "),writelist(Tail,N).

 member(N,[N|_]).
 member(N,[_|T]):- member(N,T).
```

A Sample Run

Now that you have the expert system entered into your computer, execute it and enter the following information into the knowledge base.

Object	Attributes
Apple	grow__on__trees, red__or__yellow, round
Orange	orange, grow__on__trees, round

Grape	purple, grow_on_vines, no_thorns
Raspberry	grow_on_canes, red, thorns
Pear	grow_on_trees, red_or_green, not_round
Watermelon	grow_on_vines, no_thorns, green, large
Cherry	red_or_yellow, grow_on_trees, small
Tangerine	soft_skinned, round, grow_on_trees, orange

With the system primed with knowledge, you can use it to identify different types of fruit. The following three dialogs were produced by using this system:

- First dialog

```
is/has/does it   round y
is/has/does it   red_or_yellow n
is/has/does it   grow_on_trees y
is/has/does it   orange y
it is orange
```

- Second dialog

```
is/has/does it   round n
is/has/does it   no_thorns y
is/has/does it   grow_on_vines y
is/has/does it   purple n
is/has/does it   large y
is/has/does it   green y
it is watermelon
```

- Third dialog

```
is/has/does it   round n
is/has/does it   no_thorns y
is/has/does it   grow_on_vines y
is/has/does it   purple n
is/has/does it   large y
is/has/does it   green why
I think it may be
watermelon because it has:
large
grow_on_vines
no_thorns

is/has/does it green y
it is watermelon
```

Notice the use of the **why** command in the third dialog. Try experimenting with the system; as soon as you are convinced that you understand its operation, proceed to the next section.

Finding Multiple Solutions

If you review the knowledge base, you will find that the definitions of orange and tangerine are identical, except that tangerine has the additional attribute of being soft-skinned. Therefore, even if the user really has a tangerine, the expert system as given will always report an orange because it fits the first three attributes of tangerine. This may be acceptable in some situations, but for most it will be important to find a complete solution. You will now see the way that you can modify the system so that it finds all solutions.

There are only two predicates that need to be altered substantially: **query** and **try**. **Query** must be changed to accept a list as a parameter. This list will hold names of the objects that the system has already examined, and it will prevent the knowledge base from being reexamined from the top when the user requests additional solutions. Another change to **query** is that it will report the current solution, instead of **try**. The modified **query** predicate is shown here:

```
query(L):-
  info(O,A),
  not(member(O,L)), /* not find same one */
  add(O,L,L2),       /* twice */
  trailyes(A),   /* test old yes responses*/
  trailno(A),    /* screen for no responses */
  try(O,A),
  !, write(O," fits the"),nl,
  write("current attributes"),nl,
  write("continue? "),
  readln(Q), Q=y,
  query(L2).
```

Here, each time that an object is found that fits the current set of facts, **query** prints the object's name and asks the user if it should continue. If the user types **y**, then the system calls **query** recursively. The list that is passed to **query** forces Turbo Prolog to find objects in the knowledge base that have not already been examined.

Try no longer reports the solution, so it is modified as shown:

```
try(_,[]).  /* found something */
try(O,[X|T]):-
  yes(X),!,
  try(O,T).
try(O,[X|T]):-
  write("is/has/does it ",X," "),
  readln(Q),
  process(O,X,Q),!,
  try(O,T).
```

Finally, you must alter **start** so that it passes a null list to **query**, as shown here:

```
start:-
  consult("x.dat"), /* read in info */
  fail.  /* proceed to next clause */
start:-
  assert(yes(end)),
  assert(no(end)),
  write("Enter information? (y/n): "),
  readln(A),
  A=y,
  not(enter),
  save("x.dat"),!,query([]).
start:-
  query([]),purge.
start:-
  purge.
```

Here is the entire improved expert system:

```
/* A simple backward-chaining expert system */
/* that finds multiple solutions */
domains
      list = symbol*
database
  info(symbol,list)
  /* object, list of attributes */
  yes(symbol)  /* keep trail of yes */
  no(symbol)   /* and no responses */

predicates
  append(list,list,list)
  writelist(list,integer)
  enter
```

```
    purge
    add(symbol,list,list)
    query(list)
    attributes(symbol,list)
    process(symbol, symbol, symbol)
    start
    trailyes(list)
    trailno(list)
    xtrailyes(symbol,list,list)
    xtrailno(symbol, list, list)
    try(symbol,list)
    member(symbol,list)
    xwrite(symbol)
goal
    start.
clauses
    start:-
      consult("x.dat"), /* read in info */
      fail.  /* proceed to next clause */
    start:-
      assert(yes(end)),
      assert(no(end)),
      write("Enter information? (y/n): "),
      readln(A),
      A=y,
      not(enter),
      save("x.dat"),!,query([]).
    start:-
      query([]),purge.
    start:-
      purge.

    /* enter objects and attributes */
    enter:-
      write("What is it?: "),
      readln(Object),
      Object<>"quit",
      attributes(Object,[]),
      write("more? "),!,
      readln(Q),Q=y,
      enter.

    /* actually get the attributes */
    attributes(O,List):-
      write(O," is/has/does: "),
      readln(Attribute),
      Attribute<>"quit",
      add(Attribute,List,List2),
      attributes(O,List2).
    attributes(Object,List):-
      assert(info(Object,List)),
      writelist(List,1),!,
      nl.
```

```
/* add a symbol to a list */
add(X,L,[X|L]).

/* request information from user to
   find an object */
query(L):-
  info(O,A),
  not(member(O,L)), /* not find same one */
  add(O,L,L2),      /* twice */
  trailyes(A),  /* test old yes responses*/
  trailno(A),   /* screen for no responses */
  try(O,A),
  !, write(O," fits the"),nl,
  write("current attributes"),nl,
  write("continue? "),
  readln(Q), Q=y,
  query(L2).

/* screen out all objects that don't have
   the proper attributes as already
   determined */
trailyes(A):-
  yes(T),!,
  xtrailyes(T,A,[]),!.

xtrailyes(end,_,_):-!.
xtrailyes(T,A,L):-
  member(T,A),!,
  add(T,L,L2),
  yes(X),not(member(X,L2)),!,
  xtrailyes(X,A,L2).


/* screen out all objects that have
   attributes already determined as
   not belonging to the object */
trailno(A):-
  no(T),!,
  xtrailno(T,A,[]),!.

xtrailno(end,_,_):-!.
xtrailno(T,A,L):-
  not(member(T,A)),!,
  add(T,L,L2),
  no(X),not(member(X,L2)),!,
  xtrailno(X,A,L2).


/* try a hypothesis */
try(_,[]).
try(O,[X|T]):-
```

```
    yes(X),!,
    try(O,T).
try(O,[X|T]):-
  write("is/has/does it ",X," "),
  readln(Q),
  process(O,X,Q),!,
  try(O,T).

/* process various responses */
process(_,X,y):-
  asserta(yes(X)),!.
process(_,X,n):-
  asserta(no(X)),!,fail.
process(O,X,why):-
  write("I think it may be"), nl,
  write(O," because it has: "),nl,
  yes(Z),xwrite(Z),nl,
  Z=end,!,
  write("is/has/does it ",X,"? "),
  readln(Q),
  process(O,X,Q),!.

xwrite(end).
xwrite(X):-
  write(X).

purge:-
  retract(yes(X)),
  X=end,fail.
purge:-
  retract(no(X)),
  X=end.

append([],List,List).
append([X|L1], List2, [X|L3]) if
  append(L1,List2,L3).

writelist([],_).
writelist([Head|Tail],3):-
  write(Head),nl,writelist(Tail,1).
writelist([Head|Tail],I):-
  N=I+1,
  write(Head," "),writelist(Tail,N).

  member(N,[N|_]).
  member(N,[_|T]):- member(N,T).
```

When the program is now run, the following dialog illustrates the changes:

```
is/has/does it   round y
is/has/does it   red_or_yellow n
is/has/does it   grow_on_trees y
is/has/does it   orange y
orange fits the
current attributes
continue? y
is/has/does it soft_skinned y
tangerine fits the
current attributes
continue? n
```

At this time, you may want to play with this new version a little. Try experimenting with new fruits that have similar definitions. As you will see, the program sometimes appears quite smart.

Knowledge Engineering

The expert system developed in this chapter begins its search with the first entry in the knowledge base, and simply proceeds in sequential order down the list of objects. While this process is fine for small amounts of objects, it could cause problems when you use larger knowledge bases. For example, if there were a thousand objects, and the one that you describe is number 999 and has many common attributes, then this type of expert system could take a very long time to find the solution. Trying to solve this sort of problem, along with others, leads to the field of knowledge engineering.

Knowledge engineering is the discipline that deals with the way that knowledge bases are organized, constructed, and verified. Although it is beyond the scope of this book to present a complete discussion of this topic, it is important to be aware of the difficulties that you can encounter when trying to build a knowledge base. Keep in mind that the field of knowledge engineering is quite young and that there is still a lot to be learned.

Knowledge Base Organization

The expert system developed in this chapter starts at the beginning of the knowledge base and works through it sequentially. Without heuristics, this is the best that you can expect the inference engine to do. However, as the creator of the knowledge base, you can control the organization of the information, which implies that there can be better or worse arrangements.

Often, a good way to organize the information is to place the most likely objects nearest the top and the least likely objects nearest the bottom. The trouble is deciding which objects are the most and least likely. Even a human expert may not know which solutions are most likely. You can sometimes create the knowledge base at random and let it be used for a short period while you record the number of times that each object is selected. Using these frequencies, you can then rearrange the knowledge base.

Another way to organize the information is to place near the top of the knowledge base those attributes that cause the largest part of the "tree" to be pruned. For large knowledge bases, it again may be difficult to determine what attributes have the greatest effect.

Finding the Expert

The one assumption that has been made throughout this chapter is that you can find a human expert and that you can easily extract that expert's knowledge. Unfortunately, this is seldom the case. First, it is often difficult to determine who is or is not a true expert. This is especially a problem when you know little about the subject. Second, two different experts on the same subject often have conflicting opinions —which makes it difficult to know which one to use.

When the opinions of experts differ, you can generally choose from three available options. First, you can select one expert and ignore the other. This is clearly the easiest, but it may mean that the knowledge base may contain some erroneous information. (But the amount of erroneous information is no more than the expert may provide.) A second solution is to *average* the information together: that is, to try to use only information that is common between the experts. Although this option is not as easy as the first, you can occasionally do the process without too much trouble. The disadvantage is that the knowledge base is "watered down" and does not reflect the full knowledge of either expert. The final solution is to include both experts' knowledge in the system and allow the user to decide; you might add a probability factor for each item. Although this may be acceptable in some situations, for many applications, you will want the expert system to be the authority —and you will not want to force the user to decide.

Another trouble spot is that most human experts do not know what they know; humans cannot do a memory dump in the same way that a computer can. Therefore, it can be difficult to extract all of the necessary information. Also, some experts will simply be less willing to spend the time telling you all they know about a topic.

Verifying the Knowledge Base

If you assume that you have found an expert who is cooperative and who gives a complete description of his or her subject of expertise, you are still faced with the problem of verifying that you have transcribed and entered the knowledge into the computer correctly. In essence, this means that you must test the knowledge base. The question is, How do you test a knowledge base?

As was stated in Chapter 1, exhaustive searching is impossible on anything other than extremely small sets of data because of the combinatoric explosion. This means that for most real-world expert systems, there is no way to verify completely that the knowledge base is accurate. Therefore, the best solution is to do sufficient testing so that you can be fairly confident in the knowledge base. By using statistical sampling techniques, you can devise a series of tests that will produce whatever confidence level is desired.

In another approach, you have the system check itself for consistency to see that all of the information in the knowledge base agrees with itself. Although this will not find all problems, it will find some. However, depending upon how this self-check is implemented, in some large knowledge bases, you may reach the combinatoric "brick wall," making this approach impossible.

Thus, as the use of expert systems grows, knowledge base verification will be one of the most important areas of research.

Natural-Language Processing

Many AI professionals believe that the most important task that AI can solve is natural-language processing. The reason for this belief is that, once accomplished, natural-language processing opens the door for direct human-computer dialogs, which would bypass normal programming and operating-system protocol. This means that once a computer can understand and speak a human language, then there would no longer be a need for most tasks to be programmed by software engineers.

As you will see in this chapter, natural-language processing is a "do-able" task, but the sheer size and complexity of human language has kept it from being fully accomplished. Yet, you will be surprised at how simple natural-language processing can be sometimes. You will also come to appreciate the difficulties of making the computer comprehend the meaning of a sentence. This chapter will discuss three general approaches to natural-language processing and develop examples of each approach.

What Is Natural-Language Processing?

As mentioned earlier, natural-language processing, usually abbreviated NLP, tries to make the computer able to understand commands written in standard human languages. (The remainder of this book will assume that English is the human language being processed, but you can apply all of the concepts that are presented to any other language.) A somewhat less important task that NLP tries to perform is to make the computer construct natural language-like responses. After you can make the computer understand natural language, it is a small step to generate responses. This chapter will not be concerned with constructing sentences.

For the most part, speech synthesis and recognition are not actually part of NLP. A natural-language processor does not care how a sentence is input into the computer. Its job is to extract information from that sentence. This chapter will assume that all conversations occur at a terminal.

As you can probably guess, a natural-language processor has no use on its own (except for research). However, NLP can provide front-ends for other computer programs —especially database managers and generalized problem-solvers. Also, many programmers are interested in NLP-driven operating systems, which would virtually eliminate the time that it takes to learn to use a computer. Natural-language processing is necessary to context-sensitive foreign-language translators in order to produce accurate translations. Finally, there is no doubt that NLP is essential to autonomous robots, which must effectively interact with a human world.

Approaches to Natural-Language Processing

Since the field of NLP is quite large, it is hopeless to try to cover all of it in one chapter. Instead, this chapter will focus on three different approaches to natural-language processing.

The core of any NLP system is the parser. The parser is the section of code that actually reads each sentence, word by word, to decide what is what. The three parsers that you will look at are

- State-machine parser
- Context-free recursive-descent parser
- Noise-disposal parser.

Each parser views a sentence differently and each has its own specific applications.

There are two opposite approaches to natural-language processing. One approach actually attempts to use all of the information in a sentence, just as a human would. The goal of this approach is to make the computer capable of carrying on a conversation. As you can guess, this goal is quite difficult to accomplish. The other approach tries to allow the computer to accept natural-language commands, but only to extract the information essential to that command —a much easier task to program. In this chapter, you will see that only one parser has even a chance of reaching the first goal, but that you can use all of them to accomplish the second. This chapter will be concerned only with those techniques that allow natural language to be converted into a form that the computer can use.

Restricting Language

One of the most difficult aspects of constructing an NLP-driven system is accommodating the complexity and flexibility of human language in the system. When you implement a natural-language processor, it is very tempting to try to restrict the type of sentences that the processor will understand to a subset of the natural language. If you restrict the grammar that a processor has to accept, your task becomes much easier and, if done correctly, the restriction is barely noticeable. In any case, it is necessary to restrict the grammar that is accepted by the processors in this chapter. If this is not done, the code to each example could be as long as a chapter. Therefore, for most of the examples in this chapter, assume that all sentences are declarative, and not interrogative. Thus, they generally follow the standard form

subject, *verb*, *object*.

You should also assume that all adjectives precede the noun that they modify, while all adverbs follow the verb that they modify. Finally, you should assume that all sentences must end with a period. Therefore, the following sentences are valid:

The child runs to the house.
The large child runs quickly to the window.

However, the parsers in this chapter will decide that sentences such as

The child quickly runs to the house.

are invalid because the adverb *quickly* precedes the verb *runs*. For the remainder of this chapter, this restricted grammar will be referred to as the G1 grammar.

In addition to these rules, you will need a vocabulary. In order to keep the examples simple, the chapter will keep the number of words to a minimum, but you are free to add to the list if you like. For the examples, the parsers will recognize these words, shown here with their types:

Word	*Type*
door	noun
window	noun
house	noun
child	noun
has	verb
runs	verb
plays	verb
large	adjective
quickly	adverb
the	determiner
a	determiner
to	preposition

The State-Machine NLP Parser

The state-machine parser uses the current state of the sentence to predict what type of word may come next legally. Figure 4-1 shows the state-machine that this chapter will use. A state-machine is a directed graph

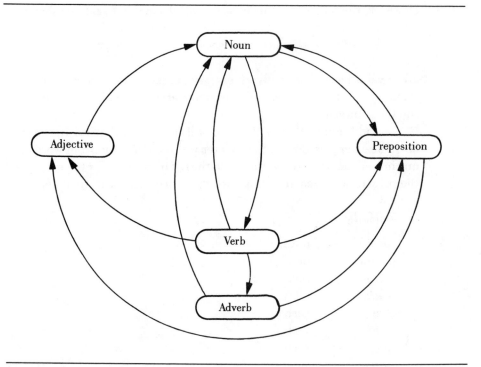

Figure 4-1.   The state-machine of the restricted G1 grammar

that shows the valid transitions from one state to another. For example, a noun can be followed by a verb or a preposition. This state-machine reflects the restricted grammar described earlier. By implementing this state-machine in Turbo Prolog, you can use it to dissect sentences into their components. You can also use it to determine whether a sentence is correctly constructed within the limitations of the G1 grammar.

Before you can implement the state-machine, you must define two databases. The first will hold the vocabulary of the words known to the system with their types. The second will hold the current state of the sentence. Here are the definitions of these databases.

```
database
  word(symbol, symbol)
      /* type, word */
  state(symbol)  /* current state of sentence*/
```

In the **goal** section of the program, each of these databases will be initialized. The program will load the **word** database with the vocabulary, and then will initialize the **state** database to contain the initial value **null**. The **goal** section is shown here:

```
goal
  /* load a small vocabulary */
  assert(word(noun, door)),
  assert(word(noun, window)),
  assert(word(noun, house)),
  assert(word(noun, child)),
  assert(word(verb, has)),
  assert(word(verb, runs)),
  assert(word(verb, plays)),
  assert(word(adjective, large)),
  assert(word(adverb, quickly)),
  assert(word(determiner, the)),
  assert(word(determiner, a)),
  assert(word(preposition, to)),
  /* initialize the state machine database */
  assert(state(null)),
  start.
```

The predicate **start** reads in a sentence entered at the keyboard and calls the routine **parse**, which breaks the sentence into its components. If **parse** returns **true**, then the sentence is correct according to the restricted grammar. If **parse** returns **false**, then the sentence is incorrect. **Start** is shown here:

```
start:-
  write("Enter sentence: "),
  readln(S),
  parse(S),
  write("Sentence OK"),nl,
  purge.
start:-purge.
```

The predicate **purge** clears the databases upon the conclusion of execution.

Before developing the state-machine parser, you will need to create a few predicates that will break a sentence into individual words. Each sentence will be represented as a string of characters. Thus, a new data type, **sentence**, is declared in the **domains** section, as follows.

```
domains
  sentence = string
```

Unfortunately, the built-in predicate **fronttoken** does not allow enough flexibility in certain situations, such as hyphenated words; therefore, you must write some routines to do this. Since you want to extract each word in the sentence one at a time, the first predicate that you need is called **next _word**, and is shown here:

```
next_word(S,S2,W):-
  find_delim(S,Count,0),!,
  Count>0,
  frontstr(Count,S,W,S3),
  strip_space(S3,S2).
```

Next _word is called with three arguments: **S** must contain the current sentence, **S2** will be bound to whatever is left of **S** after the first word is removed, and **W** will contain the word removed: that is, if **S** contains the sentence

This is a test.

then upon return from **next _word**, **S2** will be

is a test.

and **W** will contain *This*. In this way, you can use **next _word** to return each word in the sentence as a symbol. **Next _word** uses the built-in Turbo Prolog predicate **frontstr** to remove the first word from the sentence. However, because **frontstr** removes the first N characters, **next _word** must compute the length of the first word by using **find _ delim**. **Find _ delim** essentially counts characters until it encounters either a space or a period. Remember that, in the restricted grammar, there are no other punctuation marks, so only a period or a space will delimit a word. After you know the length of the word, you can use **frontstr** to remove the word from the sentence. The last step that **next _word** takes is to call **strip _ space**, which is a clean-up procedure that removes any leading spaces from the remaining sentence. The support predicates are shown here:

```
/* find a space or period */
find_delim(S,Count,C):-
  frontchar(S,CH,S2),
  CH<>' ', CH<>'.',
  C2=C+1,
  find_delim(S2,Count,C2).
find_delim(_,Count,Count).


strip_space(S,S2):-
  frontchar(S,Ch,S2),
  Ch=' '.
strip_space(S,S).
```

Now that you have all of the necessary support predicates, the main parser predicate can be written, as shown here:

```
/* check each word for correct order */
parse(S):-
  next_word(S, S2, W),
  state(X),!,
  process(W,X),!,   /* see if each word is in */
  parse(S2).        /* its proper place */
parse(S):-  /* check for proper termination */
  frontchar(S,CH,_),
  CH='.'.
```

As this shows, **parse** is recursive. Each time that it is called, a word from the sentence is removed, and the current state of the machine is determined with the line **state (X)**. This state, along with the current word, is passed to **process**, which is the routine that actually performs the state changes and checks for the legality of each word in relation to the current state. The **process** procedure is shown here:

```
/* Process each new word based on current state.
   Process is called with the current word and state.
   That is, process(word, state).  If the word
   is legal, then the new state is placed into the
   state database and processing continues. */
process(W,_):-
```

```
   word(T,W),
   T=determiner, /* do nothing */
   !.
process(W,null):-
   word(T,W),
   asserta(state(T)),!.
process(W,noun):-
   word(verb,W),
   asserta(state(verb)),!.
process(W,noun):-
   word(preposition, W),
   asserta(state(preposition)).
process(W,verb):-
   word(preposition, W),
   asserta(state(preposition)).
process(W,verb):-
   word(noun,W),
   asserta(state(noun)),!.
process(W,verb):-
   word(adverb,W),
   asserta(state(adverb)),!.
process(W,verb):-
   word(adjective, W),
   asserta(state(adjective)),!.
process(W,adverb):-  /* noun may follow adverb */
   word(noun,W),
   asserta(state(noun)),!.
process(W,adverb):-  /* preposition may follow adverb */
   word(preposition,W),
   asserta(state(preposition)),!.
process(W,adjective):- /* noun must follow adjective */
   word(noun,W),
   asserta(state(noun)),!.
process(W,preposition):-
   word(noun,W),
   asserta(state(noun)),!.
process(W,preposition):-
   word(adjective,W),
   asserta(state(adjective)),!.
process(_,_):-
   write("error in sentence"),
   nl,!,fail.
```

This is the way that **process** works: If the next word in the sentence is anything other than a verb, adverb, noun, adjective, or preposition, the first clause succeeds and no state transition occurs. The second clause starts the state-machine. Because the **state** database initially contains only a null state, and because of the second clause, the first word from the sentence will always cause **process** to return **true**. The rest of the clauses, except the last, are used to perform the proper state transitions. If no other clauses succeed, then the last clause is executed, which reports an error and then fails.

The entire state-machine parser program is shown here. You should enter it into your computer at this time.

```
/* State-machine Natural-Language Parser */
domains
  sentence = string

database
  word(symbol, symbol)
      /* type, word */
  state(symbol)  /* current state of sentence*/
predicates
  next_word(sentence,sentence, symbol)
  find_delim(sentence, integer, integer)
  parse(sentence)
  strip_space(sentence, sentence)
  process(symbol, symbol)
  purge
  start
goal
  /* load a small vocabulary */
  assert(word(noun, door)),
  assert(word(noun, window)),
  assert(word(noun, house)),
  assert(word(noun, child)),
  assert(word(verb, has)),
  assert(word(verb, runs)),
  assert(word(verb, plays)),
  assert(word(adjective, large)),
  assert(word(adverb, quickly)),
  assert(word(determiner, the)),
  assert(word(determiner, a)),
  assert(word(preposition, to)),
  /* initialize the state-machine database */
  assert(state(null)),
  start.
clauses
  start:-
    write("Enter sentence: "),
    readln(S),
    parse(S),
    write("Sentence OK"),nl,
    purge.
  start:-purge.

  /* check each word for correct order */
```

```
parse(S):-
  next_word(S, S2, W),
  state(X),!,
  process(W,X),!,
  parse(S2).
parse(S):-
  frontchar(S,CH,_),
  CH='.'.

/* find a space or period */
find_delim(S,Count,C):-
  frontchar(S,CH,S2),
  CH<>' ', CH<>'.',
  C2=C+1,
  find_delim(S2,Count,C2).
find_delim(_,Count,Count).

next_word(S,S2,W):-
  find_delim(S,Count,0),!,
  Count>0,
  frontstr(Count,S,W,S3),
  strip_space(S3,S2).

strip_space(S,S2):-
  frontchar(S,Ch,S2),
  Ch=' '.
strip_space(S,S).

/* Process each new word based on current state.
   Process is called with the current word and state.
   That is, process(word, state).  If the word
   is legal, then the new state is placed into the
   state database and processing continues. */
process(W,_):-
  word(T,W),
  T=determiner, /* do nothing */
  !.
process(W,null):-
  word(T,W),
  asserta(state(T)),!.
process(W,noun):-
  word(verb,W),
  asserta(state(verb)),!.
process(W,noun):-
  word(preposition, W),
  asserta(state(preposition)).
process(W,verb):-
  word(preposition, W),
  asserta(state(preposition)).
process(W,verb):-
  word(noun,W),
  asserta(state(noun)),!.
```

```
process(W,verb):-
  word(adverb,W),
  asserta(state(adverb)),!.
process(W,verb):-
  word(adjective, W),
  asserta(state(adjective)),!.
process(W,adverb):-  /* noun may follow adverb */
  word(noun,W),
  asserta(state(noun)),!.
process(W,adverb):-  /* preposition may follow adverb */
  word(preposition,W),
  asserta(state(preposition)),!.
process(W,adjective):- /* noun must follow adjective */
  word(noun,W),
  asserta(state(noun)),!.
process(W,preposition):-
  word(noun,W),
  asserta(state(noun)),!.
process(W,preposition):-
  word(adjective,W),
  asserta(state(adjective)),!.
process(_,_):-
  write("error in sentence"),
  nl,!,fail.

purge:-  /* purge state */
  retract(state(_)) ,fail.
purge.
```

If you run this program, you will find that it will accept correctly constructed sentences that use the vocabulary words, assuming the G1 grammar. To see how it operates, work through a simple example by using the sentence

the child runs quickly to the large house.

The diagram of the sentence shown here verifies that it follows the restricted grammar:

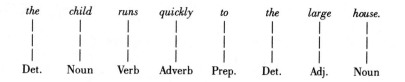

the	child	runs	quickly	to	the	large	house.
Det.	Noun	Verb	Adverb	Prep.	Det.	Adj.	Noun

Try to remember the state-machine that was presented in Figure 4-1 while you work through this sentence in the same way that the state-machine parser does. The first word extracted is *the*. Since this word is a determiner, the parser discards it and no state changes take place. The next word is *child*, a noun, which succeeds on the second clause because the initial state is null. This causes the current state of the machine to become **noun**. The state-machine has now been started. The next word is the verb *runs*. As you saw in Figure 4-1, there are two possible transitions from a noun: to a verb or to a preposition. Because *runs* is a verb, this transition succeeds and places the new state **verb** into the **state** database; that is, the state-machine is now at the node **verb**.

The next word is the adverb *quickly*. Looking at the state-machine in Figure 4-1, you can see that one valid transition from **verb** is **adverb**, so the appropriate clause succeeds, placing the system at the state **adverb**. After **adverb**, there are only two states that can follow: **noun** or **preposition**. The next word in the sentence is the preposition *to*, which causes a transition to state **preposition**; this state must be followed by either a noun or an adjective. The next word is the determiner *the*, which the parser throws away and which causes no state change. Then comes the adjective *large*, which causes a transition to **adjective**. The state **adjective** may only be followed by **noun**, which is what happens when *house* is parsed. Thus, the sentence is fully parsed.

To see what happens with a poorly written sentence, consider

the house child runs to the.

Here, there are two nouns back to back. When the parser encounters the first noun, the state-machine is placed into the **noun** state. According to the G1 grammar of the state-machine, the only valid transitions from **noun** are to either **verb** or **preposition**. Because the noun *child* follows, none of the state transition clauses of **process** succeed, leaving only the last, which is the error clause, to execute and report the error.

Try several sentences to see the effect. Remember that this state-machine is very crude and does not recognize all of the subtleties of real English, so you will be able to confuse it easily.

Analysis of the State-Machine
NLP Parser

As applied to natural language, the worst problem with the state-machine parser is its complexity. Even for the simple G1 grammar that you have been working with, you need 14 separate clauses to perform the state transitions. Although it is sometimes possible to collapse one state into another, try to imagine how many different states there would be for the entire English grammar. For this reason, state-machine parsers are never used except in situations that can utilize a strict subset of the grammar.

Another problem with state-machine parsers is that the parser does not "know" how it got to any particular state: it cannot relate a modifying phrase to a specific noun, for example. This means that you cannot call on a state-machine parser to supply any information other than its current state.

On the positive side, state-machine parsers are ideal for certain specific applications, such as operating system job-control languages and some database applications. In these environments you need only make certain that the user enters the commands in a valid format and that the computer knows each word. State-machine parsers work here because there are few valid types of sentences and, thus few states.

The Context-Free Recursive-Descent
NLP Parser

To understand context-free parsers, you must look at the construction of a sentence in a completely different way from the way that you did for the state-machine model. For the context-free parser, think of a sentence as being composed of various items, which themselves are composed of other items, and so forth until you break the sentence down to its atomic elements —noun, verb, adjective, and so on. The rules that govern how each of the parts may be constructed are called the production rules of the grammar. A context-free parser uses these production rules to analyze a sentence.

SENTENCE → NP + VP

NP → determiner + noun
NP → determiner + adjective + noun
NP → preposition + NP

VP → verb + NP
VP → verb + adverb + NP
VP → verb + adverb
VP → verb

Figure 4-2. Production rules for the G1 grammar

Figure 4-2 shows the production rules for the G1 grammar. Read the right arrow as "produces." In this figure, *NP* stands for "noun phrase," and VP stands for "verb phrase." The noun phrase is a recursive definition for a prepositional clause, and the verb phrase is indirectly recursive because it evokes a noun phrase as part of its definition.

To see how these rules can be applied to a sentence, consider this diagram:

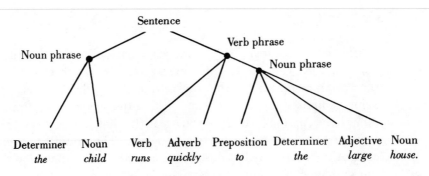

The production rules form a sort of tree. This tree is often referred to as a parse tree because it represents the way that the parser sees the sentence.

A parser that generates this type of parse tree is called "context-free" because the tree is not based upon the context of each element: this means that the rules will work for any sentence that conforms to the G1 grammar without any regard to the context of each phrase.

Here are some points to help you to understand the implications of a context-free parser. Context-free parsing is used not only by AI NLP programs, but also by virtually all computer languages. For example, you can parse languages such as Pascal, BASIC, C, Modula-2, and others with a context-free parser. The fact that you can represent even a subset of English by using production rules that a context-free parser can parse has enormous implications. First, it asserts that, in some ways, English conforms to a strict set of rules —that is, English is not just a jumble of disconnected arbitrary restrictions. Second, it lets you apply to natural language some well-understood parsing techniques that were developed for computer languages —you do not have to reinvent the wheel. Finally, because the context-free production rules are organized from phrases down to the words that actually comprise them, it is very easy to extract not only individual words, but also whole phrases. Thus, you can parse phrases as well as individual words —and know where each phrase came from. This gives you the basis from which semantic information may be gathered, which is a big step forward from the state-machine parser.

There are many ways to implement a context-free parser that uses the production rules given earlier. However, the easiest, especially when you use Turbo Prolog, is to create what is called a recursive-descent parser. A recursive-descent parser uses a collection of mutually recursive routines that *descend down* through the production rules until the sentence is completely parsed.

To create a context-free recursive-descent parser, you will use the same vocabulary database and the support predicates to extract words from a sentence as the state-machine parser used, but you will not need the additional database **state**. If you assume these routines, here is the context-free recursive-descent parser:

```
/* parse the sentence */
parse(S):-
  noun_phrase(S,S2),
  verb_phrase(S2,S3),
  terminator(S3).
/* find each piece */
noun_phrase(S,S2):- /* no adjective */
  next_word(S,S1,W),
  word(determiner,W),
  next_word(S1,S2,W2),
  word(noun,W2).
noun_phrase(S,S3):- /* with adjective */
  next_word(S,S1,W),
  word(determiner,W),
  next_word(S1,S2,W2),
  word(adjective,W2),
  next_word(S2,S3,W3),
  word(noun,W3).
noun_phrase(S,S2):- /* prepositional phrases */
  next_word(S,S1,W),
  word(preposition, W),
  noun_phrase(S1,S2).

verb_phrase(S,S3):- /* verb + adverb + NP */
  next_word(S,S1,W),
  word(verb, W),
  next_word(S1,S2,A),
  word(adverb, A),
  noun_phrase(S2,S3).
verb_phrase(S,S2):- /*  verb + NP */
  next_word(S,S1,W),
  word(verb, W),
  noun_phrase(S1,S2).
verb_phrase(S,S2):- /* verb + adverb  - no NP*/
  next_word(S,S1,W),
  word(verb, W),
  next_word(S1,S2,W2),
  word(adverb, W2).
verb_phrase(S,S2):- /* only verb - no NP */
  next_word(S,S2,W),
  word(verb, W).

/* find period */
terminator(S):-
  frontchar(S,CH,_),
  CH='.'.
```

The parser operates as follows. At the top-most level, a sentence is comprised of a noun phrase, a verb phrase, and, in this case, a period as a terminator. Therefore, the predicate **parse** calls the routine **noun _ phrase**, followed by **verb _ phrase**. If you assume that these succeed, which implies that the sentence does meet the G1 grammar rules, then the parser calls **terminator** to confirm that the sentence ends in a period. The support predicates **noun _ phrase** and **verb _ phrase** implement the context-free rules in the exact way that was described earlier. If a sentence does not conform to these rules, then either **noun _ phrase** or **verb _ phrase** will fail, which causes the sentence to be rejected.

To see exactly how the parser works, follow the way it processes this sample sentence:

the child runs quickly to the large house.

First, **parse** calls **noun _ phrase**. In the case of this sentence, the first clause succeeds because it finds both the determiner *the* and the noun *child*. Then, **parse** calls **verb _ phrase**. The first clause also succeeds because the verb *runs* is followed by the adverb *quickly*, which is followed by the prepositional noun phrase *to the large house*. This phrase fails on both the first clause and the second clause of **noun _ phrase** because it begins with the preposition *to*. However, it succeeds with the third clause, which causes **noun _ phrase** to be called recursively. This time, the second clause of **noun _ phrase** succeeds. After this, all of the recursive calls unravel and **verb _ phrase** succeeds, so that it returns to **parse**. The last step in the process is to confirm a period by using **terminator**. Finally, **parse** succeeds. This process tells you that the sentence does, indeed, satisfy the rules of the restricted grammar.

The entire program for the context-free recursive-descent NLP parser is shown here. You should enter this into your computer and try it with several sentences to understand its operation better. You may also find it interesting to trace the execution of **noun _ phrase** and **verb _ phrase**.

```
/* Context-free Natural Language
   Recursive-Descent Parser */
domains
  sentence = string

database
  word(symbol, symbol)
      /* type, word */
```

```
predicates
  next_word(sentence,sentence, symbol)
  find_delim(sentence, integer, integer)
  parse(sentence)
  strip_space(sentence, sentence)
  start
  noun_phrase(sentence, sentence)
  verb_phrase(sentence, sentence)
  terminator(sentence)
goal
  /* load a small vocabulary */
  assert(word(noun, door)),
  assert(word(noun, window)),
  assert(word(noun, house)),
  assert(word(noun, child)),
  assert(word(verb, has)),
  assert(word(verb, runs)),
  assert(word(verb, plays)),
  assert(word(adjective, large)),
  assert(word(adverb, quickly)),
  assert(word(determiner, "and")),
  assert(word(determiner, the)),
  assert(word(determiner, a)),
  assert(word(preposition, to)),
  start.
clauses
  start:-
    write("Enter sentence: "),
    readln(S),
    parse(S),!,
    write("Sentence OK"),nl.
  start:-
    write("Sentence in error"),nl.

  /* parse the sentence */
  parse(S):-
    noun_phrase(S,S2),
    verb_phrase(S2,S3),
    terminator(S3).

  /* find each piece */
  noun_phrase(S,S2):- /* no adjective */
    next_word(S,S1,W),
    word(determiner,W),
    next_word(S1,S2,W2),
    word(noun,W2).
  noun_phrase(S,S3):- /* with adjective */
    next_word(S,S1,W),
    word(determiner,W),
    next_word(S1,S2,W2),
    word(adjective,W2),
```

```
   next_word(S2,S3,W3),
   word(noun,W3).
noun_phrase(S,S2):- /* prepositional phrases */
   next_word(S,S1,W),
   word(preposition, W),
   noun_phrase(S1,S2).

verb_phrase(S,S3):- /* verb + adverb + NP */
   next_word(S,S1,W),
   word(verb, W),
   next_word(S1,S2,A),
   word(adverb, A),
   noun_phrase(S2,S3).
verb_phrase(S,S2):- /* verb + NP  */
   next_word(S,S1,W),
   word(verb, W),
   noun_phrase(S1,S2).
verb_phrase(S,S2):- /* only verb + adverb */
   next_word(S,S1,W),
   word(verb, W),
   next_word(S1,S2,W2),
   word(adverb, W2).
verb_phrase(S,S2):- /* only verb */
   next_word(S,S2,W),
   word(verb, W).

/* find period */
terminator(S):-
   frontchar(S,CH,_),
   CH='.'.

/* find space */
find_delim(S,Count,C):-
   frontchar(S,CH,S2),
   CH<>' ', CH<>'.',
   C2=C+1,
   find_delim(S2,Count,C2).
find_delim(_,Count,Count).

/* get one word at a time */
next_word(S,S2,W):-
   find_delim(S,Count,0),!,
   Count>0,
   frontstr(Count,S,W,S3),
   strip_space(S3,S2).

strip_space(S,S2):-
   frontchar(S,Ch,S2),
   Ch=' '.
strip_space(S,S).
```

By slightly modifying **parse**, **noun ___ phrase**, and **verb ___ phrase**, you can use these routines to dissect sentences into their component phrases. Unlike the state-machine parser that could only deal with words, the context-free recursive-descent parser can be used to extract phrases. This is important because it opens the door to having the computer actually comprehend, rather than simply verify, a sentence: it lets the computer work with related groups of words. If you include the code that follows here to the program just given, it will return both the noun phrase and the verb phrase for a sentence. The parser returns the phrases in a list format, which makes further processing easy. The support predicates **add** and **append** are also included. These are used to add an element to a list and to append two lists together.

```
parse(S):-
  noun_phrase(S,S2,NP),
  write("noun phrase is ",NP),nl,
  verb_phrase(S2,S3,VP),
  write("verb phrase is ",VP),nl,
  terminator(S3).

/* get each piece */
noun_phrase(S,S2,NP):- /* no adjective */
  next_word(S,S1,W),
  word(determiner,W),
  add(W,[],T),
  next_word(S1,S2,W2),
  word(noun,W2),
  append(T,[W2],NP).
noun_phrase(S,S3,NP):- /* with adjective */
  next_word(S,S1,W),
  word(determiner,W),
  add(W,[],T),
  next_word(S1,S2,W2),
  word(adjective,W2),
  append(T,[W2],T2),
  next_word(S2,S3,W3),
  word(noun,W3),
  append(T2,[W3],NP).
noun_phrase(S,S2,NP):- /* prepositional phrases */
  next_word(S,S1,W),
  word(preposition, W),
  noun_phrase(S1,S2,T),
  append([W],T,NP).

verb_phrase(S,S3,VP):- /* verb + adverb + NP*/
  next_word(S,S1,W),
```

```
    word(verb, W),
    next_word(S1,S2,A),
    word(adverb, A),
    noun_phrase(S2,S3,T),
    append([A],T,T2),
    append([W],T2,VP).
verb_phrase(S,S2,VP):- /* verb + NP */
    next_word(S,S1,W),
    word(verb, W),
    noun_phrase(S1,S2,T),
    append([W],T,VP).
verb_phrase(S,S2,VP):- /* only verb + adverb */
    next_word(S,S1,W),
    word(verb, W),
    next_word(S1,S2,A),
    word(adverb, A),
    add(W,[],T),
    append(T,[A],VP).
verb_phrase(S,S2,VP):- /* only verb */
    next_word(S,S2,W),
    word(verb, W),
    add(W,[],VP).

/* add a symbol to a list */
add(X,L,[X|L]).

/* append two lists */
append([],List,List).
append([X|L1], List2, [X|L3]):-
    append(L1,List2,L3).
```

Here is the complete program, which uses this version of the parser:

```
/* Context-free Natural Language
   Recursive-Descent Parser #2 */
domains
  sentence = string
  list = symbol*
database
  word(symbol, symbol)
      /* type, word */
predicates
  next_word(sentence,sentence, symbol)
  find_delim(Sentence, integer, integer)
  parse(sentence)
  strip_space(sentence, sentence)
  start
  noun_phrase(sentence, sentence, list)
  verb_phrase(sentence, sentence, list)
  terminator(sentence)
```

```
        add(symbol, list, list)
        append(list, list, list)
goal
    /* load a small vocabulary */
    assert(word(noun, door)),
    assert(word(noun, window)),
    assert(word(noun, house)),
    assert(word(noun, child)),
    assert(word(verb, has)),
    assert(word(verb, runs)),
    assert(word(verb, plays)),
    assert(word(adjective, large)),
    assert(word(adverb, quickly)),
    assert(word(determiner, "and")),
    assert(word(determiner, the)),
    assert(word(determiner, a)),
    assert(word(preposition, to)),
    start.
clauses
    start:-
      write("Enter sentence: "),
      readln(S),
      parse(S),
      write("Sentence OK"),nl.
    start:-
      write("Sentence in error"),nl.

    parse(S):-
      noun_phrase(S,S2,NP),
      write("noun phrase is ",NP),nl,
      verb_phrase(S2,S3,VP),
      write("verb phrase is ",VP),nl,
      terminator(S3).

    /* get each piece */
    noun_phrase(S,S2,NP):- /* no adjective */
      next_word(S,S1,W),
      word(determiner,W),
      add(W,[],T),
      next_word(S1,S2,W2),
      word(noun,W2),
      append(T,[W2],NP).
    noun_phrase(S,S3,NP):- /* with adjective */
      next_word(S,S1,W),
      word(determiner,W),
      add(W,[],T),
      next_word(S1,S2,W2),
      word(adjective,W2),
      append(T,[W2],T2),
      next_word(S2,S3,W3),
      word(noun,W3),
      append(T2,[W3],NP).
```

```
noun_phrase(S,S2,NP):- /* prepositional phrases */
  next_word(S,S1,W),
  word(preposition, W),
  noun_phrase(S1,S2,T),
  append([W],T,NP).

verb_phrase(S,S3,VP):- /*  verb + adverb + NP */
  next_word(S,S1,W),
  word(verb, W),
  next_word(S1,S2,A),
  word(adverb, A),
  noun_phrase(S2,S3,T),
  append([A],T,T2),
  append([W],T2,VP).
verb_phrase(S,S2,VP):- /* verb + NP  */
  next_word(S,S1,W),
  word(verb, W),
  noun_phrase(S1,S2,T),
  append([W],T,VP).
verb_phrase(S,S2,VP):- /* only verb + adverb */
  next_word(S,S1,W),
  word(verb, W),
  next_word(S1,S2,A),
  word(adverb, A),
  add(W,[],T),
  append(T,[A],VP).
verb_phrase(S,S2,VP):- /* only verb */
  next_word(S,S2,W),
  word(verb, W),
  add(W,[],VP).

terminator(S):-
  frontchar(S,CH,_),
  CH='.'.

/* find a space or period */
find_delim(S,Count,C):-
  frontchar(S,CH,S2),
  CH<>' ', CH<>'.',
  C2=C+1,
  find_delim(S2,Count,C2).
find_delim(_,Count,Count).

/* get the next word */
next_word(S,S2,W):-
  find_delim(S,Count,0),!,
  Count>0,
  frontstr(Count,S,W,S3),
  strip_space(S3,S2).

strip_space(S,S2):-
  frontchar(S,Ch,S2),
```

```
  Ch=' '.
strip_space(S,S).

/* add a symbol to a list */
add(X,L,[X|L]).

append([],List,List).
append([X|L1], List2, [X|L3]):-
  append(L1,List2,L3).
```

If you use this version of the parser, then with the input sentence

the child runs quickly to the house.

you will see this output display on your screen:

```
noun phrase: ["the","child"]
verb phrase: ["runs","quickly","to","the","house"]
```

Analysis of the Context-Free
Recursive-Descent NLP Parser

Context-free parsing has a lot of advantages. First, it is easy to implement in Turbo Prolog. Second, it can deal with a sentence on both the word level and the phrase level. Third, it "knows" where it is in the sentence at all times. This is different from the state-machine example, which had no idea of where it actually was in a sentence.

The main disadvantage with context-free parsing is that it cannot handle the numerous valid ways that an English sentence can be constructed. When you used the simple restricted grammar given earlier, it was easy to define a set of production rules that fully described that grammar. However, in real-world English (or any other language), the rules would be very complex. These rules could lead to a combinatoric explosion, which would make this method impossible to use. However, this is only a possibility — no one has yet proven it.

Noise-Disposal Parsers

Certain applications are only concerned with a few keywords that a sentence contains and are not concerned with all the associative words that make up a language. In essence, these types of applications are interested only in the information that the sentence contains. This idea leads to a variation of the context-free parser. In this variation, called the noise-disposal parser, all words that are not known or required are simply treated as noise and discarded. Typically, all sentences must follow a rigid format that resembles natural language.

This type of parser is actually quite common in database-type applications, such as a command processor. For example, consider a database that consists of company names and their respective stock prices. Assume that the database will accept queries such as the following:

> *show me all companies with stock prices $>$ 100.*
> *show me all.*
> *show me XYZ.*
> *show me one with stock price $<$ 100.*

As you can see, these types of queries all fit the following basic template:

> *command $<$modifier$>$ $<$name$>$ $<$operator$>$ $<$value$>$.*

Here, the *command* must always be present, but the other four elements are optional. However, note that if the operator is present, then the value must be present as well. As long as the necessary elements are present, it does not matter how many noise words are present because they have no effect.

To see an example of such a parser, you must first define a small database so that you can interrogate it. This database is called **stock** and its definition is

```
stock(symbol, integer)
/*    name,    price */
```

Next, you will need a list of words and symbols that can be used in a valid command. This example will use this list:

Word	Type
show	command
xyz	name
abc	name
ucl	name
all	modifier
one	modifier
>	operator
<	operator

Here, *xyz*, *abc*, and *ucl* are company names.

The **goal** section of the program loads the **stock** database and the **word** database, as shown here:

```
/* load a small set of valid commands */
assert(word(command, show)),
assert(word(name, xyz)),
assert(word(name, abc)),
assert(word(name, ucl)),
assert(word(modifier, all)),
assert(word(modifier, one)),
assert(word(operator, ">")),
assert(word(operator, "<")),
/* load stocks and prices */
assert(stock(end, 0)),
asserta(stock(xyz, 100)),
asserta(stock(abc, 35)),
asserta(stock(ucl, 123)),
start.
```

Notice that the sentinel **end** marks the end of the **stock** database. You will see how it is used later.

The parser is similar to the context-free parser developed in the previous section, except that it only enforces the order of the command sentence, while it discards all unnecessary words. The top level of the parser is called **process** because it is designed to be used only as a command processor for the **stock** database. It is shown here:

```
/* parse the command line */
process(S):-
  get_command(S,S2,C),
  get_modifier(S2,S3,M),
  get_name(S3,S4,N),
  get_quantity(S4,S5,O,Q),
  terminator(S5),
  perform(C,M,N,O,Q).
```

Process parses a command sentence as if it were made up of four distinct parts: the command itself, a modifier, a name, and a quantifier. All commands must end in a period. After the parser parses all pieces of the command, **perform** actually performs the command specified. The support predicates are shown here:

```
get_command(S,S2,C):-
  next_word(S,S2,C),
  word(command,C).
get_command(S,S2,C):-
  get_noise(S,S1,_),
  get_command(S1,S2,C).

get_modifier(S,S2,M):-
  next_word(S,S2,M),
  word(modifier,M).
get_modifier(S,S2,M):-
  get_noise(S,S1,_),
  get_modifier(S1,S2,M).
get_modifier(S,S2,M):-
  S2=S,
  M=all.   /* default to all */

get_name(S,S2,N):-
  next_word(S,S2,N),
  word(name,N).
get_name(S,S2,N):-
  get_noise(S,S1,_),
  get_name(S1,S2,N).
get_name(S,S,N):-
  N=none.   /* default to none */

get_quantity(S,S2,O,Q):-
```

```
      next_word(S,S1,0),
      word(operator,0),
      next_word(S1,S2,Q).
get_quantity(S,S2,0,Q):-
      get_noise(S,S1,_),
      get_quantity(S1,S2,0,Q).
get_quantity(S,S,0,Q):-
      Q=none, O=none.  /* default to none */

/* dispose of noise word */
get_noise(S,S2,X):-
      next_word(S,S2,X),
      not(word(_,X)).
```

These routines all are recursive when they encounter noise words.
Notice that optional parts of the command syntax have default cases.
This structure is necessary to maintain a consistent interface to the
routines that actually execute the commands.

The entire program is shown here. You should enter it into your
computer at this time.

```
/* Command Parser with Noise Disposal */
domains
   sentence = string
   list = symbol*

database
   word(symbol, symbol)
       /* type, word */
   stock(symbol, integer)
   /*    name,   price */

predicates
   next_word(sentence,sentence, symbol)
   find_delim(sentence, integer, integer)
   strip_space(sentence, sentence)
   start
   process(sentence)
   get_command(sentence, sentence, symbol)
   get_name(sentence, sentence, symbol)
   get_quantity(sentence, sentence, symbol, symbol)
   get_modifier(sentence, sentence, symbol)
   get_noise(sentence, sentence, symbol)
   terminator(sentence)
   perform(symbol, symbol, symbol, symbol, symbol)
   purge
goal
```

```
/* load a small set of valid commands */
assert(word(command, show)),
assert(word(name, xyz)),
assert(word(name, abc)),
assert(word(name, ucl)),
assert(word(modifier, all)),
assert(word(modifier, one)),
assert(word(operator, ">")),
assert(word(operator, "<")),
/* load stocks and prices */
assert(stock(end, 0)),
asserta(stock(xyz, 100)),
asserta(stock(abc, 35)),
asserta(stock(ucl, 123)),
start.
clauses
start:-
  write("?: "),
  readln(S),
  process(S), purge.
start:-
  write("command error"),nl,
  purge.

/* parse the command line */
process(S):-
  get_command(S,S2,C),
  get_modifier(S2,S3,M),
  get_name(S3,S4,N),
  get_quantity(S4,S5,O,Q),
  terminator(S5),
  perform(C,M,N,O,Q).

/* simple context-free parser */
get_command(S,S2,C):-
  next_word(S,S2,C),
  word(command,C).
get_command(S,S2,C):-
  get_noise(S,S1,_),
  get_command(S1,S2,C).

get_modifier(S,S2,M):-
  next_word(S,S2,M),
  word(modifier,M).
get_modifier(S,S2,M):-
  get_noise(S,S1,_),
  get_modifier(S1,S2,M).
get_modifier(S,S2,M):-
  S2=S,
  M=all.  /* default to all */

get_name(S,S2,N):-
```

```
  next_word(S,S2,N),
  word(name,N).
get_name(S,S2,N):-
  get_noise(S,S1,_),
  get_name(S1,S2,N).
get_name(S,S,N):-
  N=none.

get_quantity(S,S2,O,Q):-
  next_word(S,S1,O),
  word(operator,O),
  next_word(S1,S2,Q).
get_quantity(S,S2,O,Q):-
  get_noise(S,S1,_),
  get_quantity(S1,S2,O,Q).
get_quantity(S,S,O,Q):-
  Q=none, O=none.

/* dispose of noise word */
get_noise(S,S2,X):-
  next_word(S,S2,X),
  not(word(_,X)).

/* find a space */
terminator(S):-
  frontchar(S,CH,_),
  CH='.'.


/* do the command */
perform(show,_,N,none,_):-
  stock(N,P),
  write(N," ",P),nl.
perform(show,all,_,">",Q):-
  stock(N,P),
  str_int(Q,I),
  P>I,
  write(N," ",P),nl,
  N=end.
perform(show, one,_,">",Q):-
  stock(N,P),
  str_int(Q,I),
  P>I,
  write(N," ",P).
perform(show,all,_,"<",Q):-
  stock(N,P),
  str_int(Q,I),
  P<I,P<>0,
  write(N," ",P),nl,
  N=end.
perform(show, one,_,"<",Q):-
```

```
    stock(N,P),
    str_int(Q,I),
    P<I,P<>0,
    write(N," ",P).
perform(show, all,_,none,_):-
    stock(N,P),
    write(N," ",P),nl,
    N=end.
perform(_,_,_,_,_).   /* do nothing */

/* find a space or period */
find_delim(S,Count,C):-
  frontchar(S,CH,S2),
  CH<>' ', CH<>'.',
  C2=C+1,
  find_delim(S2,Count,C2).
find_delim(_,Count,Count).

/* get the next word */
next_word(S,S2,W):-
  find_delim(S,Count,0),!,
  Count>0,
  frontstr(Count,S,W,S3),
  strip_space(S3,S2).

strip_space(S,S2):-
  frontchar(S,Ch,S2),
  Ch=' '.
strip_space(S,S).

purge:-
  retract(stock(_,_)),fail.
purge:-
  retract(word(_,_)), fail.
purge.
```

When run, this program will correctly interpret the following queries and respond as shown here:

```
show me all companies with prices > 100.
uc1 123

show me all.
uc1 123
abc  35
xyz 100
end   0
please show me one with a price of < 50.
abc  35
```

The second query also displays the end marker of the database, which indicates that all companies have been shown. Although this simple database only has one command for simplicity, it would be easy to add others.

Analysis of the Noise-Disposal Parser

One disadvantage to a noise-disposal parser is that it is not useful outside of restricted situations, such as the database example just given, because it is based upon two assumptions. The first assumption is that the sentence follows a strict format. The second assumption is that only a few key words or symbols are important. As you know, in actual conversation, most of the words are important in some way or another.

A second disadvantage is that, in many situations, it accepts bizarre sentences, such as

the big pig show house all > 100.

This type of disadvantage does not tend to inspire confidence in the program.

The principal advantages of a noise-disposal parser are that it is simple to implement and that it gets to the information in the message quickly. In fact, there is no doubt that any successful NLP system will have at least some noise-disposal system.

5

Vision And Pattern Recognition

If a computer is to interface completely with the human world, clearly some sort of vision capability is required. In the case of an autonomous robot, vision is indispensable. Although the actual process of digitizing a television camera's signal is not part of AI, the process of interpreting those signals is. As you will see, there are several ways in which the computer can interpret those images.

Do not be concerned if you do not have a vision system connected to your computer. You will not need one for any of the examples in this chapter. Since this chapter does not cover the actual capturing of a television signal, but does cover the recognition of various patterns, you will be simulating a digitized signal for the examples.

Often the term *image processing* describes the fairly broad field of vision, pattern recognition, and image enhancement. The reason that the field is so large is that it encompasses two major subdivisions. The first subdivision is two-dimensional processing and the second subdivision is three-dimensional processing (sometimes called real-world processing). Before you can develop Turbo Prolog programs to recognize various objects, you should have a general idea of some of the key topics and problems of image processing and pattern recognition.

Filtering, Contrast, and Shading

Generally, there are two methods by which vision systems are implemented. In the first method, the goal is to reduce an image to the lines that form the outline of each object. This method uses both various filters to remove information from the image and contrast enhancers to make all parts of the image either black or white. This is sometimes called a binary image because there are no gray areas — every point in the image is either black or white.

The actual production of a binary image is generally left to a preprocessor, which is not concerned with any interpretation of the image. Although filtering of images can be done digitally, it is common in simple systems to do it by using analog circuits that produce high-contrast images similar to the one that you can create by turning the contrast control on your television set up all the way while you reduce the brightness control. However, this chapter will not cover image reduction.

The advantage of binary images is that they provide strictly defined boundaries that a computer can easily recognize by using fairly simple algorithms. In other words, it is clear where each object begins and ends. High-contrast imaging is most common in controlled environments where it is known in advance that only a few selected objects are to be viewed. For the most part, this is the type of implementation used by two-dimensional image-processing systems.

The second method by which vision systems are implemented attempts to give the computer a more humanlike view of the image. This method gives information about the brightness of part of the image to the computer. This allows two important features to be derived from the image that are not possible with a high-contrast image: surfaces and shadows. The computer can use both of these to provide three-dimensional information about images and to help resolve conflicts when one object partially blocks another. This type of imaging is usually used by three-dimensional vision systems.

Color Versus Black and White

Virtually all vision systems use black-and-white images instead of color for two reasons: first, color is not generally necessary and, second, the addition of color information places even greater demands upon both the computer and the software that are processing the image. Given the current and expected near-term state of vision technology, this situation is not likely to change. Therefore, this chapter will assume that all images are black and white.

Two-Dimensional Systems

Two-dimensional vision systems require a strictly controlled and constrained environment in order to function properly because they process all images as if the images were flat. In fact, two-dimensional image processing is sometimes called flat-image processing for this reason. Because only two dimensions are represented, a high-contrast binary image is generally used. This causes objects to be reduced to their outlines. Two-dimensional systems are quite common in such environments as automated assembly lines, where the orientation, location, or recognition of certain specific two-dimensional shapes is of interest.

Keep in mind that the actual objects that are viewed need not be flat, but are, in fact, usually three-dimensional. The only requirement of a two-dimensional system is that the three-dimensional image can be reduced to a two-dimensional image without losing its identity. For example, imagine a toy factory that manufactures only four kinds of blocks: squares, rectangles, triangles, and cylinders. As the blocks are made, they are placed on a conveyor belt for automated sorting. A TV camera that is mounted above the conveyor belt feeds a two-dimensional, top-view image of each block to a computer. It decides what type each block is and orders it to be placed in the correct bin. Figure 5-1 illustrates this situation.

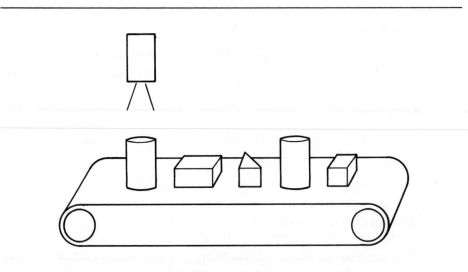

Figure 5-1. A two-dimensional vision-controlled sorting line

Figure 5-2. The computer's view of the blocks

As each block passes before the camera, its three-dimensional shape is reduced to the two dimensions that form its top view. Figure 5-2 shows the image that the computer sees. Even though one entire dimension has been discarded, there is still sufficient information for the computer to recognize each block correctly.

Keep in mind that it is essential to the success of a simple two-dimensional vision processor that the objects viewed be strictly controlled and that variations do not occur. For instance, if you fed the block sorter a pyramid with a square base, its two-dimensional image would appear as a square and it would be placed in the square's bin. If it became necessary to recognize such a pyramid, then either you would have to alter the camera's position or you would have to use a second two-dimensional system to take side views as well.

A common problem with two-dimensional systems is that a system may have difficulty recognizing an object when it is partially blocked or covered by another object. Because third-dimensional information is unavailable, the computer is given what appears to be conflicting or erroneous information and it may not always be able to resolve such a conflict correctly. As you will see in the programs given later, the way that the recognition routine is implemented controls what types of situations the computer can handle. To understand this problem, imagine that a triangular block was accidentally placed on top of a square block on the conveyor belt of the toy manufacturer. The computer would see the following:

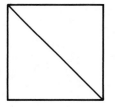

The computer cannot distinguish between two triangles next to each other that form a square shape, and, as is the case, a triangle on top of a square. Such problems lead to the use of three-dimensional imaging.

Three-Dimensional Systems

Basically, the goal of three-dimensional vision systems is to handle correctly all viewing problems that are generated by objects that interfere with — by being, for example, on top of or in front of — another object. A secondary goal is to be able to extract topographical information from an image — for instance, to allow a computer program to generate geophysical maps of the country. Three-dimensional image processing is at the forefront of AI technology because there are substantial problems that must be overcome before programmers can implement a three-dimensional vision system.

You may be surprised to learn that one-camera vision systems are sufficient for many applications that require three-dimensional information. To understand why, close one eye for a moment and look around. You can still easily recognize the objects around you. The reason for this is simple to explain but difficult to implement on a computer. You can still see with only one eye because your vision contains much more information than just the boundary lines of objects. It has information about color, shading, brightness, and distance. You still have a three-dimensional view of the world with only one eye because you can rely on the other information (at least partially) to make up for the loss of binocular vision. The rest of this discussion will assume that only one camera is used.

Three-dimensional systems must overcome several problems that did not exist in the restricted two-dimensional approach. First, the image that the computer processes contains much more information. This sounds like a simple statement, but think about it for a moment: In a high-contrast binary image, each pixel can be stored in one bit because either it is black or white. (A pixel is one discrete point of a video image.) However, to gain three-dimensional information requires information about the relative brightness of each pixel. Depending upon various constraints, there may be a few degrees of brightness to several hundred degrees of brightness. Assume that there are 256 shades of gray and that each pixel requires one byte for storage. This is eight times as much storage space as that required by the high-contrast method. To get an idea how much storage is needed, think about the following: The average American TV camera uses 525 scan lines. If you assume an equivalent horizontal resolution, then you will need 275,625 bytes to store a black-and-white picture. (If you want to store a color image, the amount of necessary storage would almost double.) Although most personal computers can easily have this amount of memory, the trouble is that it contains a lot of information for a program to digest, and may take more time to analyze an image in this form as opposed to another image in high-contrast mode. In real-world applications, this may be a problem.

A more important problem arises when you try to make the computer use all of the information that you know the image contains. Because you see either instinctively or by learning at a very young age, you do not give much thought to how you see. After all, your eyes are not significantly different from a TV camera. Therefore, your brain must do a significant amount of processing to interpret all of the images that you see every day. It is AI's job to duplicate in the computer the way that you process images. To understand the difficulty of interpreting real-world images, study the following problems and their resolutions.

Detecting Surface Direction

A photograph of the Rocky Mountains that is taken by a satellite would look similar to the sketch given in Figure 5-3. If you used a computer to analyze this sketch, how would the computer know that it is looking at

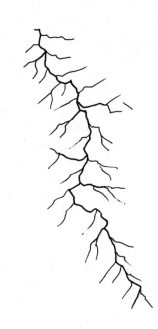

Figure 5-3.   A sketch of a satellite's view of the Rocky Mountains

mountains and not valleys? In other words, how can the computer determine that the sketch is of a mountain range and not of a large gorge, such as the Grand Canyon? In order for the computer to interpret an image of the mountains correctly, it must know the direction of the surfaces in the image.

You can determine the direction of a surface by studying the way that light is reflected by it. Figure 5-4 shows a side view of both a mountain and a valley with the sun directly overhead. As the figure shows, the light striking the mountain sides is reflected sideways, whereas the light striking the valley is first reflected to the opposite wall and then back into the sky. A program that analyzes the image can use the relative brightness of the surfaces to determine whether the computer is viewing a mountain or a valley. As you can guess, this is a fairly complex task even with a simple image, and it becomes almost overwhelming with complex ones.

Determining Surface Texture

Although you can be fooled, you can generally determine whether an object is smooth or rough by looking at it. For example, a fuzzy ball of yarn looks soft and a glass marble looks hard — even at a distance. Further, highly polished metal and glass have a different look than natural wood. Thus, you can determine the texture of an object by studying its appearance.

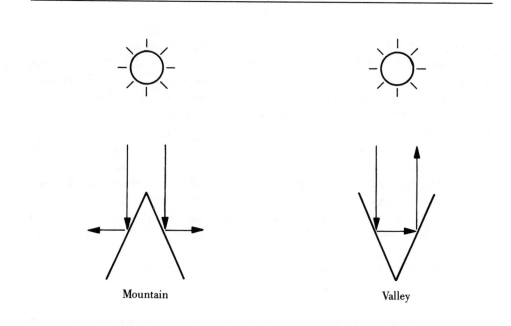

Figure 5-4.   Light reflection on a mountain and a valley

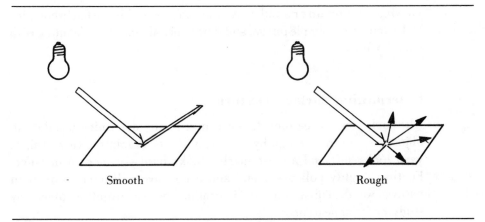

Figure 5-5.   Light reflection on smooth and rough surfaces

The key to distinguishing a smooth object from a rough one is again tied to an interpretation of the way that light is reflected by each. As shown in Figure 5-5, a smooth surface, which is characteristic of a hard object, reflects light in a uniform way, but a rough surface, which is characteristic of a soft object, scatters light. Hence, the relative brightness of a soft-textured object will be less than a hard-textured one.

In controlled situations, the computer can simply use the relative brightness of each object to determine whether the surface is smooth or rough. This type of image processing is common on automobile assembly lines where such features as welds and paint are checked for uniformity.

However, to enable the computer to recognize rough-textured objects from smooth-textured in a real-world situation requires more than simply comparing the relative brightnesses of objects. The reason is that the relative brightness of an object is also affected by its color and the reflective qualities of the material used to make the object. Therefore, the determination of texture requires two or more images of the objects from differing viewpoints in relation to the light source. In Figure 5-6, the hard-textured object when viewed from point A appears

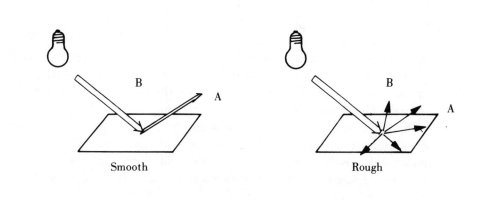

Figure 5-6.   Smooth and rough objects from two points of view, A and B

very bright because it directly reflects nearly all of the light that strikes it at the viewer. The soft-textured object only reflects a portion of the light to the viewer. However, when viewed from point B, the amount of light reflected from the hard-textured object is very small, while the amount of light reflected from the soft-textured one is nearly the same. Hence, the computer can tell the difference between the textures by comparing the change of the brightnesses. A large change indicates a smooth texture and a small change indicates a rough texture.

Common Recognition Problems

Assuming that you can solve all problems of correctly interpreting an image by using either a two- or three-dimensional system, you will still have the problem of correctly identifying the objects or features that make up the image. This is probably the harder task to accomplish, as the next few discussions will show.

Overlapping Objects

One of the toughest problems that you will encounter when trying to create a vision system is the recognition of overlapping objects. The trouble is not that the computer cannot tell that one object is in front of another. Generally, shadows and differences in shading supply sufficient clues. The real difficulty is programming the computer to recognize partial objects for what they are. For example, if you instruct the computer that a triangle has three sides and three vertices, and if the computer sees a triangle that has one of its vertices obscured by another object (or perhaps out of the camera's field of view), how does the computer know that it is still seeing a triangle, even though the third vertex is missing?

There are many approaches to this problem, but perhaps the most interesting solution, and the one closest to the way that the human eye does it, is called controlled hallucination. In this method, the computer, guided by the initial information, postulates that it is seeing a triangle and tries to verify this by using some means, such as by computing that the two lines will intersect somewhere in the region that is obscured. As you can guess, this is a tricky process to program in all but highly controlled environments.

Recognition of Objects
By Classification

Another difficult problem is programming the computer to recognize classes of objects — that a tree is a tree or that a house is a house. It is far easier to make the computer recognize a *specific* object than it is to make the computer recognize objects in a certain classification. The reason for this is that you can give specific objects a strict set of limitations to which they must conform, but you must keep a class definition quite general and loose to cover all slight variances.

As of this writing, it is not clear how you can solve this problem for the general case. Later as the chapter develops some programs that perform pattern recognition, you will see that it is possible to determine simple geometric shapes based upon a class definition, but the techniques that can be applied to these types of objects do not translate to highly complex objects.

Optical Illusions

No overview of image processing is complete without a brief mention of optical illusions and their effect on computerized vision systems. Curiously, many optical illusions that may fool you do not affect a computer analysis of the same image. For example, lines A and B in Figure 5-7 are exactly the same length, but A appears to be longer. However, a computer would not make the same mistake.

However, the reverse is also true: the computer may be confused by images that you can interpret. For example, when you look down a

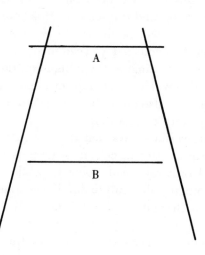

Figure 5-7.   A simple optical illusion

long, straight road, it appears to narrow and finally disappear at the "vanishing point": that is, things look smaller to you the farther away they are. You are accustomed to this effect and think little of it. However, in less-than-perfect vision systems, the computer is likely to think that faraway objects are simply small.

Thus, you must be aware that a different set of optical illusions will exist for the computer than exist for you. Further, many features that you take for granted must be explicitly programmed before the computer can interpret an image correctly.

Now that you have completed this overview of the main topics and problems associated with smart vision systems, you are ready to see how you can use Turbo Prolog to tackle some of these problems.

Two-Dimensional Pattern Recognition

Because of the complexity of three-dimensional images and the associated techniques that are necessary to recognize three-dimensional objects, they are beyond the scope of this book and this discussion of pattern recognition will be limited to two-dimensional images. As the overview just given indicated, you can solve most practical problems that require image processing by using high-contrast, flat images. It is this type of image that will be used in the examples. (Some of the techniques discussed here can also be applied to the more complex realm of three-dimensional pattern recognition.)

There are various ways that the computer can recognize objects. Some ways work better in certain situations than others. Also, some methods work only on specific objects, while others work on a general class. Therefore, it is difficult to develop an objective set of criteria that determines whether one approach is better than another. However, the answers to the following questions will help you determine to what situations you can apply a specific recognition technique and what its limitations are:

1. Does the technique correctly resolve objects on top of other objects?

2. Does the orientation of the objects affect recognition?

3. Does the exact size of the object affect recognition? (That is, does it only work with specific objects?)

4. How efficient is the technique?

5. Can the program be confused and make mistakes?

With these questions as a backdrop, here are three separate pattern recognition methods.

The Situation

Imagine that your task is to design pattern recognition routines that will correctly identify triangles and squares. At first, there will only be one type of triangle —isosceles. Later, you will try to add a right triangle. There is always only one type of square.

At first, you may think that this task seems too simple but, as you will soon see, it illustrates much of the difficulty of creating pattern recognition routines.

Simulating a Video Image

As stated in the beginning of this chapter, because you probably do not have a vision system attached to your computer, and because various types of vision hardware work differently, you will simulate a visual image. You can do this by using the memory that holds the screen display information of your computer. The IBM PC and its compatibles use memory mapped video. In this method, each character position on the screen corresponds to a byte in a reserved portion of RAM. Whatever is in this area of memory is displayed on the screen. The reverse is also true —whatever is displayed on the screen is also in memory. To simulate a vision image, you will first clear the screen and then display the outlines of simple objects. This represents a high-contrast, flat image. Then the recognition portion of the program will scan the video memory and attempt to identify the objects. As you will see, the recognition portion of the programs has no direct knowledge of what has been placed on the screen.

Fortunately, Turbo Prolog contains a rich set of built-in predicates that you can use to control the display. Before routines can be developed that will recognize patterns, you will need some way of placing objects on the screen. The following routines will first ask you for the coordinates of the starting location of each object by using the *row,column* format. Then the actual objects will be drawn on the screen. All of the arguments are integers.

```
/* place objects on the screen  */
  position:-
    write("starting coordinates for triangle: "),
    readint(R),write(","),readint(C),
    write("starting coordinates for square: "),
    readint(R1),write(","),readint(C1),
    clear,
    make_triangle(R,C,5),
    make_square(R1,C1,5).

  make_triangle(R,C,N):-
    make_left(R,C,N),
    make_right(R,C,N),
    make_base(R,C,N).
  make_left(R,C,N):-
    N<>0,
    cursor(R,C),
    write("*"),
    R1=R+1,
    C1=C-1,
    N1=N-1,
    make_left(R1,C1,N1).
  make_left(_,_,_).
  make_right(R,C,N):-
    N<>0,
    cursor(R,C),
    write("*"),
    R1=R+1,
    C1=C+1,
    N1=N-1,
    make_right(R1,C1,N1).
  make_right(_,_,_).
  make_base(R,C,N):-
    R1=R+N, C1=C-N,
    cursor(R1,C1),
    write("***********").

  make_square(R,C,N):-
    make_top_bottom(R,C,N),
```

```
    make_leftside(R,C,N),
    make_rightside(R,C,N).

make_top_bottom(R,C,N):-
    cursor(R,C),
    write("**********"),
    R1=R+N,
    cursor(R1,C),
    write("**********").

make_leftside(R,C,N):-
    N<>0,
    cursor(R,C),
    write("*"),
    N1=N-1,
    R1=R+1,
    make_leftside(R1,C,N1).
make_leftside(_,_,_).

make_rightside(R,C,N):-
    N<>0,
    C1=C+9,
    cursor(R,C1),
    write("*"),
    N1=N-1,
    R1=R+1,
    make_rightside(R1,C,N1).
make_rightside(_,_,_).
```

These routines will place on a blank screen a triangle and a square. They use asterisks to form the images. This means that you do not need any special graphics adapters to run the routines and that they will work with all combinations of hardware. Now that you have a way of simulating a video image, you are ready to proceed to pattern recognition.

The Recognition-by-Angles Program

In a tightly controlled environment, it is possible to identify a triangle or a square correctly by measuring the angle at a vertex. Limiting the types of triangles to an isosceles makes it simple to discern a triangle from a square: you only have to check two points at any vertex. If the points are at right angles, the object has to be a square. If they are at 60-degree angles, the object must be a triangle.

Before you can implement a pattern recognizer based upon this approach, you need a way to scan the screen for points that form the outlines of the objects. To do this, the built-in predicate **scr __ char** is used. Given the row and column, **scr __ char** will return what character is in that location. The predicate **find __ point** shown here will search the screen, starting at the location passed to it, and return the row and column of a point that contains an asterisk.

```
/* find the next point that is an * */
find_point(A,B,R,C):-
  scr_char(A,B,Ch),
  Ch='*',
  R=A,C=B.
find_point(A,B,R,C):-
  B1=B+1,
  B1<80,!,
  find_point(A,B1,R,C).
find_point(A,_,R,C):-
  A1=A+1,
  A1<20,!,
  find_point(A1,0,R,C).
find_point(_,_,_,_):-fail.
```

As a matter of convention, the routines will always scan the screen by beginning with the upper left-hand corner, location 0,0, and proceeding left to right, line by line. The routine that recognizes triangles is shown here.

```
find_triangle(R,C):-
  find_point(0,0,A,B),
  A1=A+1,
  B1=B-1,
  scr_char(A1,B1,Ch),
  Ch='*',
  B2=B+1,
  scr_char(A1,B2,Ch2),
  Ch2='*',
  R=A, C=B.
```

The operation of this routine is based upon Turbo Prolog's automatic backtracking. Each time that **find __ point** returns with the location of an asterisk, the routine checks to see if there is another asterisk also on the diagonal. If there is, the object must be a triangle and the clause succeeds. If not, through backtracking, **find __ point** is re-executed and a new point is tried. Eventually, the routine discovers the triangle.

The procedure to find a square is exactly the same as that used to find a triangle, except that each time the procedure locates an asterisk, it checks to see if there is another asterisk at right angles with the first asterisk. This routine is shown here.

```
find_square(R,C):-
  find_point(0,0,A,B),
  A1=A+1,
  scr_char(A1,B,Ch),
  Ch='*',
  R=A, C=B.
```

The entire Recognition-by-Angles program is shown here. You should enter it into your computer at this time.

```
/* Recognition by Angles */
predicates
  start
  clear
  make_triangle(integer, integer, integer)
  make_left(integer, integer, integer)
  make_right(integer, integer, integer)
  make_base(integer, integer, integer)
  make_square(integer,integer, integer)
  make_top_bottom(integer,integer, integer)
  make_rightside(integer, integer, integer)
  make_leftside(integer, integer, integer)
  position
  recognize
  find_triangle(integer, integer).
  find_square(integer, integer)
  find_point(integer, integer, integer, integer)
goal
  start.

clauses
  start:-
    clear,
    position,
    recognize.

  /* attempt to find objects */
  recognize:-
    find_triangle(R,C),
    cursor(0,0),
    write("triangle at ",R," ",C),nl,
    find_square(R1,C1),
    write("square at ",R1," ",C1),nl.

  /* must be on diagonal */
  find_triangle(R,C):-
```

```
    find_point(0,0,A,B),
    A1=A+1,
    B1=B-1,
    scr_char(A1,B1,Ch),
    Ch='*',
    B2=B+1,
    scr_char(A1,B2,Ch2),
    Ch2='*',
    R=A,  C=B.

/* must be right angle */
find_square(R,C):-
    find_point(0,0,A,B),
    A1=A+1,
    scr_char(A1,B,Ch),
    Ch='*',
    R=A,  C=B.

/* find the next point that is an * */
find_point(A,B,R,C):-
    scr_char(A,B,Ch),
    Ch='*',
    R=A,C=B.
find_point(A,B,R,C):-
    B1=B+1,
    B1<80,!,
    find_point(A,B1,R,C).
find_point(A,_,R,C):-
    A1=A+1,
    A1<20,!,
    find_point(A1,0,R,C).
find_point(_,_,_,_):-fail.

/* place objects on the screen   */

position:-
    write("starting coordinates for triangle: "),
    readint(R),write(","),readint(C),
    write("starting coordinates for square: "),
    readint(R1),write(","),readint(C1),
    clear,
    make_triangle(R,C,5),
    make_square(R1,C1,5).


make_triangle(R,C,N):-
    make_left(R,C,N),
    make_right(R,C,N),
    make_base(R,C,N).
make_left(R,C,N):-
    N<>0,
    cursor(R,C),
```

```
      write("*"),
      R1=R+1,
      C1=C-1,
      N1=N-1,
      make_left(R1,C1,N1).
make_left(_,_,_).
make_right(R,C,N):-
      N<>0,
      cursor(R,C),
      write("*"),
      R1=R+1,
      C1=C+1,
      N1=N-1,
      make_right(R1,C1,N1).
make_right(_,_,_).
make_base(R,C,N):-
      R1=R+N, C1=C-N,
      cursor(R1,C1),
      write("**********").

make_square(R,C,N):-
      make_top_bottom(R,C,N),
      make_leftside(R,C,N),
      make_rightside(R,C,N).

make_top_bottom(R,C,N):-
      cursor(R,C),
      write("**********"),
      R1=R+N,
      cursor(R1,C),
      write("**********").

make_leftside(R,C,N):-
      N<>0,
      cursor(R,C),
      write("*"),
      N1=N-1,
      R1=R+1,
      make_leftside(R1,C,N1).
make_leftside(_,_,_).

make_rightside(R,C,N):-
      N<>0,
      C1=C+9,
      cursor(R,C1),
      write("*"),
      N1=N-1,
      R1=R+1,
      make_rightside(R1,C,N1).
make_rightside(_,_,_).

clear:-
      makewindow(1,6,0,"",0,0,25,80).
```

Analysis of the Recognition-by-Angles Program   Run the program and enter the coordinates **10,10** for the triangle and **12,55** for the square. You will then see a display similar to the one shown in Figure 5-8. As the figure shows, the recognition routines correctly identified the triangle and the square.

Analyze the program's performance by using the questions given earlier. Does this approach correctly recognize an object placed on top of another? To see this, run the program again and enter **10,10** as the coordinates of both objects. The display that appears will be similar to that shown in Figure 5-9. Once again, the routine correctly discovered the square and the triangle.

Does the orientation of the objects affect recognition? Unfortunately, the way that the program is implemented, in order to identify the objects, requires that they be in one of a few positions —they may not be rotated at random. In the example given, there is no possibility of rotation, so this requirement is not a meaningful limitation, but it does prevent the routines from being applied to more varied problems. However, it is possible to design a version of the Recognition-by-Angles program that would allow the objects to be rotated.

Does the exact size of the objects affect recognition? The answer is no, because all that the routines do is confirm the angle of the intersection between two sides. Thus, the Recognition-by-Angles program can be applied to differently sized objects.

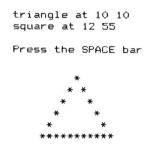

```
triangle at 10 10
square at 12 55

Press the SPACE bar
```

Figure 5-8.   The display of the Recognition-by-Angles program

```
triangle at 10 10
square at 10 10

Press the SPACE bar


        *********
       ***        *
      *  *  *      *
     *   *   *      *
    *    *    *      *
   ***************
```

Figure 5-9.   The display of the overlapping of a triangle and a square

How efficient is the program? Because of its simplicity and the restriction on orientation, the recognizer is quite efficient.

Can the program be confused? Within the restrictions of the example just given, the program will not make mistakes. But, if another type of shape were allowed, then it could make mistakes. For example, the program could easily mistake a right triangle for a square if the triangle's orientation were such that the program tested as the first point the vertex opposite the hypotenuse.

As this analysis shows, you can only apply the Recognition-by-Angles program to very tightly controlled situations with a minimum number of widely varied objects. To use the program in other situations would probably produce unreliable results.

The Recognition-by-Key-Points Program

Because a right triangle could confuse the Recognition-by-Angles program, this section will add a right triangle to the isosceles triangle and the square that were just tested, and create a program that identifies all three objects. (You will find the additional display code given in the complete listing of this program.)

One way for the program to identify objects that always have the

Figure 5-10.   The key points for the triangles and the square

same size is to examine only a few key points. The key locations are
chosen in such a way that one and only one object will satisfy the
conditions. Figure 5-10 shows the three objects that the program must
identify, as well as their key points.

The revised routines **find_triangle** and **find_square** are
shown here.

```
find_triangle(R,C):-
  find_point(R,C,A,B),
  is_triangle(A,B),
  write("triangle at ",A," ",B," "),
  R1=A+1, C1=C+1,
  find_triangle(R1,C1).
find_triangle(_,_).
```

```
/* check for proper * locations */
is_triangle(R,C):- /* inverted right triangle */
  R1=R+9,
  R1<24,
  scr_char(R1,C,Ch),
  Ch='*',
  C1=C+9,
  C1<80,
  scr_char(R,C1,Ch1),
  Ch1='*',
  C2=C+1,
  R2=R1-1,
  scr_char(R2,C2,Ch2),
  Ch2='*'.
is_triangle(R,C):-  /* standard isosceles */
  R1=R+5,
```

```
C1=C-5,
R1<24, C1>0,
scr_char(R1,C1,Ch),
Ch='*',
C2=C+5,C2<80,
scr_char(R1,C2,Ch1),
Ch1='*'.

find_square(R,C):-
  find_point(R,C,A,B),
  A1=A+5,B1=B+9,
  A1<25, B1<81,
  scr_char(A1,B,Ch),
  Ch='*',
  scr_char(A1,B1,Ch1),
  Ch1='*',
  scr_char(A,B1,Ch2),
  Ch2='*',
  A2=A+1, B2=B+1,
  write("square at ",A,' ',B,' '),
  find_square(A2,B2).
find_square(_,_).
```

Because the routine **find _triangle** must now find two (or more) triangles, it has been broken into two sections to take better advantage of Turbo Prolog's backtracking features. The **is _triangle** section performs the identification process. Notice that the routines themselves report the position of the object: This is necessary because more than one triangle may be present.

The entire Recognition-by-Key-Points program is shown here, which you should now enter into your computer.

```
/* recognition by selected sampling of
   key points */
predicates
  start
  clear
  make_triangle(integer, integer, integer)
  make_left(integer, integer, integer)
  make_right(integer, integer, integer)
  make_base(integer, integer, integer)
  make_square(integer,integer, integer)
  make_top_bottom(integer,integer, integer)
  make_rightside(integer, integer, integer)
  make_leftside(integer, integer, integer)
  make_rt_left(integer, integer, integer)
  make_rt_right(integer, integer, integer)
  make_right_triangle(integer, integer, integer)
```

```
    position
    recognize
    find_triangle(integer, integer).
    find_square(integer, integer)
    find_point(integer, integer, integer, integer)
    is_triangle(integer, integer)

goal
  start.

clauses
  start:-
    clear,
    position,
    recognize.

  /* attempt to find objects */
  recognize:-
    cursor(0,0),
    find_triangle(0,0),
    cursor(1,0),
    find_square(0,0).


  find_triangle(R,C):-
    find_point(R,C,A,B),
    is_triangle(A,B),
    write("triangle at ",A," ",B," "),
    R1=A+1, C1=C+1,
    find_triangle(R1,C1).
  find_triangle(_,_).

  /* check for proper * locations */
  is_triangle(R,C):- /* inverted right triangle */
    R1=R+9,
    R1<24,
    scr_char(R1,C,Ch),
    Ch='*',
    C1=C+9,
    C1<80,
    scr_char(R,C1,Ch1),
    Ch1='*',
    C2=C+1,
    R2=R1-1,
    scr_char(R2,C2,Ch2),
    Ch2='*'.
  is_triangle(R,C):-  /* standard isosceles */
    R1=R+5,
    C1=C-5,
    R1<24, C1>0,
    scr_char(R1,C1,Ch),
    Ch='*',
```

```
        C2=C+5,C2<80,
        scr_char(R1,C2,Ch1),
        Ch1='*'.


    find_square(R,C):-
        find_point(R,C,A,B),
        A1=A+5,B1=B+9,
        A1<25, B1<81,
        scr_char(A1,B,Ch),
        Ch='*',
        scr_char(A1,B1,Ch1),
        Ch1='*',
        scr_char(A,B1,Ch2),
        Ch2='*',
        A2=A+1, B2=B+1,
        write("square at ",A,' ',B,' '),
        find_square(A2,B2).
    find_square(_,_).

    find_point(A,B,R,C):-
        scr_char(A,B,Ch),
        Ch='*',
        R=A,C=B.
    find_point(A,B,R,C):-
        B1=B+1,
        B1<80,!,
        find_point(A,B1,R,C).
    find_point(A,_,R,C):-
        A1=A+1,
        A1<24,!,
        find_point(A1,0,R,C).
    find_point(_,_,_,_):-fail.

/* place objects on the screen */


    position:-
        write("coordinates for isosceles triangle: "),
        readint(R),write(","),readint(C),
        write("coordinates for right triangle: "),
        readint(R2),readint(C2),
        write("coordinates for square: "),
        readint(R1),write(","),readint(C1),
        clear,
        make_triangle(R,C,5),
        make_square(R1,C1,5),
        make_right_triangle(R2,C2,10).


    make_triangle(R,C,N):-
        make_left(R,C,N),
```

```
  make_right(R,C,N),
  make_base(R,C,N).
make_left(R,C,N):-
  N<>0,
  cursor(R,C),
  write("*"),
  R1=R+1,
  C1=C-1,
  N1=N-1,
  make_left(R1,C1,N1).
make_left(_,_,_).
make_right(R,C,N):-
  N<>0,
  cursor(R,C),
  write("*"),
  R1=R+1,
  C1=C+1,
  N1=N-1,
  make_right(R1,C1,N1).
make_right(_,_,_).
make_base(R,C,N):-
  R1=R+N,  C1=C-N,
  cursor(R1,C1),
  write("***********").

make_right_triangle(R,C,N):-
  make_rt_left(R,C,N),
  C1=C+9,
  make_rt_right(R,C1,N),
  cursor(R,C),
  write("*********").

make_rt_left(R,C,N):-
  N<>0,
  cursor(R,C),
  write("*"),
  R1=R+1,
  N1=N-1,
  make_rt_left(R1,C,N1).
make_rt_left(_,_,_).
make_rt_right(R,C,N):-
  N<>0,
  cursor(R,C),
  write("*"),
  R1=R+1,
  C1=C-1,
  N1=N-1,
  make_rt_right(R1,C1,N1).
make_rt_right(_,_,_).

make_square(R,C,N):-
  make_top_bottom(R,C,N),
```

```
     make_leftside(R,C,N),
     make_rightside(R,C,N).

make_top_bottom(R,C,N):-
     cursor(R,C),
     write("*********"),
     R1=R+N,
     cursor(R1,C),
     write("*********").

make_leftside(R,C,N):-
     N<>0,
     cursor(R,C),
     write("*"),
     N1=N-1,
     R1=R+1,
     make_leftside(R1,C,N1).
make_leftside(_,_,_).

make_rightside(R,C,N):-
     N<>0,
     C1=C+9,
     cursor(R,C1),
     write("*"),
     N1=N-1,
     R1=R+1,
     make_rightside(R1,C,N1).
make_rightside(_,_,_).

clear:-
     makewindow(1,6,0,"",0,0,25,80).
```

Analysis of the Recognition-by-Key-Points Program   Run the program and enter the following coordinates:

Isosceles triangle	4,10
Right triangle	11,55
Square	12,30

You will see a display similar to the one shown in Figure 5-11. Clearly, the key-point method of recognition works for this restricted situation.

To understand the limitations of the program, you must answer the five criteria questions. Does the program correctly resolve objects that are on top of each other? To find out, run the program with all objects placed at location 10,10. As shown in Figure 5-12, the program now

```
triangle at 4 10 triangle at 11 55
square at 12 30
Press the SPACE bar
```

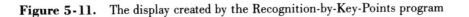

Figure 5-11. The display created by the Recognition-by-Key-Points program

thinks that there is only one triangle and one square. The program fails to find the second triangle because, as implemented, it tries one point only once. Hence, after it finds the first triangle at location 10,10, it does not try 10,10 again for the second triangle. The reason that the program finds the square is that the **find _ square** routine begins its search from the top. However, if the second triangle had been shifted even one location in any direction, it would have been found.

Does the orientation of the objects affect recognition? As you can see, each object must be oriented precisely as shown, or the program will not identify it. The angle-based recognizer given earlier could accommodate certain variations in rotation, but the key-point recognizer given here cannot.

Does the exact size of each object affect recognition? Because each object must be exactly the correct size for the recognizer to work, the recognizer will fail if the sizes of the objects change.

How efficient is the program? Because it examines only a few points to determine the identity of an object, it is quite efficient — nearly as

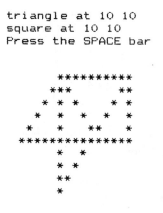

```
triangle at 10 10
square at 10 10
Press the SPACE bar


        *********
        ***      **
       * * *    * *
      *  *  *  *  *
     *   *   **   *
     ***************
           *  *
           *  *
           **
           *
```

Figure 5-12. The display of three objects at location 10,10

efficient as the Recognition-by-Angles program.

Can the program be easily confused? If you experiment with the program, you will find that you can make it think that there are three triangles present. This can happen if you arrange the positions of the triangles and the square in such a way that there are isolated points that appear to the recognizer to form a triangle.

It seems that apart from being able to recognize a greater variety of triangles, you have lost more than you have gained with this approach. It requires an even more restrictive environment than the angle-based version and it is easy to confuse.

The Delta-D Recognizer

The last recognition method that this chapter will examine is based upon change of direction. For example, starting at any point of a triangle, if you follow the lines until you return to the starting point, you will have changed direction three times. If you follow the lines of a square, you will change direction four times. The number of times that the direction changes is equal to the number of vertices in the shape. (A circle can either be thought of as having infinite direction changes, as in calculus, or as having zero changes.) Each time that a vertex is encountered, there is a change in the direction. These changes are often called delta values in mathematics and in computer science. Because the program presented here is based on a change in direction, this method is sometimes called the delta-D recognizer, where the *D* stands for direction.

For the delta-D recognizer to operate, it must be able to follow the shape of an object. For the example given earlier, this means that the program has to be able to follow a straight line until it intersects with another. At the intersection, the program must correctly find the next straight line and follow it. Although there are many ways to solve this problem, the solution given in this section requires the use of the three databases shown here.

```
database
  point(integer,integer)
  increments(integer,integer)
  turns(symbol)
```

The **point** database is used to keep a list of all points visited so that the routines can know when they are back at the starting point, and to avoid redundant solutions. The **increments** database is used to help find the connecting line at an intersection. (Its use will be explained later.) Finally, the **turns** database simply keeps a count of the number of changes of direction.

Here is the routine **follow ____ shape** with the support predicate **follow**:

```
/* follow a shape until back at
   starting point counting the
   number of changes in direction */
follow_shape(R,C):-
  assert(point(R,C)),
  R1=R+1,
  scr_char(R1,C,Ch),
  Ch='*',
  follow(R1,C,1,0),!.
follow_shape(R,C):-
  R1=R+1,C1=C+1,
  scr_char(R1,C1,Ch),
```

```
       Ch='*',
       follow(R1,C1,1,1),!.
/* follow each line */
follow(R,C,_,_):-
   point(Y,X),
   R=Y,C=X.  /* back at start */
follow(R,C,I,J):-/* keep going in same direction */
   R1=R+I,
   C1=C+J,
   scr_char(R1,C1,Ch),
   Ch='*',
   assert(point(R,C)),
   follow(R1,C1,I,J).
follow(R,C,_,_):-/* try horizontal */
   assert(turns(once)), /* change direction */
   increments(I,J),
   R1=R+I, C1=C+J,
   not(point(R1,C1)),
   scr_char(R1,C1,Ch),
   Ch='*',
   follow(R1,C1,I,J).
```

In the predicate **follow**, the first clause simply follows a line by proceeding in the direction indicated by the increment arguments **I** and **J**. If there is no asterisk, which indicates a turn, at the next location, then the second clause is tried. The second clause uses the **increments** database and Turbo Prolog's backtracking to find the direction of the next line. In the goal section of the program, the **increments** database is loaded with all of the possible values that **I** and **J** could assume. The program repeatedly tries different sets of these increments until it discovers another asterisk. This new set of increments is then used in a recursive call to **follow**, and an item is added to the **turns** database.

The revised **find — triangle** and **find — square** predicates are shown here.

```
find_triangle(R,C):-
   find_point(R,C,A,B),
   is_triangle(A,B),
   write("triangle at ",A," ",B," "),
   C1=C+1,
   find_triangle(A,C1).
find_triangle(_,_).

is_triangle(R,C):-
```

```
  follow_shape(R,C),
  purge(O,N),!,
  N=2.
is_triangle(_,_):-
  purge(O,_), fail.

find_square(R,C):-
  find_point(R,C,A,B),
  is_square(A,B),
  write("square at ",A," ",B," "),
  C1=C+1,
  find_square(A,C1).
find_square(_,_).

is_square(R,C):-
  follow_shape(R,C),
  purge(O,N),!,
  N=3.
is_square(_,_):-
  purge(O,_), fail.
```

The routines work as follows. Each time that an asterisk is found, the routine follows the shape that the asterisk is part of and notes each change in direction. Upon return from **follow __ shape**, the **turns** database will contain some number of items that represents the number of turns. The **purge** routine is used both to clear the database for future use and to count the number of items in it. As implemented here, the **follow __ shape** routine does not count the final turn; if the object is a triangle, there must be two items in the **turns** database, and there must be three if it is a square.

The entire delta-D recognizer program is shown here. You should enter this into your computer at this time.

```
/* recognition by counting vertices:
   the delta-D recognizer */
database
  point(integer,integer)
  increments(integer,integer)
  turns(symbol)
predicates
  start
  clear
  make_triangle(integer, integer, integer)
  make_left(integer, integer, integer)
  make_right(integer, integer, integer)
  make_base(integer, integer, integer)
```

```
    make_square(integer,integer, integer)
    make_top_bottom(integer,integer, integer)
    make_rightside(integer, integer, integer)
    make_leftside(integer, integer, integer)
    make_rt_left(integer, integer, integer)
    make_rt_right(integer, integer, integer)
    make_right_triangle(integer, integer, integer)
    purge(integer, integer)
    purge_points
    position
    recognize
    find_triangle(integer, integer).
    find_square(integer, integer)
    find_point(integer, integer, integer, integer)
    is_square(integer, integer)
    is_triangle(integer, integer)
    follow_shape(integer, integer)
    follow(integer, integer, integer, integer)
goal
    assert(increments(1,1)),
    assert(increments(-1,1)),
    assert(increments(1,-1)),
    assert(increments(1,0)),
    assert(increments(0,1)),
    assert(increments(-1,-1)),
    assert(increments(-1,0)),
    assert(increments(0,-1)),
    start.

clauses
    start:-
      clear,
      position,
      recognize.

    /* attempt to find objects */
    recognize:-
      cursor(0,0),
      find_triangle(0,0),
      cursor(1,0),
      purge_points, /* clear the points database */
      find_square(0,0),
      purge_points.

    find_triangle(R,C):-
      find_point(R,C,A,B),
      is_triangle(A,B),
      write("triangle at ",A," ",B," "),
      C1=C+1,
      find_triangle(A,C1).
    find_triangle(_,_).
```

```
is_triangle(R,C):-
  follow_shape(R,C),
  purge(0,N),!,
  N=2.
is_triangle(_,_):-
  purge(0,_), fail.

find_square(R,C):-
  find_point(R,C,A,B),
  is_square(A,B),
  write("square at ",A," ",B," "),
  C1=C+1,
  find_square(A,C1).
find_square(_,_).

is_square(R,C):-
  follow_shape(R,C),
  purge(0,N),!,
  N=3.
is_square(_,_):-
  purge(0,_), fail.

find_point(A,B,R,C):-
  scr_char(A,B,Ch),
  Ch='*',
  R=A,C=B.
find_point(A,B,R,C):-
  B1=B+1,
  B1<80,!,
  find_point(A,B1,R,C).
find_point(A,_,R,C):-
  A1=A+1,
  A1<24,!,
  find_point(A1,0,R,C).
find_point(_,_,_,_):-fail.

/* follow a shape until back at
   starting point counting the
   number of changes in direction */
follow_shape(R,C):-
  assert(point(R,C)),
  R1=R+1,
  scr_char(R1,C,Ch),
  Ch='*',
  follow(R1,C,1,0),!.
follow_shape(R,C):-
  R1=R+1,C1=C+1,
  scr_char(R1,C1,Ch),
  Ch='*',
  follow(R1,C1,1,1),!.

/* follow each line */
```

```
  follow(R,C,_,_):-
    point(Y,X),
    R=Y,C=X.   /* back at start */

  follow(R,C,I,J):-/* keep going in same direction */
    R1=R+I,
    C1=C+J,
    scr_char(R1,C1,Ch),
    Ch='*',
    assert(point(R,C)),
    follow(R1,C1,I,J).
  follow(R,C,_,_):-/* try horizontal */
    assert(turns(once)), /* change direction */
    increments(I,J),
    R1=R+I, C1=C+J,
    not(point(R1,C1)),
    scr_char(R1,C1,Ch),
    Ch='*',
    follow(R1,C1,I,J).

  purge(0,N):-
    retract(turns(_)),
    N1=0+1,
    purge(N1,N).
  purge(0,0).

  purge_points:-
    retract(point(_,_)),
    fail.
  purge_points.
/* place objects on screen */

  position:-
    write("coordinates for isosceles triangle: "),
    readint(R),write(","),readint(C),
    write("coordinates for right triangle: "),
    readint(R2),readint(C2),
    write("coordinates for square: "),
    readint(R1),readint(C1),
    clear,
    make_triangle(R,C,5),
    make_square(R1,C1,5),
    make_right_triangle(R2,C2,10).


  make_triangle(R,C,N):-
    make_left(R,C,N),
    make_right(R,C,N),
    make_base(R,C,N).
  make_left(R,C,N):-
    N<>0,
```

```
      cursor(R,C),
      write("*"),
      R1=R+1,
      C1=C-1,
      N1=N-1,
      make_left(R1,C1,N1).
   make_left(_,_,_).
   make_right(R,C,N):-
      N<>0,
      cursor(R,C),
      write("*"),
      R1=R+1,
      C1=C+1,
      N1=N-1,
      make_right(R1,C1,N1).
   make_right(_,_,_).
   make_base(R,C,N):-
      R1=R+N,  C1=C-N,
      cursor(R1,C1),
      write("**********").

   make_right_triangle(R,C,N):-
      make_rt_left(R,C,N),
      C1=C+9,
      make_rt_right(R,C1,N),
      cursor(R,C),
      write("*********").

   make_rt_left(R,C,N):-
      N<>0,
      cursor(R,C),
      write("*"),
      R1=R+1,
      N1=N-1,
      make_rt_left(R1,C,N1).
   make_rt_left(_,_,_).
   make_rt_right(R,C,N):-
      N<>0,
      cursor(R,C),
      write("*"),
      R1=R+1,
      C1=C-1,
      N1=N-1,
      make_rt_right(R1,C1,N1).
   make_rt_right(_,_,_).

   make_square(R,C,N):-
      make_top_bottom(R,C,N),
      make_leftside(R,C,N),
      make_rightside(R,C,N).

   make_top_bottom(R,C,N):-
      cursor(R,C),
```

```
      write("*********"),
      R1=R+N,
      cursor(R1,C),
      write("*********").

make_leftside(R,C,N):-
    N<>0,
    cursor(R,C),
    write("*"),
    N1=N-1,
    R1=R+1,
    make_leftside(R1,C,N1).
make_leftside(_,_,_).

make_rightside(R,C,N):-
    N<>0,
    C1=C+9,
    cursor(R,C1),
    write("*"),
    N1=N-1,
    R1=R+1,
    make_rightside(R1,C,N1).
make_rightside(_,_,_).

clear:-
    makewindow(1,6,0,"",0,0,25,80).
```

Analysis of the Delta-D Recognizer   Run the program and enter
these coordinates:

Isosceles triangle	4,10
Right triangle	11,55
Square	12,30

You will see a display similar to the one shown in Figure 5-13. Clearly,
the delta-D method of recognition works for our restricted situation.

To understand the weaknesses of the program, you must answer the
five criteria questions. Does the program correctly recognize objects that
are on top of each other? This question points to the worst feature of the
delta-D recognizer: it completely falls apart when an object is on top of
another. To see this, run the program again with all objects located at
10,10. The result is shown in Figure 5-14: As you can see, the program
fails to find any triangles, and it identifies the square only by accident.

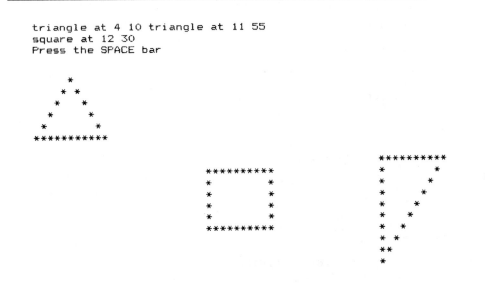

Figure 5-13. The display created by the delta-D program

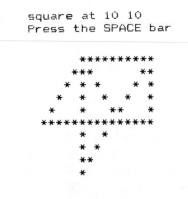

Figure 5-14. The display of three objects at location 10,10

The reason that it cannot discern the triangles is that it finds too many changes of direction because it follows many different lines.

Does the orientation of the objects affect recognition? One of the best features of the program is that it will operate correctly no matter what position the objects are in. This feature makes the delta-D recognizer attractive in many real-world situations.

Does the exact size of each object affect recognition? Another good point about the delta-D approach is that it does not care what size the objects are. This means that it can be used to recognize a class of objects.

How efficient is the program? Because the delta-D recognizer is much more general than the previous two approaches, it does not operate as efficiently. However, the trade-off of efficiency for reliability is generally worthwhile.

Can the program be easily confused? As implemented, the delta-D recognizer can be easily confused by overlapping objects, but it will not mistake one type of object for another, given the constraints of the situation.

In the final analysis, the delta-D recognition method provides the greatest generality of the three programs given so far, as long as the environment in which it is applied is tightly controlled.

Generalized Systems

As the discussions and examples given so far have illustrated, no one approach to interpreting images is going to be adequate for all situations. A combination of many different approaches that are applied selectively by a smart program will probably result in a system that can be used in common real-world situations. You might find it interesting to try this on your own.

Robotics

When people hear the word *robot,* the mental response is usually a visual image of the hardware; that is, the mechanical and electronic devices that make up the physical being of the robot. However, the deeper a person digs into the workings of a robot, the more apparent it becomes that what forms the robot is the linkage of software with the hardware. The software gives the device its intelligence, and it is this intelligence that separates a robot from other forms of automation. This chapter is not concerned with the hardware beyond a brief overview. Instead, it focuses on the software that forms the intelligence that drives the hardware.

There are basically two types of robots. The first type includes the fixed-place, industrial assembly robots, such as those used to assemble cars. This kind of robot must be operated only in a highly controlled environment that has been explicitly designed for it. The second type consists of autonomous robots. These robots are designed to operate in the real world —the world around you. Aside from some very simple models, autonomous robots do not yet exist. The reason for this is that the creation of a truly autonomous robot requires solving several of AI's toughest problems. This reason is also what makes autonomous robots so enticing to AI programmers.

This chapter begins with an overview of the current state of robotics, including a quick look at the ways that a robot can be built and the specialized robotic control languages used to program it. The last part of the chapter develops a simple but expandable robot simulator that can serve as a starting point for your own research on autonomous robotics.

Robot Arms

Virtually all industrial robots are simply robot arms that have grippers attached to the end. The robotic arm is the fundamental manipulative device of any robot —industrial or autonomous. As such, it is important for you to understand a few of the complex problems that you will encounter if you attempt to control a robot arm. For example, when you reach for a glass of water, the movement seems to be effortless and without thought. However, it is, in fact, a complicated task that requires the coordination of several muscles. Remember that a baby needs several months to learn it.

The common robot arm is modelled on the human arm. Most robot arms are six-axis arms because they allow the greatest freedom of movement. Figure 6-1 shows a sketch of a six-axis arm. Each axis, or joint as it is commonly called, is operated by its own separate motor or, as is the case of large arms, hydraulic cylinder.

As Figure 6-1 shows, a six-axis robot arm actually contains two coordinate frames of reference. First, the base and the two pieces of the arm form an X-Y-Z coordinate system and, second, the grip allows fine movements within that system. Therefore, reaching any specific point in space requires the help of five joints in the arm. The movement along the sixth axis is the rotation of the grip itself, which affects only orientation.

The major difficulty of controlling an arm of this type is not in making the movement precise —the hardware takes care of that —but rather in coordinating the six joints. To understand the problem, imagine that you want the robot arm to reach inside a partially open window, and that the robot is initially positioned with its arm outstretched and facing away from the window. If you move each joint separately, starting with the base and working up to the grip, the window is smashed because the robot, with its arm extended, is rotated first, causing it to strike the window. For a robot arm to work properly, all joints must work together, simultaneously, like a human arm.

However, just moving all of the joints at once does not completely solve all of the problems. For example, it is often necessary that the robot arm extend its gripper toward an object in a straight line in order to reach inside a narrow object. To accomplish this requires the use of fairly complex trigonometry. Figure 6-2 shows a graphic representation of this situation. As you can see, for the gripper to reach point C, both joints A and B must be moved. Although moving joint A does cause the arm to extend more fully, it also causes the arm to be lowered. This necessitates making a compensating move by joint B. Furthermore, because the lengths of the pieces that compose the arm may be different, the joints A and B may have to be instructed to move at different rates in order to move the arm in a straight line. This same type of problem

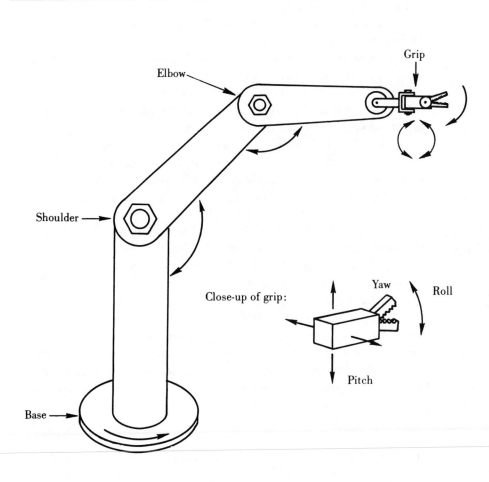

Figure 6-1.   A six-axis robot arm, with a close-up of the grip

occurs on a more complex scale if the robot must change its complete orientation within a prescribed spatial area. For instance, many compensating moves might be required if the robot arm had to reach around a corner.

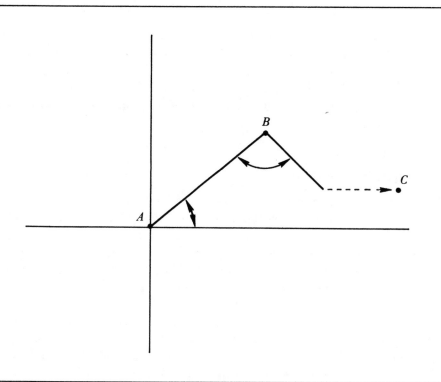

Figure 6-2.   A graph of a straight-line motion

A variation of the straight-line motion problem occurs when the robot must move its grip in a straight horizontal line in front of it. The only way that this can be done is by turning the base of the robot. However, as the base rotates, the other joints must make compensating moves.

The Industrial Robot

In the field of robotics, most efforts have been applied to creating and improving industrial assembly robots. Because these robots are used in a controlled environment, they can be considerably less smart than autonomous robots.

For now and for the foreseeable future, industrial robots can only perform those tasks that they have been explicitly programmed to do. There are two ways that robots can be taught new skills: first, they can be taught by using a teach pendant or, second, they can be programmed by using a robotic-control language. This section will examine both methods.

The Teach Pendant

The most common method of programming a robot to perform a new task is through the use of the teach pendant. The teach pendant is a hand-held control box that allows an operator to move the various joints of the robot. (It is similar to the controllers that are used with model cars, boats, and airplanes.) Although each manufacturer of robots has a slightly different style of teach pendant, all teach pendants are similar to the sketch shown in Figure 6-3.

The teach pendant is not linked directly to the robot, but rather through the robot's main control computer. If you wanted to teach the robot a task, you could use the teach pendant to guide the robot through the necessary sequence of moves that make up the task. As you move each joint, the computer records each position. After teaching has been completed, the robot can now perform the job on its own without the need for further assistance.

Robotic-Control Languages

The teach pendant is an excellent method for teaching the robot simple tasks such as welding and palletizing. However, if the task becomes more complex and external event synchronization becomes more important, or if the robot needs to recognize and respond differently to many possible occurrences, the teach pendant system quickly becomes overburdened. It is for this reason that robotic-control languages were developed.

A robotic-control language is a computer language that is specifi-

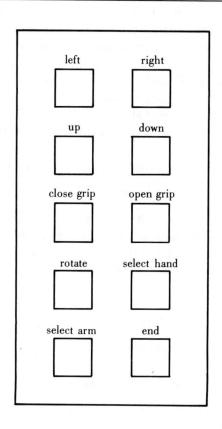

Figure 6-3.   A hand-held teach pendant

cally designed to control a robot. In addition to containing the expected commands such as loop-control and conditional statements, a robotic-control language also includes commands that control the motion of the robot. It is the control of motion that sets robotic-control languages apart from other, general-purpose programming languages. A robotic-control language contains a built-in database that is used to hold the spatial information about each move that the robot will make.

It is important to understand that a robotic-control language is not designed to replace the teach pendant, but rather to supplement it. Hence, a robotic-control language must provide an interface to the teach pendant. The typical method is to teach the robot the necessary spatial information by using the pendant, and then to use the control language to prescribe how the robot should use that information. Generally, each specific location is given a symbolic name so that the program can refer to it.

The typical robotic-control language has a syntax similar to BASIC. Although not elegant, this syntax is easy to learn. (It has only been recently that more structured, Pascal-like robotic-control languages have been developed.) The most common robotic-control language is called VAL. It was the first language ever developed for robotic control, created by Unimation. To get the flavor of a VAL program, examine the one shown here. You could use it to make a robot remove boxes from a conveyor belt.

```
REMARK  WAIT FOR OBJECT
10 WAIT 2
    REMARK  OBJECT PRESENT, REMOVE IT
    MOVE POS1
    MOVE POS2
    CLOSEI  REMARK CLOSE THE GRIP
    MOVE BOX1
    OPENI   REMARK DROP THE OBJECT
GOTO 10
```

Using this program, the robot will wait until input signal 2 is active: this means that it will do nothing until the number 2 signal line goes high. This signal tells the robot that an object is on the conveyor. Next, the robot will move over the object, and then come down on top of it. Then, it will close its grip, move the object off the conveyor, and release the object. Finally, the program will loop and wait for the next object.

VAL only supports uppercase letters. The three positions **POS1**, **POS2**, and **BOX1** are the symbolic names that are given to locations explicitly taught by using the teach pendant.

All industrial robots provide some way of inputting and outputting signals for synchronization; for example, the **WAIT** command in the VAL program just given uses input signal 2. A typical robot will have access to approximately eight input and output lines. Industrial robots do not generally have any sensors as part of themselves. If a robot needs some form of sensor, it is provided as a stand-alone device that simply connects to the robot by means of an input signal. The programmer then must properly interpret the meaning of the signal lines.

Autonomous Robots

An autonomous robot is much more complex than industrial robots because it must be much smarter. If an autonomous robot is to operate successfully in the uncontrolled environment of the real world, it will need various skills that the industrial robot does not require; for example, it will need sensors that allow it to hear and see and it must understand natural language and what the language means. As the preceding chapters have shown, giving the robot these two capabilities is no small feat. In addition, the robot must be able to solve problems, which is perhaps the most complicated programming task of all. This is necessary so that the robot can adapt to various situations because clearly you cannot program the robot in advance for every possible occurrence.

The major roadblock preventing the creation of an autonomous robot is the fact that programmers have not yet developed the necessary software techniques. Also, a robot of this type will probably require some parallel processing, which is still in its infancy. (Parallel processing uses two or more CPUs to obtain greater speed.)

Assuming that one can overcome the technical problems, there still is the question of the autonomous robot's interpretation under the law. If the robot commits a crime, whether accidental or intended, is the robot guilty or is the owner? Perhaps the guilty party is the manufacturer of the robot or even the person who programmed it. In addition, does an autonomous robot have any rights or is it simply a mechanical slave? These questions will need to be answered much further in the future.

Because autonomous robots present such an interesting area of research and speculation, the robot simulator developed in the next section uses a simple autonomous robot.

Creating a Robot Simulator

It is not necessary to have a robot in order to experiment with robotics. The actual hardware that forms the robot is incidental because it is the software that defines the robot. Without software, a robot is simply an expensive doorstop.

You might be surprised to learn that robot simulators are actually quite common in industry because they allow production engineers to lay out assembly lines, and even entire factories, in advance. Some of these simulators are very complex and require fast, expensive computers to operate. However, you can implement a fairly simple simulator by using Turbo Prolog that will allow you to see what it is like to program a robot.

The robot simulator developed in this chapter is easily the longest program in this book. It contains several features, including a robotic-control language parser; several databases that are used to store program and spatial information; display and motion simulation routines; a simple editor; and various support predicates. Before you can explore the program, you must understand what it does and what its limitations are.

The Simulator Specifications

The robot simulator environment consists of a world that is filled with only four objects: a square, two triangles, and the robot. The rest of the screen is blank. The square and triangles are the same ones that were used in Chapter 5, and the same display routines as given there will be used with the simulator. The robot is autonomous and is represented on the screen by a # sign. (Again, since no graphics modes are used, you can run this program on any computer.) The robot can go anywhere as long as there is no other object: that is, the square and triangles are obstacles and the robot must go around, not through, them. Finally, the robot has the ability to sense an obstacle in its immediate proximity, and the ability to find triangles and squares.

There are two ways to program the robot. The first is through the use of its own robotic-control language. The control language is simple but easily expandable, and consists of the following commands:

moveto

move

findt

finds

label

goto

ifsense/then

Moveto

The **moveto** command tells the robot to go to the specified row,column location on the screen. The upper-left corner of the screen is location 0,0. This means that the rows are numbered from 0 to 24, and the columns are numbered from 0 to 79. For example,

```
moveto 12 60
```

causes the robot to move to location 12,60. Notice that there is no comma between the numbers; you must use a space.

Move

The **move** command causes the robot to move one position in a specified direction, which must be either left, right, up, or down. For example,

```
move up
move left
```

first causes the robot to move up one row and left one column from its previous position. The directions are screen-relative: that is, as you look at the screen, the top is up and the bottom is down.

Findt and Finds

The commands **findt** and **finds** tell the robot to find a triangle or a square, respectively. To do this, the robot uses the delta-D pattern recognizer that was developed in Chapter 5. The robot can only find an object if it is located above the object. After it finds the object, the robot will position itself one column to the left of the uppermost right corner of the object.

Label

To keep the parser as simple as possible, the keyword **label** must precede all labels. A label can be any sequence of characters. For example, the following are valid label statements:

```
label one
label box37
```

Goto

The **goto** statement causes program execution to be transferred to the specified label. For example,

```
goto five
```

transfers control to the code that follows label five.

Ifsense

The only program-control statement is **ifsense**. It determines whether there is an object either to the immediate right, left, above, or below the robot as specified. If there is an object, then the statement that follows the **then** is executed; if there is no object, execution resumes with the next line of the program. You must specify the direction of the sense by using the keywords **up, down, left,** or **right.**

For example, the following program will cause the robot to move along the side of an object.

```
label one
  move down
  ifsense right then goto one
```

Teaching the Robot

You can issue the **teach** command at any time as you type in a program. The command causes the editor screen to be replaced by the environment screen. The robot is positioned at its home position of 0,0. At this point, you can use the numeric keypad to move the robot by using the arrow keys. In addition, you may use the HOME key to send the robot to location 0,0. Each move is recorded and actually becomes part of the program. To stop teaching the robot, you press the END key.

Because the teach routines use the standard predicate **readchar**, it is necessary to use the NUMLOCK key because **readchar** cannot read the arrow keys directly. (To do so would have required using system calls through the **bios** predicate, which would be an unnecessary complication to an already complex program.)

The Program

Because you must have some way to enter a program, a good place to start development is with the program editor. The editor is very simple: it lets you enter one line at a time and then stores each line in a database. You can terminate editing by entering a blank line. After you complete editing, the program is converted into a list, which is saved for possible use by the **goto** statement.

The editor needs the following domains and database declarations:

```
domains
  sentence = string
  prog = sentence*
  list = symbol*
database
  program(sentence)
  store_program(prog)
  xyposition(integer, integer)
```

The **program** database holds the program as a series of sentences and is used by the parser. **Store_program** stores the program as a list and is used by the **goto** statement. Finally, **xyposition** holds the current row,column position of the robot.

As shown, the routine **get_program** actually reads in the program text. The first clause prompts you with a semicolon and reads a line of text. This process repeats until you enter either a blank line or the teach command. The support routine **make_list** converts the text into a list that is saved in the **store_program** database. **Re_store** returns the program back to the **program** database so that the parser can use it.

```
/* enter the program */
get_program(P):-
  write(": "),
  readln(S),
  S<>"",
  assertz(program(S)),
  S<>"teach",
  get_program(P).
get_program(P):-
  /* convert to a list */
  retract(program("teach")),
  clear,
  position,
  teach,
  clear,
  get_program(P).
get_program(P):-
  make_list([],P),
  assert(store_program(P)),
  re_store(P).

make_list(T,S):-
  retract(program(X)),
  append(T,[X],S1),
  make_list(S1,S).
```

```
make_list(S,S).

/* put in database */
re_store(P):-
  get_line(P,P2,S),
  assertz(program(S)),
  re_store(P2).
re_store(_).

/* return the first line and
   the rest of the list */
get_line([S|P2],P2,S).
```

The **teach** predicate, shown here, reads characters from the keypad and uses **record** to place the correct instructions into the **program** database. The predicate **is _clear** (not shown here, but given later in the complete program listing) is used to determine if the requested move is possible. It returns true if the specified location is blank; it returns false if the location is not blank.

```
/* teach the robot some movements */
teach:-  /* use cursor keys to teach
            the robot */
  readchar(C),
  C<>'1',
  record(C),
  teach.
teach.

/* record each move */
record('2'):-
  xyposition(R,C),
  R1=R+1,
  is_clear(R1,C),
  retract(xyposition(R,C)),
  assert(xyposition(R1,C)),
  moveto(R1,C,R,C),
  assertz(program("move down")).
record('8'):-
  xyposition(R,C),
  R1=R-1,
  is_clear(R1,C),
  retract(xyposition(R,C)),
  assert(xyposition(R1,C)),
  moveto(R1,C,R,C),
  assertz(program("move up")).
record('4'):-
  xyposition(R,C),
  C1=C-1,
  is_clear(R,C1),
```

```
  retract(xyposition(R,C)),
  assert(xyposition(R,C1)),
  moveto(R,C1,R,C),
  assertz(program("move left")).
record('6'):-
  xyposition(R,C),
  C1=C+1,
  is_clear(R,C1),
  retract(xyposition(R,C)),
  assert(xyposition(R,C1)),
  moveto(R,C1,R,C),
  assertz(program("move right")).
record('7'):-
  assertz(program("moveto 0 0")),
  retract(xyposition(R,C)),
  assert(xyposition(0,0)),
  moveto(0,0,R,C).
record(_).
```

The robotic programs are executed by a parser that is designed to
work with the syntax of the control language described earlier. The
parser consists of the two predicates **parse**, which is the top-level
routine, and **command**, which handles the specific actions. These
routines are shown here:

```
/* command processor */
parse:-
  retract(program(S)),
  next_word(S,S2,C),
  command(C,S2),!,
  cursor(0,0),
  parse.

command(moveto,S):-
  /* move to specific row and column */
  next_word(S,T,R),
  next_word(T,_,C),
  str_int(R,Ri),   /* convert to integers */
  str_int(C,Ci),
  xyposition(Y,X),
  moveto(Ri,Ci,Y,X),
  purge_xy,
  assert(xyposition(Ri,Ci)),
  purge_points.
command(findt,_):-
  /* find a triangle */
  xyposition(R,C),
  find_triangle(R,C,R1,C1),
  retract(xyposition(Y,X)),
  C2=C1-1,
```

```
    purge_points,
    moveto(R1,C2,Y,X),
    assert(xyposition(R1,C2)).
command(finds,_):-
  /* find a square */
  xyposition(R,C),
  find_square(R,C,R1,C1),
  retract(xyposition(Y,X)),
  C2=C1-1,
  purge_points,
  moveto(0,0,Y,X),
  moveto(R1,C2,0,0),
  assert(xyposition(R1,C2)).
command(move,S):-
  /* move in indicated direction */
  next_word(S,_,D),
  do_move(D),
  purge_points.
command(ifsense,S):-
  /* look for object */
  next_word(S,S2,D),
  next_word(S2,S3,T),
  T=then,
  ifsense(D,S3),
  purge_points.
command(label,_).   /* for use with gotos */
command(goto,S):-
  /* goto a label */
  next_word(S,_,Name),
  store_program(P),  /* get copy */
  find_label(Name,P,_).
command(_,_):-
  write("error in program"),
  nl, fail.
```

The entire program is shown here. The simulation of the robot and the routines that actually carry out each command make up a substantial part of the program, and you should study them carefully. Enter this program into your computer at this time.

```
/* Robot Simulator */
domains
  sentence = string
  prog = sentence*
  list = symbol*
database
  point(integer,integer)
  increments(integer,integer)
  turns(symbol)
```

```
    xyposition(integer, integer)
    program(sentence)
    store_program(prog)
predicates
    start
    run
    clear
    teach
    record(char)
    make_triangle(integer, integer, integer)
    make_left(integer, integer, integer)
    make_right(integer, integer, integer)
    make_base(integer, integer, integer)
    make_square(integer,integer, integer)
    make_top_bottom(integer,integer, integer)
    make_rightside(integer, integer, integer)
    make_leftside(integer, integer, integer)
    make_rt_left(integer, integer, integer)
    make_rt_right(integer, integer, integer)
    make_right_triangle(integer, integer, integer)
    purge(integer, integer)
    purge_points
    purge_program
    purge_increments
    purge_storeprogram
    purge_xy
    position
    make_list(prog,prog)
    append(prog, prog, prog)
    find_triangle(integer, integer, integer, integer)
    find_square(integer, integer, integer, integer)
    find_point(integer, integer, integer, integer)
    is_square(integer, integer)
    is_triangle(integer, integer)
    follow_shape(integer, integer)
    follow(integer, integer, integer, integer)
    find_delim(sentence, integer, integer)
    find_label(symbol, prog, prog)
    next_word(sentence, sentence, symbol)
    strip_space(sentence, sentence)
    parse
    re_store(prog)
    get_line(prog, prog, sentence)
    command(symbol, sentence)
    moveto(integer, integer, integer, integer)
    do_move(symbol)
    is_clear(integer, integer)
    get_program(prog)
    ifsense(symbol, sentence)
goal
    assert(increments(1,1)),
```

```
        assert(increments(-1,1)),
        assert(increments(1,-1)),
        assert(increments(1,0)),
        assert(increments(0,1)),
        assert(increments(-1,-1)),
        assert(increments(-1,0)),
        assert(increments(0,-1)),
        assert(xyposition(0,0)),
        clear,
        start.

clauses
    start:-
        cursor(0,0),
        write("enter program: "),nl,
        get_program(_),
        clear,
        position,
        retract(xyposition(_,_)),
        assert(xyposition(0,0)),
        run.

    /* execute the program */
    run:-
        parse.
    run:-
        purge_xy,
        purge_program,
        purge_increments,
        purge_storeprogram,
        cursor(22,0),
        write("run completed"),nl.

    /* enter the program */
    get_program(P):-
        write(": "),
        readln(S),
        S<>"",
        assertz(program(S)),
        S<>"teach",
        get_program(P).
    get_program(P):-
        /* convert to a list */
        retract(program("teach")),
        clear,
        position,
        teach,
        clear,
        get_program(P).
    get_program(P):-
        make_list([],P),
```

```prolog
    assert(store_program(P)),
    re_store(P).

make_list(T,S):-
    retract(program(X)),
    append(T,[X],S1),
    make_list(S1,S).
make_list(S,S).

/* put in database */
re_store(P):-
    get_line(P,P2,S),
    assertz(program(S)),
    re_store(P2).
re_store(_).

/* return the first line and
    the rest of the list */
get_line([S|P2],P2,S).

/* teach the robot some movements */
teach:-  /* use cursor keys to teach
            the robot */
    readchar(C),
    C<>'1',
    record(C),
    teach.
teach.

/* record each move */
record('2'):-
    xyposition(R,C),
    R1=R+1,
    is_clear(R1,C),
    retract(xyposition(R,C)),
    assert(xyposition(R1,C)),
    moveto(R1,C,R,C),
    assertz(program("move down")).
record('8'):-
    xyposition(R,C),
    R1=R-1,
    is_clear(R1,C),
    retract(xyposition(R,C)),
    assert(xyposition(R1,C)),
    moveto(R1,C,R,C),
    assertz(program("move up")).
record('4'):-
    xyposition(R,C),
    C1=C-1,
    is_clear(R,C1),
    retract(xyposition(R,C)),
    assert(xyposition(R,C1)),
```

```
   moveto(R,C1,R,C),
   assertz(program("move left")).
record('6'):-
   xyposition(R,C),
   C1=C+1,
   is_clear(R,C1),
   retract(xyposition(R,C)),
   assert(xyposition(R,C1)),
   moveto(R,C1,R,C),
   assertz(program("move right")).
record('7'):-
   assertz(program("moveto 0 0")),
   retract(xyposition(R,C)),
   assert(xyposition(0,0)),
   moveto(0,0,R,C).
record(_).


/* command processor */
parse:-
   retract(program(S)),
   next_word(S,S2,C),
   command(C,S2),!,
   cursor(0,0),
   parse.

command(moveto,S):-
   /* move to specific row and column */
   next_word(S,T,R),
   next_word(T,_,C),
   str_int(R,Ri),   /* convert to integers */
   str_int(C,Ci),
   xyposition(Y,X),
   moveto(Ri,Ci,Y,X),
   purge_xy,
   assert(xyposition(Ri,Ci)),
   purge_points.
command(findt,_):-
   /* find a triangle */
   xyposition(R,C),
   find_triangle(R,C,R1,C1),
   retract(xyposition(Y,X)),
   C2=C1-1,
   purge_points,
   moveto(R1,C2,Y,X),
   assert(xyposition(R1,C2)).
command(finds,_):-
   /* find a square */
   xyposition(R,C),
   find_square(R,C,R1,C1),
   retract(xyposition(Y,X)),
   C2=C1-1,
```

```
     purge_points,
     moveto(0,0,Y,X),
     moveto(R1,C2,0,0),
     assert(xyposition(R1,C2)).
command(move,S):-
   /* move in indicated direction */
   next_word(S,_,D),
   do_move(D),
   purge_points.
command(ifsense,S):-
   /* look for object */
   next_word(S,S2,D),
   next_word(S2,S3,T),
   T=then,
   ifsense(D,S3),
   purge_points.
command(label,_).   /* for use with gotos */
command(goto,S):-
   /* goto a label */
   next_word(S,_,Name),
   store_program(P),  /* get copy */
   find_label(Name,P,_).
command(_,_):-
   write("error in program"),
   nl, fail.

/* dissect each line */
/* find a space or period */
find_delim(S,Count,C):-
   frontchar(S,CH,S2),
   CH<>' ', CH<>'.',
   C2=C+1,
   find_delim(S2,Count,C2).
find_delim(_,Count,Count).

/* get the next word */
next_word(S,S2,W):-
   find_delim(S,Count,0),!,
   Count>0,
   frontstr(Count,S,W,S3),
   strip_space(S3,S2).

strip_space(S,S2):-
   frontchar(S,Ch,S2),
   Ch=' '.
strip_space(S,S).

/*****************************************/
/*    actually perform the commands      */
/*****************************************/
/* do the goto */
find_label(N,P,P2):-
   get_line(P,P2,S),
   next_word(S,S2,L),
```

```
    L=label,
    next_word(S2,_,Name),
    N=Name,
    purge_program,
    re_store(P2). /* reset program to label */
find_label(N,P,P2):-
    get_line(P,P3,_),
    find_label(N,P3,P2).

/* move to the specified row and column */
moveto(R,C,Rcurrent,Ccurrent):-
    R=Rcurrent, C=Ccurrent,
    assert(point(R,C)).
moveto(R,C,Rcurrent,Ccurrent):-
    Rcurrent<R,
    R1=Rcurrent+1,
    is_clear(R1,Ccurrent),!, /* no objects in way */
    cursor(Rcurrent,Ccurrent),
    write(' '),
    cursor(R1,Ccurrent),
    write('#'),
    sound(5,100),
    moveto(R,C,R1,Ccurrent).
moveto(R,C,Rcurrent,Ccurrent):-
    Ccurrent<C,
    C1=Ccurrent+1,
    is_clear(Rcurrent,C1),!, /* no objects in way */
    cursor(Rcurrent,Ccurrent),
    write(' '),
    cursor(Rcurrent,C1),
    write('#'),
    sound(5,200),
    moveto(R,C,Rcurrent,C1).
moveto(R,C,Rcurrent,Ccurrent):-
    Rcurrent>R,
    R1=Rcurrent-1,
    is_clear(R1,Ccurrent),!, /* no objects in way */
    cursor(Rcurrent,Ccurrent),
    write(' '),
    cursor(R1,Ccurrent),
    write('#'),
    sound(5,300),
    moveto(R,C,R1,Ccurrent).
moveto(R,C,Rcurrent,Ccurrent):-
    Ccurrent>C,
    C1=Ccurrent-1,
    is_clear(Rcurrent,C1),!, /* no objects in way */
    cursor(Rcurrent,Ccurrent),
    write(' '),
    cursor(Rcurrent,C1),
    write('#'),
    sound(5,400),
    moveto(R,C,Rcurrent,C1).
moveto(R,C,Rcurrent,Ccurrent):-
```

```
      R=Rcurrent,
      R1=R+1,
      moveto(R1,C,Rcurrent,Ccurrent),
      retract(point(Y,X)),
      moveto(R,C,Y,X).
moveto(R,C,Rcurrent,Ccurrent):-
      R=Rcurrent,
      R1=R-1,
      moveto(R1,C,Rcurrent,Ccurrent),
      retract(point(Y,X)),
      moveto(R,C,Y,X).
moveto(R,C,Rcurrent,Ccurrent):-
      C=Ccurrent,
      C1=C+1,
      moveto(R,C1,Rcurrent,Ccurrent),
      retract(point(Y,X)),
      moveto(R,C,Y,X).

/* move in the specified direction */
do_move(left):-
      xyposition(R,C),
      C1=C-1,
      moveto(R,C1,R,C),
      purge_xy,
      assert(xyposition(R,C1)).
do_move(right):-
      xyposition(R,C),
      C1=C+1,
      moveto(R,C1,R,C),
      purge_xy,
      assert(xyposition(R,C1)).
do_move(up):-
      xyposition(R,C),
      R1=R-1,
      moveto(R1,C,R,C),
      purge_xy,
      assert(xyposition(R1,C)).
do_move(down):-
      xyposition(R,C),
      R1=R+1,
      moveto(R1,C,R,C),
      purge_xy,
      assert(xyposition(R1,C)).

/* if object then take action */
ifsense(left,S):-
      xyposition(R,C),
      C1=C-1,
      scr_char(R,C1,Ch),
      Ch<>' ',
      next_word(S,S2,W),
      command(W,S2).
ifsense(right,S):-
      xyposition(R,C),
```

```
        C1=C+1,
        scr_char(R,C1,Ch),
        Ch<>' ',
        next_word(S,S2,W),
        command(W,S2).
     ifsense(up,S):-
        xyposition(R,C),
        R1=R-1,
        scr_char(R1,C,Ch),
        Ch<>' ',
        next_word(S,S2,W),
        command(W,S2).
     ifsense(down,S):-
        xyposition(R,C),
        R1=R+1,
        scr_char(R1,C,Ch),
        Ch<>' ',
        next_word(S,S2,W),
        command(W,S2).
     ifsense(_,_).

     /* no object in location R,C */
     is_clear(R,C):-
        R<25, R>-1, C<80, C>-1,
        scr_char(R,C,Ch),
        Ch=' '.

/*******************************/
/* Delta-D recognizer from     */
/* chapter 5                   */
/*******************************/

     find_triangle(R,C,A,B):-
        find_point(R,C,A,B),
        is_triangle(A,B).

     is_triangle(R,C):-
        follow_shape(R,C),
        purge(0,N),!,
        N=2.
     is_triangle(_,_):-
        purge(0,_), fail.

     find_square(R,C,A,B):-
        find_point(R,C,A,B),
        is_square(A,B).

     is_square(R,C):-
        follow_shape(R,C),
        purge(0,N),!,
        N=3.
     is_square(_,_):-
        purge(0,_), fail.

     find_point(A,B,R,C):-
```

```
    scr_char(A,B,Ch),
    Ch='*',
    R=A,C=B.
find_point(A,B,R,C):-
  B1=B+1,
  B1<80,!,
  find_point(A,B1,R,C).
find_point(A,_,R,C):-
  A1=A+1,
  A1<24,!,
  find_point(A1,0,R,C).
find_point(_,_,_,_):-fail.

/* follow a shape until back at
   starting point counting the
   number of changes in direction */
follow_shape(R,C):-
  assert(point(R,C)),
  R1=R+1,
  scr_char(R1,C,Ch),
  Ch='*',
  follow(R1,C,1,0),!.
follow_shape(R,C):-
  R1=R+1,C1=C+1,
  scr_char(R1,C1,Ch),
  Ch='*',
  follow(R1,C1,1,1),!.

/* follow each line */
follow(R,C,_,_):-
  point(Y,X),
  R=Y,C=X.   /* back at start */
follow(R,C,I,J):-/* keep going in same direction */
  R1=R+I,
  C1=C+J,
  scr_char(R1,C1,Ch),
  Ch='*',
  assert(point(R,C)),
  follow(R1,C1,I,J).
follow(R,C,_,_):-/* try horizontal */
  assert(turns(once)), /* change direction */
  increments(I,J),
  R1=R+I, C1=C+J,
  not(point(R1,C1)),
  scr_char(R1,C1,Ch),
  Ch='*',
  follow(R1,C1,I,J).

purge(0,N):-
  retract(turns(_)),
  N1=0+1,
  purge(N1,N).
purge(0,0).

purge_points:-
  retract(point(_,_)),
  fail.
```

```
purge_points.

purge_program:-
  retract(program(_)),
  fail.
purge_program.

purge_storeprogram:-
  retract(store_program(_)),
  fail.
purge_storeprogram.

purge_xy:-
  retract(xyposition(_,_)),
  fail.
purge_xy.

purge_increments:-
  retract(increments(_,_)),
  fail.
purge_increments.

/* place objects on screen */

position:-
  R=4, C=10,
  R2=11, C2=50,
  R1=10, C1=30,
  clear,
  make_triangle(R,C,5),
  make_square(R1,C1,5),
  make_right_triangle(R2,C2,10).


make_triangle(R,C,N):-
  make_left(R,C,N),
  make_right(R,C,N),
  make_base(R,C,N).
make_left(R,C,N):-
  N<>0,
  cursor(R,C),
  write("*"),
  R1=R+1,
  C1=C-1,
  N1=N-1,
  make_left(R1,C1,N1).
make_left(_,_,_).
make_right(R,C,N):-
  N<>0,
  cursor(R,C),
  write("*"),
  R1=R+1,
  C1=C+1,
  N1=N-1,
  make_right(R1,C1,N1).
make_right(_,_,_).
```

```
make_base(R,C,N):-
  R1=R+N, C1=C-N,
  cursor(R1,C1),
  write("***********").

make_right_triangle(R,C,N):-
  make_rt_left(R,C,N),
  C1=C+9,
  make_rt_right(R,C1,N),
  cursor(R,C),
  write("**********").

make_rt_left(R,C,N):-
  N<>0,
  cursor(R,C),
  write("*"),
  R1=R+1,
  N1=N-1,
  make_rt_left(R1,C,N1).
make_rt_left(_,_,_).
make_rt_right(R,C,N):-
  N<>0,
  cursor(R,C),
  write("*"),
  R1=R+1,
  C1=C-1,
  N1=N-1,
  make_rt_right(R1,C1,N1).
make_rt_right(_,_,_).

make_square(R,C,N):-
  make_top_bottom(R,C,N),
  make_leftside(R,C,N),
  make_rightside(R,C,N).

make_top_bottom(R,C,N):-
  cursor(R,C),
  write("**********"),
  R1=R+N,
  cursor(R1,C),
  write("**********").

make_leftside(R,C,N):-
  N<>0,
  cursor(R,C),
  write("*"),
  N1=N-1,
  R1=R+1,
  make_leftside(R1,C,N1).
make_leftside(_,_,_).

make_rightside(R,C,N):-
  N<>0,
  C1=C+9,
```

```
   cursor(R,C1),
   write("*"),
   N1=N-1,
   R1=R+1,
   make_rightside(R1,C,N1).
make_rightside(_,_,_).

clear:-
   makewindow(1,6,0,"",0,0,25,80).

append([],List,List).
append([X|L1], List2, [X|L3]):-
   append(L1,List2,L3).
```

Using the Simulator

The robot simulator is a complex program that uses a significant amount of recursion. For this reason, it is necessary to set the stack size, via Turbo Prolog's **setup** command, to 4000 before running the program. Remember to save the setup and reload it to activate the new stack size.

When you run the simulator program, you will first be instructed to enter a program. You do this by simply entering one line at a time. For a simple example, enter the following program.

```
moveto 12 70
moveto 0 0
finds
```

Then enter a blank line. The environment screen will replace the editor screen and you will see the robot move about as instructed. You will also hear different sounds as it changes direction. Figure 6-4 shows this screen and the robot's path.

When you run the program, the robot correctly goes around the objects that lie in its path. You should study the **moveto** predicate to see how this is accomplished.

Here is another example: the next program will make the robot follow the side of the square.

```
moveto 10 29
label one
move down
ifsense right then goto one
```

As long as there is an object to the robot's right, the robot proceeds to move down. Figure 6-5 shows the path that the robot takes.

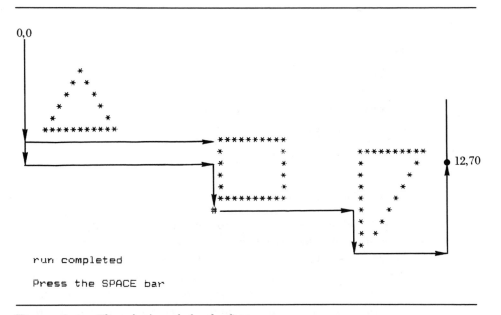

Figure 6-4.   The robot's path for the first program

The next step you should take is to try teaching the robot by using the teach command. Remember —to begin teaching, you simply type the keyword **teach** after the semicolon prompt of the editor.

Expanding the Simulator

In a book, long listings can become oppressive and generally should be avoided. Even with the few commands that the simulator can accept, in its present form, its length is dangerously close to the limit. Because of this, the simulator did not include more functionality. However, it is easy for you to add more commands to the control language by simply following the format of the other commands given here.

One particularly interesting change is to add other types of single-character objects to the environment and allow the robot to pick them up. This would necessitate the addition of close and open grip com-

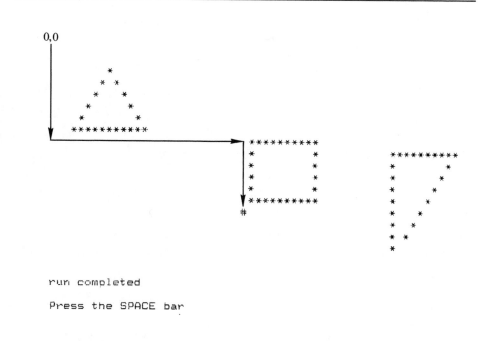

Figure 6-5.   The robot's path as it follows the side of the square

mands, as well as another sensing statement. Also, you might want to try sprinkling "energy pellets" about and making the robot find them.

You can add variables to the simulator by creating another database. For example, the format for this database would be

```
variable(symbol, integer)
```

Therefore, a statement like **A = 1** would result in a **retract (variable(A, _))**, followed by **assert(variable(A, 1))**.

Finally, you will probably want a way to save and load your programs. You can do this by using **save** and **consult**. You could also read and write files by using Turbo Prolog's built-in file predicates.

Machine Learning

Closely tied to intelligence is learning. In fact, intelligence cannot exist without the ability to learn because learning is the means of acquiring new knowledge. Learning allows you both to adapt to and use to your advantage various situations and events. Thus, the ability to learn is a powerful tool. It is not surprising that many programmers want to create a program that can use this tool in the way that people do. A program that could do this would in theory be the last program ever written because it could learn to perform various tasks on its own simply by being taught.

In this chapter, you will explore the various ways in which a computer can learn. (These learning methods also apply to a person.) In addition, the chapter will develop a fairly simple program that illustrates a sophisticated method of achieving machine learning.

Two Kinds of Learning

A surprising paradox is that it is both very easy and extremely difficult for a computer to learn. The reason for this is that there are two distinctly different types of learning: rote learning and cognitive learning. At this point, you may be tempted to suggest that there are several other types of learning, such as learning by analogy, learning by example, learning by observation, and the like. However, these refer to methods by which knowledge can be acquired and not to the actual mechanisms that enable learning to occur. It is the basis of learning that is the focus of this section.

Learning by Rote

Much of what you learn is simply made up of facts that you acquire through memorization or repetition. This process is called learning by rote. Some examples of facts that you may learn by this method might be that the capital of Illinois is Springfield, that 1+1 is 2, or that the distance from New York to Chicago is 1500 miles. But rote learning is not restricted only to facts; it also can be applied to a sequence of actions —

such as a task. A factory worker, for instance, can learn to remove red and yellow boxes from an assembly line, and then place them in the proper bins. The memorized sequence is as follows:

1. Pick up red or yellow boxes.

2. Place in proper bins.

The same idea applies to the way that most children are taught long division or multiplication. Each child memorizes a specific sequence of actions and then applies the sequence on demand.

The key to rote learning is specialization. By necessity, all things that you can learn by rote are specific. The capital of Illinois is specific. The distance from New York to Chicago is specific, as are the factory worker's task and the method used to solve long division. Although such a method might be applied to a wide variety of problems, such as long division, which could be used to divide any two numbers, the actual sequence of steps that make up the task is not generalized. Thus, sequences learned by rote are more properly called procedures.

A computer can easily learn anything that you can learn by rote. In fact, it is the normal manner in which a computer operates: it is programmed! Since computers are very good at following instructions, they can easily follow a procedure or store some item of information in a database. For example, just as you might tell a student that water is liquid between 32 degrees and 212 degrees, so you can enter the same information into a database program and, when you ask when water is liquid, both the student and the computer will respond in the same way.

As another example, the robot simulator that was developed in Chapter 6 was able to be taught various actions. As the robot was taught, it remembered the individual instructions. Further, the robot was able to act upon that knowledge later —it could demonstrate what it had learned.

In summary, rote learning involves the memorization of either specific facts or procedures. It does not require any generalizations to be derived or any high-level thinking. Because computers can already easily learn by rote, the next section looks at another way to learn.

Cognitive Learning

The most important way that you learn, which is the hardest to implement on a computer, is cognitive learning. In this form of learning, you use your reason to analyze, organize, and correlate specific pieces of knowledge. The product of this mental effort is the creation of class descriptions. A class description is simply a generalization that is derived from the examination of a few specific examples. For example, through your knowledge of a few specific dogs, you are able to create a generalized concept of a dog that allows you to recognize virtually any specific dog as a dog. The point is that you have learned the class description of a dog. Generally, a class description defines all objects of its type.

It is amazing how quickly you can learn a generalization. Consider the four objects shown in Figure 7-1. One of them does not belong. Clearly, the triangle is not of the same classification as the squares, even though the squares are of three different sizes. You knew that the triangle, and not one of the squares, was odd, because you could easily create a classification that would fit all three squares, but would not

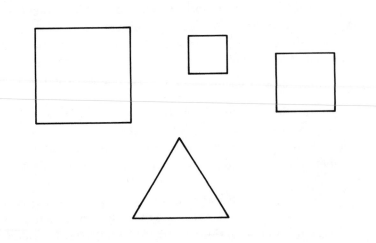

Figure 7-1.   Which figure does not belong?

apply to the triangle. In a simple situation like this, you created that general category without even thinking about it.

You can also form class descriptions for procedures. You can then adapt these generalized procedures to a variety of similar situations. For example, you know the general procedure to sweep a floor — any floor — with just about any broom. Further, you can easily drive your car on any road, along any route, even if you have never seen it before. You can do these things because you can generalize the basic procedural elements that define these tasks. It is the ability to generalize procedures that currently separates humans from robots. A robot can only know a specific task; it is not able to generalize it.

Your ability to learn a classification is not restricted to objects or procedures, but can apply to ideas and concepts as well. For example, most philosophies and religions attempt to give their followers a generalized code of conduct and beliefs, and allow the individual to interpret specific events according to this code. Consider the concepts of good and evil. These are general classifications that are used to describe specific events. These concepts represent class descriptions of certain actions with moral implications.

Clearly, the ability to learn class descriptions is fundamental to the creation of a computer that thinks the way that humans do. It is the emulation of this type of learning that this chapter deals with.

How Class Descriptions Are Learned

Many times, this book has noted that one of the largest hurdles to overcome when trying to create an intelligent computer is the fact that you have very little understanding of your own thought processes. The same is true of cognitive learning. Usually, you have virtually no idea of how you can create generalized class descriptions of individual objects. However, in the course of trying to find a way to emulate this type of learning in a computer, some insight into human thought processes may have been uncovered.

Professor Patrick Henry Winston, the director of the artificial intelligence laboratory at the Massachusetts Institute of Technology, made the major breakthrough toward understanding cognitive learning. He is one of the world's leading authorities on AI, and his book *Artificial Intelligence* (Menlo Park, Calif.: Addison-Wesley, 1984) is recommended reading to the serious student of AI. His method of learning class descriptions is sometimes called "hit-and-near-miss" for reasons that you will soon see.

Examples and Near-Misses

To help you understand the hit-and-near-miss procedure, you will now study a traditional example that illustrates its key points. Imagine that you are teaching someone to recognize an arch that is constructed out of blocks. You first build the arch shown in Figure 7-2a and then tell the person that this structure is an arch. Next, you remove the top block and place it next to the other two blocks, as shown in Figure 7-2b, and inform the student that this is not an arch. This implies that an arch must have a block on top. You next build an arch like the one shown in Figure 7-2c and tell the person that this is an arch. Then you construct the structure shown in Figure 7-2d and say that this is not an arch. This implies that the side supports may not touch. Finally, you build the arch in Figure 7-2e, which has a cylinder instead of a block on top, and indicate that this is still an arch. At this point, the student will have this class description for an arch: it must have either a block or a cylinder on top of two other blocks that do not touch, and the support blocks may be standing up or lying down.

This example illustrates this key point: you can create a class description by using selected examples of objects (or concepts, or ideas, or procedures) either that are part of the class or that only differ in a few ways. As long as the student is told which objects are part of the class and which objects are near-misses, the student can construct a class description by observing the similarities and differences that are associated with each example.

As a class description is developed, the role played by the correct examples is different from that played by the near-misses. Each correct

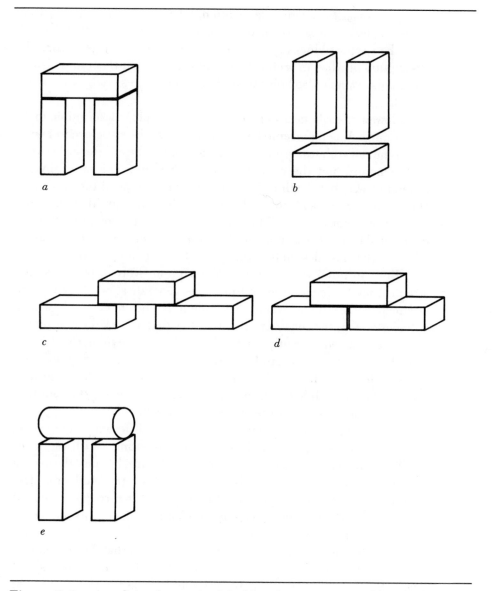

Figure 7-2.   A traditional example of the hit-and-near-miss procedure: *a*, an arch; *b*, a near-miss — no top; *c*, another arch; *d*, a near-miss — blocks touching; and *e*, an arch

example causes the current description to be broadened or generalized. For example, in the case of an arch, when you show the student the arch with the support blocks lying down, the student must generalize the description of what an arch is to accept the fact that this too is also an arch. This example also holds true when the student sees the arch with a cylinder.

However, each near-miss causes a developing description to be constrained. When presented with the fact that the structure in Figure 7-2*b* is not an arch, the student has to determine the difference between that structure and the current class description. The only obvious difference was that the third block is no longer on top of the other two. Hence, the student adds to the description the constraint that all arches must have a block on top. The student follows the same process when confronted with the near-miss in which the sides touch: the constraint is added to the class description that the sides must not touch.

Keep in mind that as a class description evolves, previous constraints may be generalized and previous generalizations may be constrained. For example, when the student is shown the arch with a cylinder on top, the constraint that requires that a block must be on top has to be changed to require that either a block *or* a cylinder may be on top. Had you shown the student several arches, each having different types of tops, eventually the constraint would have been changed to require that an arch have something on top. In a case like this, another class description is substituted for a long OR list.

If you look at this procedure from a slightly different point of view, you can see that each correct object presents the student with a series of attributes that an object of its class *may have*. Hence, because the person is told that a specific object is part of a class, the student's class description must include objects of this type. It is through the use of near-misses that the student can learn what an object of its class *must have* or *must not* have.

Fundamental to this learning process is the fact that the near-misses must differ from the actual thing in only a few, obvious ways — preferably one. Otherwise, the student would not be able to discern what the constraining factor is. For example, if you showed the first arch and then pointed to a bird flying outside the window and said that the bird was not an arch, the student could add no meaningful information to the class description of an arch!

The Hit-and-Near-Miss Procedure

It is now time to translate the example just given of the hit-and-near-miss method of learning class descriptions into an algorithm that a computer can use. Although you will ultimately want to transform the following procedure into its Turbo Prolog declarative version, first study it in its procedural form.

The hit-and-near-miss algorithm makes two assumptions: First, there is a teacher that presents either samples that are part of the class or near-misses, and never lies about the samples. Second, the first example must be a valid sample because it is the one that forms the initial model. Given these assumptions, the hit-and-near-miss algorithm is as follows.

```
observe the sample and form the initial model
repeat
      observe sample
      if hit then generalize
      else restrict
until done
```

At this point, it is not important how the sample is observed or how the initial model is formed. However, it is crucial to your understanding of the algorithm that you see how the model is generalized and restricted. Here are the procedures to accomplish this in their simplest forms. (For the complete form of these procedures, you should refer to Winston's book that was mentioned earlier.)

```
procedure restrict:
      determine the difference between the near-miss
      and the evolving model
      if the model has an attribute not found
      in the near-miss, then require this
      attribute
```

if the near-miss has an attribute not found
in the model, then forbid this attribute

procedure generalize:
determine the difference between the example
and the evolving model
reconcile the difference by enlarging the model

As you can see, although easy to describe, the procedures **generalize** and **restrict** are tricky to implement. The most difficult aspect is to reconcile the differences and enlarge the model, as required by the **generalize** procedure. To understand why this is so, think back to the arch example. If a computer was shown the arch with the cylinder, the structure would have invoked the **generalize** procedure. Because the only difference between the current description and the sample was the shape of what was on top of the arch, the **generalize** procedure must change the model so that it allows either a cylinder or a block to be on top. However, what is the best way to do this? There are two approaches. The first approach is to create an OR list. In this case, the part of the model that deals with the top of the arch becomes "must have block OR cylinder on top." This approach is the easiest but has a serious flaw when the computer encounters a large number of variations. The second approach is for the computer to create a new class of attributes and to use the class name in the model, while storing the actual attributes that form the class elsewhere. In this case, the what's-on-top part of the model becomes "must have BC on top," where BC is the class name that refers to the class of objects that can be on top. At this point, BC contains only "block" and "cylinder"; however, it could be enlarged without changing the description of the model.

Two Important Principles

Although not completely necessary for the proper operation of the hit-and-near-miss procedure, there are two principles that, when applied, greatly enhance its efficiency and reliability. The first is called "no guessing" and is invoked when the computer cannot confidently discern the difference between the current model and the near-miss; that is, when there is doubt about what should be learned then the computer should *learn nothing*. Although this principle may sound conservative, it helps avoid errors. This principle need not be invoked if the teacher always supplies near-misses with obvious differences.

The second principle is called no altering. If the teacher supplies a correct example that fails to match the current definition, then the computer creates a separate special-case classification rather than trying to expand the current classification to cover it. For example, the definition of an automobile may contain the constraint that it has an internal combustion engine. Hence, the computer should treat an electric car as a member of a special-case classification.

Because both of these principles are invoked only in situations of conflict that can be avoided if the teacher is careful about the examples, they will not be added to the program that is developed later in this chapter. However, you will need to implement them for any application to be used in the real world.

Later in this chapter, you will see a simple implementation of the hit-and-near-miss approach to learning class definitions. However, before you can develop any programs, you should understand the various ways that a computer can represent and store knowledge.

Knowledge Representation

Aside from the obvious difficulty of devising a program that can learn, a secondary problem is creating a way to store the acquired knowledge inside the computer. Both the nature of the knowledge and the preference of the programmer determine the way that knowledge is represented. There are several techniques that have evolved in the field of knowledge representation. The most important are as follows:

- Trees

- Lists

- Networks.

This section will explore each of these techniques.

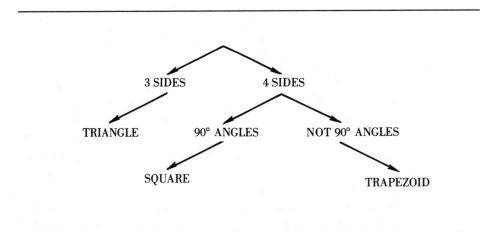

Figure 7-3.   A knowledge tree of squares, triangles, and trapezoids

Trees

If you think back to the way that a backward-chaining expert system operates, you can clearly see that the most efficient way to represent knowledge for this type of expert system is as a tree. As the expert system progresses through the tree, it prunes away large sections and finds the proper piece of knowledge quickly. To understand how knowledge can be represented as a tree, consider the tree, which is shown in Figure 7-3, that is used to store information about squares, triangles, and trapezoids. As this figure shows, an expert system that uses this knowledge tree will always ask its user to answer relevant questions as it moves through the tree.

Trees are hierarchical in nature and, hence, may only be used to store hierarchical knowledge. However, this is not too great a restriction because much knowledge falls into this category. The greatest disadvantage to using trees is the difficulty of constructing and maintaining them so that they stay efficient. The level of overhead associated with trees may make them unattractive when you want to store fairly small amounts of knowledge.

Lists

As you probably know by now, lists are important to successful Turbo Prolog programming. What you may not know is that lists have always been AI's traditional method of knowledge representation. The primary reason for this is that LISP (LISt Processing), the first AI language, was designed to handle lists efficiently. What makes lists particularly attractive for knowledge representation is that they are so easy to work with in Turbo Prolog.

To understand how knowledge is represented in lists, imagine a card catalog in a library. If you are looking for a book about a specific topic, you will scan each card, rejecting those that do not pertain to what you are seeking and stopping when you find the book that you want. In other words, knowledge stored as a list requires a sequential search to retrieve it. Figure 7-4 shows how you can store the knowledge about triangles, squares, and trapezoids as a list.

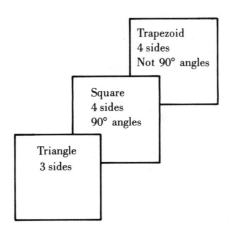

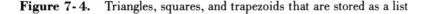

Figure 7-4.   Triangles, squares, and trapezoids that are stored as a list

Even though lists can only be processed sequentially, they are important because you can use them to represent any and all types of knowledge. It is this great flexibility that made them important to AI in the first place. Also, remember that, by using various indexing schemes, you can make lists almost as efficient as trees.

Networks

The representation of knowledge as a network is as fascinating and powerful as it is complex. It is possible that network representation of knowledge will be the standard one day, but only after "black-box" routines are available for general use. The knowledge network is based on two conditions. First, the knowledge in the network is represented by nodes in a nonhierarchical graph: unlike the tree, all nodes in the network have the same importance and any one of them could be used as a starting point. The second condition is that the nodes are arranged so that similar types of knowledge are grouped close to each other; that is, adjacent nodes have near-miss relationships. For example, Figure 7-5 shows a network of geometric shapes.

You access the network model by entering the network at an appropriate point and then proceeding along the network until the proper node is reached. In theory, this method should be quite efficient because each transition to a new node is made because it is in the direction of increasing similarity —which is a form of hill climbing. (Actually, the method samples each node that connects to the current node and selects the one that is most consistent with the evidence.) Although this procedure will work no matter where you enter the network, it is best to enter at a node that is somewhat close to the goal. Hence, most network models also contain lists of indexes that help select the entry node for each situation. As a worst case, if you accidentally chose the most dissimilar node, the network degenerates into a list.

An advantage to the network method of knowledge representation is that it can easily and efficiently handle both hierarchical and nonhierarchical knowledge. The nonhierarchical knowledge will tend to be on the outer boundary of the network, with the hierarchical knowledge located nearer the center (in an abstract sense).

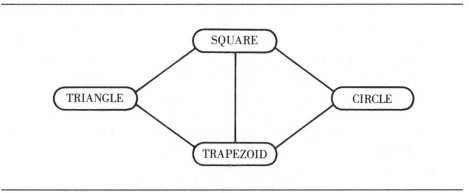

Figure 7- 5.   A network of geometric shapes

Many AI researchers believe that the network model most closely resembles a human's method of knowledge representation. But this is not known conclusively as of this writing.

Implementing the Hit-and-Near-Miss Procedure

Of the three possible ways that knowledge can be represented, the easiest and quickest when using Turbo Prolog is the list. So, it is this method that will be used by the implementation of the hit-and-near-miss class description learning program that is developed here. As was stated during the description of the hit-and-near-miss algorithm, the program described in this chapter is the simplest version. However, even this simple version presents some fairly challenging problems if you implement it in the most general manner. Unfortunately, the solution to some of these problems requires a great deal of code and clouds the fundamental logic of each predicate. Hence, the version developed here will correctly learn class descriptions, assuming that the teacher follows a strict format, which will be explained later.

The key to implementing the class definition learning procedure is to maintain two lists for each classification. The first list contains those attributes that the classification requires, and the second list holds attributes that the classification *may have*. Although only the required list is needed to define the class, the "may have" list is used to evolve the model. As the computer learns new attributes, it places them first in the "may have" list and, if it is studying a near-miss, it only moves the attributes to the required list if it learns that they must be part of the definition.

Each classification is stored in a database that holds its name and lists. The necessary declarations are shown here.

```
domains
  attribute = attr(string,string,string)
  list = attribute*

database
  class(symbol,list,list)
     /* name, must, can */
```

Note that **list** is a list of compound objects that use the functor **attr**. The use of a compound object here greatly simplifies the argument lists of some other predicates, as you will see.

The main loop of the learner is shown here.

```
/* this is the main learning loop */
learn(ClassName):-
  example(ClassName,[],E),
  retract(class(ClassName,R,C)),
  generalize(E,C,Can,R,R2),
  nearmiss(ClassName,[],M),
  restrict(E,M,R2,Req),
  reconcile(Req,Can,Newcan),
  assert(class(ClassName,Req,Newcan)),!,
  write("More? (y/n)"),
  readln(Q), Q=y,
  learn(ClassName).
```

The loop works like this. The predicate **example** is used to read in a user-input example that belongs to the class specified by **ClassName**. The current model is extracted from the database and generalized using

generalize. Next, **nearmiss** reads in the user's near-miss description of an object. The predicate **restrict** is used to restrict the model as defined by the hit-and-near-miss procedure. **Reconcile** performs a little cleanup before the loop replaces the updated definition in the database. This cycle repeats until there are no more examples and near-misses.

The entire program is shown here. You should enter it into your computer at this time.

```
/* A simple implementation of the "hit and miss"
   class description learning procedure
*/
domains
  attribute = attr(string,string,string)
  list = attribute*

database
  class(symbol,list,list)
    /* name, must, can */

predicates
  start
  learn(symbol)
  restrict(list,list,list,list)
  generalize(list,list,list,list,list)
  add(attribute,list)
  member(attribute,list)
  append(list,list,list)
  example(symbol,list,list)
  nearmiss(symbol, list, list)
  remove(attribute, list, list)
  reconcile(list,list,list)
  display_knowledge
  writelist(list,integer)
goal
  start.

clauses

  start:-
    write("learn or display? (l/d) "),
    readln(Q),
    Q=l,
    write("class name: "),
    readln(Name),
    assert(class(Name,[],[])),
    learn(Name).
  start:-
    display_knowledge.
```

```
/* this is the main learning loop */
learn(ClassName):-
  example(ClassName,[],E),
  retract(class(ClassName,R,C)),
  generalize(E,C,Can,R,R2),
  nearmiss(ClassName,[],M),
  restrict(E,M,R2,Req),
  reconcile(Req,Can,Newcan),
  assert(class(ClassName,Req,Newcan)),!,
  write("More? (y/n)"),
  readln(Q), Q=y,
  learn(ClassName).

/* get attributes of a correct example */
example(Name,L,E):-
  write("E: subject "),
  readln(S),
  S<>"",
  write("E: verb "),
  readln(V),
  write("E: object "),
  readln(O),
  add(attr(S,V,O),L,E2),
  example(Name,E2,E).
example(_,E,E).

/* get attributes of a near-miss */
nearmiss(Name,L,E):-
  write("M: subject "),
  readln(S),
  S<>"",
  write("M: verb "),
  readln(V),
  write("M: object "),
  readln(O),
  add(attr(S,V,O),L,E2),
  nearmiss(Name,E2,E).
nearmiss(_,E,E).

/* restrict the definition */
restrict(_,[],Req,Req).
restrict(E,[M|Mt],Req,Req2):-
  /* if part of description continue */
  remove(M,E,Et),
  restrict(Et,Mt,Req,Req2).
restrict(E,[attr(S,V,O)|Mt],Req,Req2):-
  /* check for negation of a trait */
  fronttoken(V,_,V2), /* remove the not */
  frontchar(V2,_,V3),
  remove(attr(S,V3,O),E,Et),
  add(attr(S,V3,O),Req,R), /* add to requirements list */
  restrict(Et,Mt,R,Req2).
restrict(_,_,Req,Req).
```

```
/* generalize the model */
generalize([],C,C,R,R).
generalize([attr(S,V,O)|Et],C,C2,R,R2):-
  /* create new class if common
     verb is encountered in required list
     with different subject
  */
  member(attr(_,V,O),R),
  remove(attr(X̄,V,O),R,T),
  X<>S,
  fronttoken(Nc," ",X),
  fronttoken(NewClass,S,Nc),
  add(attr(NewClass,V,O),T,T2),
  generalize(Et,C,C2,T2,R2).
generalize([attr(S,V,O)|Et],C,C2,R,R2):-
  /* create new class if common
     verb is encountered in may have
     list with different subject
  */
  member(attr(_,V,O),C),
  remove(attr(X̄,V,O),C,T),
  X<>S,
  fronttoken(Nc," ",X),
  fronttoken(NewClass,S,Nc),
  add(attr(NewClass,V,O),T,T2),
  generalize(Et,T2,C2,R,R2).
generalize([E|Et],C,C2,R,R):-
  /* otherwise add to may have list */
  not(member(E,C)),
  add(E,C,C3),
  generalize(Et,C3,C2,R,R).

generalize([_|T],C,C2,R,R2):-
  generalize(T,C,C2,R,R2).

append([],List,List).
append([X|L1], List2, [X|L3]):-
  append(L1,List2,L3).

/* clean up the may have list */
reconcile([],C,C).
reconcile([R|T],C,C2):-
  remove(R,C,C3),
  reconcile(T,C3,C2).
reconcile([_|T],C,C2):-
  reconcile(T,C,C2).


writelist([],_).
writelist([attr(S,V,O)|Tail],3):-
  write(S," ",V," ",O),nl,
  nl,writelist(Tail,1).
writelist([attr(S,V,O)|Tail],I):-
```

```
    N=I+1,
    write(S," ",V," ",O),nl,
    writelist(Tail,N).

  member(N,[N|_]).
  member(N,[_|T]):- member(N,T).

  add(X,L,[X|L]).

remove(X,[X|T],L):-
  remove(X,T,L),!.
remove(X,[X|T],T).
remove(X,[H|T],[H|L]):-
  remove(X,T,L).

display_knowledge:-
  class(Name,R,C),
  write(Name," requires: "),nl,
  writelist(R,1),nl,
  write("can have: "),nl,
  writelist(C,1),nl,
  fail.
display_knowledge.
```

The predicate **restrict** moves attributes from the **may have** list to the required list. When **generalize** determines that a new class of objects must be created, it creates a new class name that consists of the previous name and the new name that are connected by an underscore.

Using the Program

As stated earlier, this program requires that you (the teacher) follow a strict format so that you do not confuse the student (the computer). First, all object descriptions must be entered in the following format:

    subject verb object

For example, here are some valid descriptions:

    tires are round

    table has four legs

    gravity pulls down

The program will prompt you for the subject, verb, and object separately so you can use sequences of words for each part without fear of confusing the system. You can enter as many attributes for each example or near-miss as desired. An empty response at the prompt for the subject stops entry. So that you can remember whether you are entering an example or a near-miss, either an **E** or an **M** precede the prompts, indicating an example or a miss, respectively.

Second, the differences between the correct examples and the near-misses must be represented as NOT relationships. For example, if the sample has the color red and the class description requires the color red, then a near-miss must not contain the color red. For example, to create the classification "red blocks," you might first tell the computer that red blocks are blocks, and they are red. For a near-miss, you would say that red blocks are blocks and are not red.

To see how the program actually works, you should run the program at this time and enter the following information.

```
learn or display? (l/d) l
class name: arch
E: subject: side 1
E: verb: left of
E: object: side 2
E: subject: brick
E: verb: on top of
E: object: sides
E: subject: <cr>
M: subject: side 1
M: verb: left of
M: object: side 2
M: subject: brick
M: verb: not on top of
M: object: sides
M: subject: <cr>
More? (y/n) y
E: subject: side 1
E: verb: left of
E: object: side 2
E: subject: cylinder
E: verb: on top of
E: object: sides
E: subject: <cr>
M: subject: <cr>
More? (y/n) n
```

```
arch requires:
cylinder_brick on top of sides

can have:
side 1 left of side 2
```

Directions for Further Development

As the program is currently written, it does use an OR list approach to creating classifications inside classifications. You should try to rewrite the program so that it uses symbolic names for these secondary classifications and actually places these classifications into the **class** database, along with what they may be.

Another improvement you may find interesting to add is to create a third list that holds a *must-not-have* relationship. Although not technically required, the list would make it easier for the teacher to enter information into the knowledge base.

Finally, if you are extremely ambitious, you should try to use the hit-and-near-miss procedure as a means of capturing information for use by the expert system that was developed in Chapter 3.

When reading this chapter, you may have guessed that machine learning is, in the language of computer programmers, a "do-able" task. The main problem is one of magnitude: there is simply so much to learn that it strains a current computer's storage facilities.

8 Logic and Uncertainty

221

This chapter deals with two important concepts that are closely related to machine intelligence. The first concept is logic, in both its propositional and predicate forms. The second concept is uncertainty —or, more accurately, the resolution of uncertainty in logical statements. Clearly, much knowledge, especially if it is gained from observation, is probabilistic to some extent; that is, one can believe something to be true while still allowing the possibility of error. For a computer to think and reason like a human, the integration of this uncertainty with logic is required.

To help illustrate the concepts of logic, this chapter will develop two programs: the first performs certain logical transformations and the second implements a subset of Turbo Prolog. Finally, as an example of the linkage of logic and uncertainty, this chapter will modify the expert system that was developed in Chapter 3 so that it includes a certainty coefficient with each attribute. The expert system will then use these certainty values to give a confidence factor about the solution.

Logic

Logic lies at the heart of Turbo Prolog. In some ways, Turbo Prolog is simply an implementation of a special form of logic. Programmers have long felt that if a computer could be made to understand logic, then it could be made to think, since logic seems to be at the core of intelligence. Because of the importance of logic to both AI and Turbo Prolog, a short history of logic is in order.

A Short History of Logic

The first known logician was Aristotle (384—322 B.C.), the Greek philosopher and natural scientist. He developed much of the theory of what has come to be called syllogistic or classical logic. Syllogistic logic essentially deals with deriving the truth (or falsehood) from a philosophical argument. This type of logic is still used broadly because it is the basis for virtually all legal argumentation. Study this short argument:

John is a man.
All men used to be boys.
Therefore, John used to be a boy.

Common sense tells us that John was a boy before he became a man. After being converted to syllogistic form, this argument becomes

$J \rightarrow M$
all $M \rightarrow B$
hence: $J \rightarrow B$

where the symbols J, M, and B stand for John, Man, and Boys, respectively. Read the $\rightarrow$ as "implies" or "is."

In many ways, syllogistic logic is simply a formalization of common sense. However, because syllogistic logic is based in natural language, it suffers from the inherent flaws of natural language. Natural language is often imprecise and can be misunderstood. Also, people tend to hear or read selectively, which can cause further confusion. This lack of precision eventually led to the invention of symbolic logic.

Symbolic logic began with G. W. Leibniz (1646–1717), but was forgotten when he died. The entire field was rediscovered by the person generally given credit for its invention, George Boole (1815–1864). This type of logic generally is called Boolean logic. Symbolic logic deals with the abstraction of concepts into symbols and the interconnection of these symbols by certain operators. For example, study the following:

If   P is true
        Q is false
Then   P or Q is true
        P and Q is false

Symbolic logic forms the basis of most procedural programming languages, and is, of course, the form of logic that this chapter will focus on.

Within symbolic logic, there are two distinct but interlocking branches. The first is propositional logic and the other is predicate calculus. Propositional logic deals with the truthfulness or falseness of a proposition, while predicate calculus also includes relationships between objects and classes of objects.

Propositional Logic

Propositional logic deals with the determination of the truthfulness or falseness of various propositions. A proposition is a properly formed statement that is either true or false. Propositional logic uses operators to connect propositions. These are the most common operators:

AND
OR
NOT
IMPLIES
EQUIVALENT

Assume the two propositions P and Q. The following truth table shows the value of the outcome of each operation when you apply the operations to the different values of P and Q.

P	Q	P and Q	P or Q	not P	P implies Q	P equivalent Q
T	T	T	T	F	T	T
T	F	F	T	F	F	F
F	T	F	T	T	T	F
F	F	F	F	T	T	T

These operations should be familiar to you since virtually all programming languages use propositional logic as the basis for program control.

You may create complex expressions by using these operators, such as

A AND B OR C AND NOT D

This expression is evaluated from left to right. If you add parentheses to an expression, they function in the same way as they do in mathematics: they raise the precedence of the expression within. The following expression uses parentheses to show the way to evaluate the expression that was just given.

(A AND B) OR (C AND NOT D)

Here, the parentheses are used to alter the natural evaluation order.

A AND (B OR (C AND NOT D))

There are a number of different transformation laws that govern the manipulation of expressions. The first law is commutativity, which states that

P AND Q ←→ Q AND P

and

P OR Q ←→ Q OR P

where ←→ means "is the same as."
The associative law states that

(P AND Q) AND R ←→ P AND (Q AND R)

and

(P OR Q) OR R ←→ P OR (Q OR R)

One of the more important laws is DeMorgan's theorem, which states

NOT(P OR Q) ←→ NOT P AND NOT Q

and

$$NOT(P \text{ AND } Q) \longleftrightarrow NOT\ P \text{ OR } NOT\ Q$$

The distributive laws are as follows.

$$P \text{ AND } (Q \text{ OR } R) \longleftrightarrow (P \text{ AND } Q) \text{ OR } (P \text{ AND } R)$$

and

$$P \text{ OR } (Q \text{ AND } R) \longleftrightarrow (P \text{ OR } Q) \text{ AND } (P \text{ OR } R)$$

There are other transformation laws that may be performed but the ones that were just given are all that are necessary.

Because Turbo Prolog itself is based in logic, it is quite easy to write a Turbo Prolog program that will apply these transformation rules. For example, the following program performs both associative and DeMorgan's transformations. The program is quite short and its operation should be obvious. The key predicate **transform** does most of the work, while the program uses **is_and_or** and **opposite** to simplify the coding of **transform**.

```
/* A simple propositional logic
   transformation program.
*/
predicates
  transform(string)
  start
  is_and_or(symbol)
  opposite(symbol, symbol)

goal
  start.

clauses
  start:-
    write("enter expression: "),nl,
    readln(E),
    transform(E).

  transform(S):- /* associative */
    fronttoken(S,T,S1),
    T="(",
    fronttoken(S1,P,S2),
```

```
    fronttoken(S2,Op,S3),
    is_and_or(Op),
    fronttoken(S3,Q,S4),
    fronttoken(S4,")",S5),
    fronttoken(S5,Op2,S6),
    Op2=Op,
    fronttoken(S6,R,_),
    write(P," ",Op,"(",Q," ",Op2," ",R,")"),
    nl.
transform(S):- /* DeMorgan's - OR */
    fronttoken(S,T,S1),
    T="not",
    fronttoken(S1,"(",S1a),
    fronttoken(S1a,P,S2),
    fronttoken(S2,Op,S3),
    is_and_or(Op),
    opposite(Op,Op2),
    fronttoken(S3,Q,S4),
    fronttoken(S4,")",_),
    write("not ",P," ",Op2," not ",Q),
    nl.

is_and_or(O):-
    O="and".
is_and_or(O):-
    O="or".

opposite(O,P):-
    O="and",
    P="or".

opposite(O,P):-
    O="or",
    P="and".
```

To use this program, enter a valid expression. The program will display its transformation. For example, if you entered

```
not (a and b)
```

the transformation displayed would be (by DeMorgan's law)

```
not a or not b
```

You might find it interesting to implement the rest of the transformation rules. Also, instead of simply printing the answer, you could have the clause **transform** produce a string that the program passes to **transform** recursively —thus, allowing multiple transformations.

Although propositional logic forms the basis for both intelligence and computer languages, you cannot use it by itself to represent human knowledge of the world. Because it lacks the ability to represent relationships between objects, it is limited to only determining the truthfulness or falseness of a given instance and cannot be used on classifications. This lacking leads to predicate calculus, which the next section discusses.

Predicate Calculus

Predicate calculus has nothing to do with the branch of higher math called calculus. Predicate calculus, sometimes called predicate logic, is simply an extension of propositional logic.

The basis for predicate calculus is the predicate, which is essentially a function that returns either a value of true or false depending upon its argument. You should be familiar with this concept because it is also the basic building block of Turbo Prolog. (For the moment, however, forget what you know about Prolog so that you can form a clear picture of predicate calculus. Later, you can relate this picture to Turbo Prolog.) A simple predicate might be *is—hard*. When you evaluate this with the argument *rock*, *is—hard* will return true. However, if you evaluate it with the argument *cotton*, it will return false. In predicate calculus, this would be written as

is—hard(rock) → true
is—hard(cotton) → false

You could write these two predicates and arguments in propositional logic as

a rock is hard
cotton is not hard

The fundamental difference between predicate logic and propositional logic is the separation of the attribute from the object that possibly possesses it: that is, in predicate calculus, it is possible to create a function that determines the hardness of any given object. However, in propositional logic, you must generate a new statement for each case.

It is important to understand that predicates can have several arguments. For example, the predicate *equal* requires two arguments and returns true only if both arguments are the same.

Perhaps the greatest improvement that predicate calculus offers over propositional logic is the use of variables. Predicate calculus uses variables to generalize predicates, as shown here:

man (X) → not woman (X)

You should read this as "if X is a man, then X is not a woman."

Another important aspect to predicate calculus is the quantifier. Predicate calculus uses two quantifiers, which are shown here with their standard notation.

Meaning	*Predicate Calculus Notation*
for all	$\forall$
there exists	$\exists$

The "for all" quantifier translates a sentence such as

All cats are animals.

into its predicate calculus equivalent:

$\forall$ X. cat (X) → animal (X)

"There exists" represents a concept such as

There is a person called Tom.

in an expression like this:

$$\exists \, X. \; \text{person}(X) \; \text{and} \; \text{name}(X, \text{Tom})$$

Notice that "name" uses two arguments in order to link a name with a person.

While there are other aspects of predicate calculus, this discussion should be sufficient to show you that Turbo Prolog represents an implementation of predicate calculus as a programming language.

A Baby Prolog

In the early days of microcomputers, there were no full-featured computer languages because there had not been enough time to develop one. To fill the void, various industrious individuals created subset implementations of certain languages. These subset languages were generally called "tiny," as in "tiny BASIC" or "tiny Pascal." Following this tradition, this section will develop a Turbo Prolog program that is a very small subset of Prolog—so much so that even "tiny" is an overstatement. Hence, it will be called "baby Prolog." This program illustrates how predicate logic can be implemented as a computer program and how Turbo Prolog operates.

In predicate calculus or Prolog, the basic form of a predicate is

<predicate __name> (<arg __list>)

However, in order to keep the program simple, baby Prolog will accept only predicates that consist of exactly two arguments. All predicate names and arguments must consist solely of letters; you may not use the underscore. For example, the following are valid for baby Prolog:

    likes(sharon,kathy)
    has(car,tom)
    true(a,b)

Clauses in baby Prolog can be either facts or conditional statements that use the **if** keyword. For example, the following program declares three facts and ends with a conditional statement:

```
true(a,b)
true(b,c)
false(a,c)
true(x,y) if true(a,b)
```

Baby Prolog also allows one variable, called **X**, to be used in place of either argument, as shown here:

```
likes(tom,linda)
likes(tom,betty)
is(happy,tom) if likes(tom,X)
```

The predicate **is (happy,tom)** will succeed as long as **tom** likes someone because the variable **X** will match any argument. As you can see, within its restrictions, baby Prolog roughly operates like Prolog.

One of the easiest ways to implement baby Prolog is to store each clause in a database. The database is shown here.

```
database
  facts(symbol,symbol,symbol,symbol,string)
     /*     name,   arg1,   arg2,    if, expression */
```

As indicated, the database holds the name of the predicate and the two arguments, and, in the case of an **if**, it will place the **if** in the fourth position and the conditional expression in the last field. (Keep in mind that Turbo Prolog does not store your programs in this way. This method only works in very restricted situations.) Each clause that you enter will have its own entry in the database.

Baby Prolog allows you to enter programs by using Turbo Prolog's editor, which it accesses through the built-in **edit** predicate. After you create a program, baby Prolog converts the program into the internal database format by using the predicate **process** shown here:

```
/* process the facts and clauses
   into internal format
*/
process(T):-
  /* end of program */
  T="";T="\n".
process(T):-
  /* an if condition */
  fronttoken(T,Tok,S),
  fronttoken(S,"(",S1),
  fronttoken(S1,Tok2,S2),
  fronttoken(S2,",",S3),
  fronttoken(S3,Tok3,S4),
  fronttoken(S4,")",S5),
  fronttoken(S5,Tok4,S6),
  Tok4="if",
  next_line(S6,S7,L),
  assert(facts(Tok,Tok2,Tok3,Tok4,L)),
  process(S7).
process(T):-
  /* facts */
  fronttoken(T,Tok,S),
  fronttoken(S,"(",S1),
  fronttoken(S1,Tok2,S2),
  fronttoken(S2,",",S3),
  fronttoken(S3,Tok3,S4),
  fronttoken(S4,")",S5),
  assert(facts(Tok,Tok2,Tok3,null,"")),
  process(S5).
```

The built-in predicate **fronttoken** removes one token at a time from each line.

Once the program has been processed, a second editor screen appears and you can create a list of goals, which will be evaluated according to the program that you have created. The predicate **eval** performs the actual evaluation and **eval — driver** sets up the calls to **eval**. Both predicates are shown here.

```
eval_driver(A):-
  A="";A="\n".
eval_driver(A):-
  /* evaluate a line at a time */
  next_line(A,A2,L),
  write(L," "),
  eval(L,_),nl,
  eval_driver(A2).
eval_driver(_).
```

```
eval(A,T):-
  /* evaluate an if clause */
  fronttoken(A,Function,A2),
  fronttoken(A2,"(",A3),
  fronttoken(A3,Arg,A4),
  fronttoken(A4,",",A5),
  fronttoken(A5,Arg2,A6),
  fronttoken(A6,")",_),
  facts(Function,Arg,Arg2,"if",A7), /* make sure valid */
  eval(A7,T).
eval(A,T):-
  /* evaluate a variable for first arg */
  fronttoken(A,Function,A2),
  fronttoken(A2,"(",A3),
  fronttoken(A3,Arg,A4),
  fronttoken(A4,",",A5),
  fronttoken(A5,Arg2,A6),
  fronttoken(A6,")",_),
  Arg="X",
  facts(Function,X,Arg2,_,_),
  write("X = ",X),nl,
  T=true,
  write(T).
eval(A,T):-
  /* evaluate a variable for second arg */
  fronttoken(A,Function,A2),
  fronttoken(A2,"(",A3),
  fronttoken(A3,Arg,A4),
  fronttoken(A4,",",A5),
  fronttoken(A5,Arg2,A6),
  fronttoken(A6,")",_),
  Arg2="X",
  facts(Function,Arg,X,_,_),
  write("X = ",X),nl,
  T=true,
  write(T).
eval(A,T):-
  /* evaluate a function with args */
  fronttoken(A,Function,A2),
  fronttoken(A2,"(",A3),
  fronttoken(A3,Arg,A4),
  fronttoken(A4,",",A5),
  fronttoken(A5,Arg2,A6),
  fronttoken(A6,")",_),
  facts(Function,Arg,Arg2,_,_),
  T=true,
  write(T).
eval(_,false):-
  write("false").
```

The entire baby Prolog program is shown here.

```
/* A baby prolog interpreter that illustrates
   various aspects of predicate calculus.

   All predicates must have the forms:

       function_name(arg,arg)
or
       function_name(arg,arg) if <predicate>

*/

database
  facts(symbol,symbol,symbol,symbol,string)
  /*    name,  arg1,  arg2,    if, expression */

predicates
  clear
  window_init
  process(string)
  baby_prolog(string)
  run
  eval(string,symbol)
  eval_driver(string)
  next_line(string,string,string)
  strip_CR(string,string)
  find_CR(string,integer,integer)
  purge
  disp_facts
 clauses
  run:-
    clear,
    window_init,
    baby_prolog("").

  baby_prolog(T):-
    shiftwindow(2),
    edit(T,Text),
    shiftwindow(3),
    process(Text),
    edit("",A),
    eval_driver(A), !,
    write("more? "),
    readln(Q),
    Q=y, baby_prolog(Text).
  baby_prolog(_).

  /* process the facts and clauses
     into internal format
  */
  process(T):-
    T="";T="\n".
  process(T):-
```

```
      /* an if condition */
      fronttoken(T,Tok,S),
      fronttoken(S,"(",S1),
      fronttoken(S1,Tok2,S2),
      fronttoken(S2,",",S3),
      fronttoken(S3,Tok3,S4),
      fronttoken(S4,")",S5),
      fronttoken(S5,Tok4,S6),
      Tok4="if",
      next_line(S6,S7,L),
      assert(facts(Tok,Tok2,Tok3,Tok4,L)),
      process(S7).
process(T):-
      /* facts */
      fronttoken(T,Tok,S),
      fronttoken(S,"(",S1),
      fronttoken(S1,Tok2,S2),
      fronttoken(S2,",",S3),
      fronttoken(S3,Tok3,S4),
      fronttoken(S4,")",S5),
      assert(facts(Tok,Tok2,Tok3,null,"")),
      process(S5).

  /* set up for eval */
eval_driver(A):-
   /* evaluate a line at a time */
   A="";A="\n".
eval_driver(A):-
   next_line(A,A2,L),
   write(L," "),
   eval(L,_),nl,
   eval_driver(A2).
eval_driver(_).


eval(A,T):-
   /* evaluate an if clause */
   fronttoken(A,Function,A2),
   fronttoken(A2,"(",A3),
   fronttoken(A3,Arg,A4),
   fronttoken(A4,",",A5),
   fronttoken(A5,Arg2,A6),
   fronttoken(A6,")",_),
   facts(Function,Arg,Arg2,"if",A7), /* make sure valid */
   eval(A7,T).
eval(A,T):-
   /* evaluate a variable for first arg */
   fronttoken(A,Function,A2),
   fronttoken(A2,"(",A3),
   fronttoken(A3,Arg,A4),
   fronttoken(A4,",",A5),
   fronttoken(A5,Arg2,A6),
   fronttoken(A6,")",_),
```

```
    Arg="X",
    facts(Function,X,Arg2,_,_),
    write("X = ",X),nl,
    T=true,
    write(T).
eval(A,T):-
    /* evaluate a variable for second arg */
    fronttoken(A,Function,A2),
    fronttoken(A2,"(",A3),
    fronttoken(A3,Arg,A4),
    fronttoken(A4,",",A5),
    fronttoken(A5,Arg2,A6),
    fronttoken(A6,")",_),
    Arg2="X",
    facts(Function,Arg,X,_,_),
    write("X = ",X),nl,
    T=true,
    write(T).
eval(A,T):-
    /* evaluate a function with args */
    fronttoken(A,Function,A2),
    fronttoken(A2,"(",A3),
    fronttoken(A3,Arg,A4),
    fronttoken(A4,",",A5),
    fronttoken(A5,Arg2,A6),
    fronttoken(A6,")",_),
    facts(Function,Arg,Arg2,_,_),
    T=true,
    write(T).
eval(_,false):-
    write("false").

clear:-
    makewindow(1,6,0,"",0,0,25,80).

window_init:-
    makewindow(2,7,0,"",10,0,10,80),
    makewindow(3,7,0,"",1,0,9,80).

    /* return a line */
find_CR(S,Count,C):-
    frontchar(S,CH,S2),
    CH<>'\n',
    C2=C+1,
    find_CR(S2,Count,C2).
find_CR(_,Count,Count).

/* get the next line */
next_line(S,S2,L):-
    find_CR(S,Count,0),!,
    Count>0,
    frontstr(Count,S,L,S3),
    strip_CR(S3,S2).
```

```
strip_CR(S,S2):-
  frontchar(S,Ch,S2),
  Ch='\n'.
strip_CR(S,S).

purge:-
  retract(facts(_,_,_,_,_)),
  fail.
purge.

disp_facts:-
  clear,
  facts(A,B,C,D,E),
  write(A," ",B," ",C," ",D," ",E),nl,
  fail.
disp_facts:-
  write("hit return"),
  readln(_).
```

There is no internal goal in this program in order to allow you flexibility when you run it. To use the program, select the run option in Turbo Prolog and then type **run** when prompted for a goal in the dialog window. You will see the screen clear and the first editor window will appear. Enter the following simple program:

```
likes(herb,sherry)
likes(tom,linda) if has(car,tom)
has(car,herb)
has(car,tom) if works(car,tom)
works(car,tom)
```

Then, press the F10 key to quit editing. Next, the second editor window will appear and you can enter some goals. Try these:

```
likes(herb,sherry)
likes(tom,linda)
```

After you press F10, the program will evaluate each goal and report whether it is true or false. Your screen will look like the one shown in Figure 8-1.

When prompted for more, enter **y** and add the following line to the program:

```
is(happy,linda) if likes(X,linda)
```

```
   Text:    36  Free:65339   Indent   Insert
likes(herb,sherry) true
likes(tom,linda) true
more?


   Text:   112  Free:65263   Indent   Insert
likes(herb,sherry)
likes(tom,linda) if has(car,tom)
has(car,herb)
has(car,tom) if works(car,tom)
works(car,tom)


F8:Previous line   F9:Edit   S-F9:View windows   S-F10:Resize window   Esc:Stop exec
```

Figure 8-1.   The first sample execution

Next, enter the following goal:

```
is(happy,linda)
```

```
   Text:    16  Free:65359   Indent   Insert
is(happy,linda) X = tom
true
more?


   Text:   146  Free:65229   Indent   Insert
likes(herb,sherry)
likes(tom,linda) if has(car,tom)
has(car,herb)
has(car,tom) if works(car,tom)
works(car,tom)
is(happy,linda) if likes(X,linda)


F8:Previous line   F9:Edit   S-F9:View windows   S-F10:Resize window   Esc:Stop exec
```

Figure 8-2.   The second sample execution

Your screen will now look like Figure 8-2.

You should experiment with other programs until you feel confident in the operation of baby Prolog. You may find it interesting to expand baby Prolog so that it is more flexible and accommodates different aspects of predicate calculus.

Uncertainty

One of the most pleasing aspects of logic is that it is certain. Things represented by logic are only either true or false. However, the real world is not like that: there are many gray areas. More importantly, the validity of most observations is governed by a probability factor that is associated with it. For example, if you see a large bird flying overhead, it *could* be an eagle, but it *might* be a hawk. For the most part, humans handle the uncertainty of natural observation without much trouble because we are accustomed to it. However, making a computer deal with uncertainty takes some effort.

In the language of programmers, it is a nontrivial task to link logic with uncertainty because they are opposites. When they are united, the result is sometimes called fuzzy logic because the truth value is based on likelihoods, rather than facts.

Resolving or dealing with uncertainty is critical to machine intelligence because it is required for real-world interfacing. Think back to the chapter on pattern recognition: one of the most difficult problems encountered, but not solved, was the recognition of an object that was only partially in view. For example, if the computer sees the following scene, would it report that the object is a triangle?

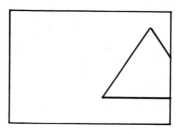

Troubles of this nature are pervasive when you try to make the computer adapt to a natural environment.

One of the most important areas that requires the processing of uncertainty is the expert system. If the expert system is to give good advice, then it must also report the probability of that advice being accurate. This section will add this capability to the expert system that was developed in Chapter 3. However, first, here is a review of the fundamentals of classical probability theory. As you will shortly see, you will need to bend these rules when you apply them to AI decision making.

Basic Probability Theory

In part, the number of possible events that could occur determines the probability of a specific event occurring. The set of all possible events that are related to a certain situation is called the event space. If the likelihood of each event in the event space occurring is the same for all events, and if no events are duplicates, then the probability (P) of a specific event X happening is equal to

$$P_x = \frac{1}{N}$$

where N is the number of possible events. For example, the odds of a flipped coin coming up heads is 1/2 because there are two possible events — heads and tails — and both are equally likely to occur. The probability of throwing a 3 by using one die is 1/6 because there are six possible outcomes and all are equally likely.

The part of probability that is of most interest to AI programmers is the computation of the likelihood that a sequence or combination of events will occur. In formal probability theory, the probability of a combination of events is equal to the product of the probabilities of each of those events. For example, the odds of a coin coming up heads three times in a row after it is tossed is

$$\frac{1}{2} \times \frac{1}{2} \times \frac{1}{2} = \frac{1}{8}$$

or one-eighth. It is important to understand that the events that form the sequence or combination need not be related. For example, the odds of both having a coin come up heads and rolling a 4 with a die are

$$\frac{1}{2} \times \frac{1}{6} = \frac{1}{12}$$

All probabilities are between 0 and 1, inclusive. An event with odds of 1 is a certainty; for example, death is a certainty. An event with odds of 0 is an impossibility; for example, living forever would be considered an impossibility. It is not possible to have a probability of less than 0 or greater than 1.

Applying the Classical Probability Theory to Expert Systems

As stated earlier, few observations are certain —rather, they are probable. However, some types of information are more likely to be true than others, and a successful expert system must take into account the probability of such information. Before you can examine the effects of using the classical probability theory as a method of resolving uncertainty, the expert system from Chapter 3 must be modified so that each piece of information that it knows carries with it a probability factor.

First, you need to alter the knowledge base. The knowledge base is held in the database **info**, which consists of an object's name and a list of attributes that are associated with it. However, now that list of attributes must also contain a probability factor. To allow for this, you must change the attribute list from being a list of symbols to being a list of functors. This database, along with the domains declaration and the support databases, is shown here.

```
domains
        attribute = attr(symbol,real)
        alist = attribute*
        list = symbol*
database
  info(symbol,alist)
  /* object, list of attributes */
  yes(attribute)  /* keep trail of yes */
```

```
no(attribute)     /* and no responses */
odds(real)        /* used to help compute
                     the current odds of
                     success
                  */
```

As you enter each attribute about an object, you are also requested to give a probability factor that reflects the likelihood that that attribute is associated with that particular object. To understand the meaning of this factor, consider the attributes that describe an illness, like a cold. Not everyone experiences colds the same way: Some people have runny noses, others sneeze, and so on. If you were to enter the symptoms for a cold into the knowledge base of an expert system, then you must specify the probability of each. For example, you may give a runny nose a 90% likelihood, whereas you may give a sore throat only a 40% chance of being a symptom. The predicate **attributes** inputs the list of attributes and probabilities that are associated with each object:

```
/* actually get the attributes */
attributes(O,List):-
  write(O," is/has/does: "),
  readln(Attribute),
  Attribute<>"quit",
  write("probability? (0-1) "),
  readreal(P),
  add(attr(Attribute,P),List,List2),
  attributes(O,List2).
attributes(O,List):-
  assert(info(O,List)),
  writelist(List,1),!,
  nl.
```

Although many minor changes to the code of the expert system are necessary to accommodate a list of functors instead of a list of symbols, the crucial change is the way that negative responses are handled by the **process** predicate, which builds the **yes** and **no** databases based upon the answer to each question. This predicate is shown here:

```
/* process various responses */
process(_,X,y):-
  asserta(yes(X)),!.
```

```
process(_,attr(X,P),n):-
  /* enter into database,
     but don't fail - continue */
  P<0.5,
  asserta(no(attr(X,P))),!.
process(_,X,n):-
  asserta(no(X)),!,fail.
process(0,attr(X,P),why):-
  write("I think it may be"), nl,
  write(0," because it has: "),nl,
  yes(attr(Z,P)),xwrite(attr(Z,P)),nl,
  Z=end,!,
  write("is/has/does it ",X,"? "),
  readln(Q),
  process(0,attr(X,P),Q),!.
```

In the expert system given in Chapter 3, if it received a negative response to an attribute, it placed that attribute in the **no** database and the clause failed, which cancelled the current line of reasoning and which caused a new object to be tried. However, this new probabilistic version still places the attribute in the **no** database, but the clause will only fail if the probability of finding this attribute is greater than 50%. (This percentage is chosen arbitrarily and you can change it if you like.) In this way, attributes that may be associated with an object can still form part of the description of the object, but, if the probability of finding that attribute is low enough, not having that attribute is insufficient to reject the object.

One new routine is needed that can compute the final probability of the expert's judgment as being correct. The predicate is called **compute __ odds** and is shown here, assuming the classical probability theory model.

```
compute_odds([]).
compute_odds([attr(_,P)|T]):-
  retract(odds(N)),!,
  N1=N*P,
  asserta(odds(N1)),
  compute_odds(T).
```

The predicate **compute odds** is passed the attribute list for the current solution and it computes the likelihood that it is correct. However, using the standard probability method provides completely unsatisfactory results!

The entire program is shown here. You should enter it into your computer at this time.

```
/* A backward-chaining expert system */
/* with probabilistic certainty factors
   that finds multiple solutions. */
domains
      attribute = attr(symbol,real)
      alist = attribute*
      list = symbol*
database
  info(symbol,alist)
  /* object, list of attributes */
  yes(attribute)   /* keep trail of yes */
  no(attribute)    /* and no responses */
  odds(real)       /* used to help compute
                      the current odds of
                      success
                   */
predicates
  append(list,list,list)
  append(alist,alist,alist)
  writelist(alist,integer)
  enter
  purge
  add(symbol,list,list)
  add(attribute,alist,alist)
  query(list)
  attributes(symbol,alist)
  process(symbol, attribute, symbol)
  start
  trailyes(alist)
  trailno(alist)
  xtrailyes(attribute,alist,alist)
  xtrailno(attribute,alist,alist)
  try(symbol,alist)
  member(symbol,list)
  amember(attribute,alist)
  xwrite(attribute)
  compute_odds(alist)
goal
  start.
clauses
  start:-
    consult("x.dat"), /* read in info */
    fail.  /* proceed to next clause */
  start:-
    write("Enter information? (y/n): "),
    readln(A),
    A=y,
```

```
    not(enter),
    save("x.dat"),!,
    assert(yes(attr(end,0))),
    assert(no(attr(end,0))),
    assert(odds(1)),
    query([]).
start:-
    assert(yes(attr(end,0))),
    assert(no(attr(end,0))),
    assert(odds(1)),
    query([]),purge.
start:-
    purge.

/* enter objects and attributes */
enter:-
    write("What is it?: "),
    readln(Object),
    Object<>"quit",
    attributes(Object,[]),
    write("more? "),!,
    readln(Q),Q=y,
    enter.

/* actually get the attributes */
attributes(O,List):-
    write(O," is/has/does: "),
    readln(Attribute),
    Attribute<>"quit",
    write("probability? (0-1) "),
    readreal(P),
    add(attr(Attribute,P),List,List2),
    attributes(O,List2).
attributes(O,List):-
    assert(info(O,List)),
    writelist(List,1),!,
    nl.

/* add a symbol to a list */
add(X,L,[X|L]).

/* request information from user to
   find an object */
query(L):-
    info(O,A),
    not(member(O,L)), /* not find same one */
    add(O,L,L2),      /* twice */
    trailyes(A),   /* test old yes responses*/
    trailno(A),    /* screen for no responses */
    try(O,A),
    !, write(O," fits the"),nl,
    write("current attributes"),nl,
    compute_odds(A),!,
    retract(odds(P)),!,
    assert(odds(1)),
```

```
write("with probability ",P),nl,
write("continue? "),
readln(Q), Q=y,
query(L2).


/* screen out all objects that don't have
   the proper attributes as already
   determined */
trailyes(A):-
  yes(T),!,
  xtrailyes(T,A,[]),!.

xtrailyes(attr(end,_),_,_):-!.
xtrailyes(T,A,L):-
  amember(T,A),!,
  add(T,L,L2),
  yes(X),not(amember(X,L2)),!,
  xtrailyes(X,A,L2).


/* screen out all objects that have
   attributes already determined as
   not belonging to the object */
trailno(A):-
  no(T),!,
  xtrailno(T,A,[]),!.

xtrailno(attr(end,_),_,_):-!.
xtrailno(T,A,L):-
  not(amember(T,A)),!,
  add(T,L,L2),
  no(X),not(amember(X,L2)),!,
  xtrailno(X,A,L2).


/* try a hypothesis */
try(_,[]).
try(O,[attr(X,_)|T]):-
  yes(attr(X,_)),!,
  try(O,T).
try(O,[attr(X,P)|T]):-
  write("is/has/does it ",X," "),
  readln(Q),
  process(O,attr(X,P),Q),!,
  try(O,T).

/* process various responses */
process(_,X,y):-
  asserta(yes(X)),!.
process(_,attr(X,P),n):-
  P<0.5,
  asserta(no(attr(X,P))),!.
```

```
                    /* but don't fail - continue */
        process(_,X,n):-
          asserta(no(X)),!,fail.
        process(0,attr(X,P),why):-
          write("I think it may be"), nl,
          write(0," because it has: "),nl,
          yes(attr(Z,P)),xwrite(attr(Z,P)),nl,
          Z=end,!,
          write("is/has/does it ",X,"? "),
          readln(Q),
          process(0,attr(X,P),Q),!.

        xwrite(attr(end,_)).
        xwrite(attr(Z,P)):-
          write(Z," with probability ",P).

        purge:-
          retract(yes(attr(X,_))),
          X=end,fail.
        purge:-
          retract(no(attr(X,_))),
          X=end, fail.
        purge:-
          retract(odds(_)), fail.
        purge.

        append([],List,List).
        append([X|L1], List2, [X|L3]) if
          append(L1,List2,L3).

        writelist([],_).
        writelist([Head|Tail],3):-
          write(Head),nl,writelist(Tail,1).
        writelist([Head|Tail],I):-
          N=I+1,
          write(Head," "),writelist(Tail,N).

         amember(attr(N,_),[attr(N,_)|_]).
         amember(N,[_|T]):- amember(N,T).

         member(N,[N|_]).
         member(N,[_|T]):- member(N,T).

        /* compute odds
           using probability model */
        compute_odds([]).
        compute_odds([attr(_,P)|T]):-
          retract(odds(N)),!,
          N1=N*P,
          asserta(odds(N1)),
          compute_odds(T).
```

The first time that you run this program, enter **y** when it prompts you to enter information. Then, enter the following facts and probabilities.

Object	Attributes
apple	grow __on __trees 1, red 0.4, edible 0.9
orange	grow __on __trees 1, orange 0.9, edible 0.9
plum	grow __on __trees 1, purple 0.5, edible 0.8
grape	grow __on __trees 0.01, purple 0.5, edible 0.8

In the description of grapes, the knowledge base contains the fact that grapes have only 1% chance of growing on trees. The reason for this is not that they do grow on trees —of course, they grow on vines —but it allows a user the chance of mistakenly identifying a very large vine for a tree. (And, it helps illustrate the point!)

Given this information, here is one dialog that can take place.

```
is/has/does it edible? y
is/has/does it red? y
is/has/does it grow_on_trees? y
apple fits the current attributes
with probability 0.36
continue? n
```

Here is another possible dialog:

```
is/has/does it edible? y
is/has/does it red? n
is/has/does it grow_on_trees? y
apple fits the current attributes
with probability 0.36
continue? y
is/has/does it orange? n
is/has/does it purple? y
plum fits the
current attributes
with probability 0.4
continue? y
grape fits the
current attributes
with probability 0.004
continue? n
```

The way that the first dialog is generated is straightforward because the responses are all positive and point directly to **apple**. The trouble is that the expert system, which uses the classic probability model, only gives a 36% chance $(1 \times 0.4 \times 0.9)$ that this solution is correct. However, this seems wrong — and it is! The classical probability model is designed to handle a sequence of events. However, the probability that is associated with each attribute in the knowledge base is simply the likelihood that the attribute is associated with a specific object. Therefore, the certainty coefficients that are associated with the knowledge base cannot be analyzed by using techniques of standard probability theory. Indeed, it is an unusual expert system that would use the classical probability model.

The second dialog shows how the expert system can use the probability associated with each attribute to resolve possible omissions in the attribute list. When you answer no to the question about whether the object is red, the system stores the response in the **no** database. However, because there is only a 40% chance of an apple being red (it could also be yellow or green), the system does not abort this line of reasoning. The system then continues on to find both **plum** and **grape** as possible solutions.

As the odds of success indicate, the classical probability model does not work well when you apply it to the resolution of uncertainty of information. Now you will look at two other more successful methods of resolving this problem.

The Weakest-Link Approach

When a certainty factor is associated with a specific attribute, it means that there is a discrete likelihood that the attribute belongs to an example of the object in question. Therefore, one approach suggests that the certainty of a solution should be the smallest certainty coefficient that is associated with the object. This concept is analogous to a chain being only as strong as its weakest link.

To make the probabilistic expert system resolve uncertainty in this way requires only a change to the predicate **compute __odds** as shown here.

```
/* compute odds
   using weakest link method */
compute_odds([]).
compute_odds([attr(_,P)|T]):-
  odds(N),
  N>P,
  retract(odds(_)),
  asserta(odds(P)),
  compute_odds(T).
compute_odds([_|T]):-
  compute_odds(T).
```

In this version, the lowest certainty factor becomes the odds of the entire solution being correct.

If you substitute this predicate in the expert system, here is a possible dialog that can be generated.

```
is/has/does it edible? y
is/has/does it red? y
is/has/does it grow_on_trees? y
apple fits the current attributes
with probability 0.4
continue? n
```

Here is another dialog that the system can generate:

```
is/has/does it edible? y
is/has/does it red? n
is/has/does it grow_on_trees? y
apple fits the current attributes
with probability 0.4
continue? y
is/has/does it orange? n
is/has/does it purple? y
plum fits the
current attributes
with probability 0.5
continue? y
grape fits the
current attributes
with probability 0.2
continue? n
```

As you can see, the solutions are the same as the standard probability model, but the probabilities have been altered, in this case upward.

The main advantage of the weakest-link method is that it gives the probability of success as if all attributes that are associated with the object are interdependent: that is, as if the likelihood of a solution is based upon a combination of factors. On the other hand, there are situations in which the most compelling argument is more important than the weakest link. This is the strongest-link approach.

The Strongest-Link Method

In certain applications, the probability that a solution is correct is based not on its weakest supporting evidence, but rather on its strongest supporting evidence. This is similar to a debate in which one argument is sufficient on its own to decide the issue. For example, why is it not good to leave loaded guns where children can find them? There are several reasons, such as the child might shoot the gun and make a loud and disturbing noise, or the child might shoot the gun and damage property. But the most compelling reason is that the child might shoot the gun and wound or kill someone. Clearly, it is the last argument that means the most.

When applied to an expert system, the strongest-link method simply implies that the probability of a solution being correct is the same as the attribute with the greatest probability. To implement this approach, you must modify the **compute __odds** predicate, as shown here:

```
/* find greatest probability */
compute_odds([]).
compute_odds([attr(_,P)|T]):-
   odds(N),
   N<P,
   retract(odds(_)),
   asserta(odds(P)),
   compute_odds(T).
compute_odds([_|T]):-
   compute_odds(T).
```

In addition to this change, you must change the initial seed value of the **odds** database from 1, which is used by both the classical probability model and the weakest-link method, to a 0. There are two places where you must do this. The first is in **start** and the second is in **query**. To avoid confusion, the entire strongest-link expert system is shown here.

```
/* A backward-chaining expert system */
/* with strongest link approach
   that finds multiple solutions. */
domains
       attribute = attr(symbol,real)
       alist = attribute*
       list = symbol*
database
  info(symbol,alist)
  /* object, list of attributes */
  yes(attribute)  /* keep trail of yes */
  no(attribute)   /* and no responses */
  odds(real)      /* used to help compute
                     the current odds of
                     success
                  */
predicates
  append(list,list,list)
  append(alist,alist,alist)
  writelist(alist,integer)
  enter
  purge
  add(symbol,list,list)
  add(attribute,alist,alist)
  query(list)
  attributes(symbol,alist)
  process(symbol, attribute, symbol)
  start
  trailyes(alist)
  trailno(alist)
  xtrailyes(attribute,alist,alist)
  xtrailno(attribute,alist,alist)
  try(symbol,alist)
  member(symbol,list)
  amember(attribute,alist)
  xwrite(attribute)
  compute_odds(alist)
goal
  start.
clauses

  start:-
    consult("x.dat"), /* read in info */
    fail.  /* proceed to next clause */
```

```
start:-
  write("Enter information? (y/n): "),
  readln(A),
  A=y,
  not(enter),
  save("x.dat"),!,
  assert(yes(attr(end,0))),
  assert(no(attr(end,0))),
  assert(odds(0)), query([]).
start:-
  assert(odds(0)),
  assert(yes(attr(end,0))),
  assert(no(attr(end,0))),
  query([]),purge.
start:-
  purge.

/* enter objects and attributes */
enter:-
  write("What is it?: "),
  readln(Object),
  Object<>"quit",
  attributes(Object,[]),
  write("more? "),!,
  readln(Q),Q=y,
  enter.

/* actually get the attributes */
attributes(O,List):-
  write(O," is/has/does: "),
  readln(Attribute),
  Attribute<>"quit",
  write("probability? (0-1) "),
  readreal(P),
  add(attr(Attribute,P),List,List2),
  attributes(O,List2).
attributes(O,List):-
  assert(info(O,List)),
  writelist(List,1),!,
  nl.

/* add a symbol to a list */
add(X,L,[X|L]).

/* request information from user to
   find an object */
query(L):-
  info(O,A),
  not(member(O,L)), /* not find same one */
  add(O,L,L2),       /* twice */
  trailyes(A),  /* test old yes responses*/
  trailno(A),   /* screen for no responses */
```

```
try(O,A),
!, write(O," fits the"),nl,
write("current attributes"),nl,
compute_odds(A),!,
retract(odds(P)),!,
assert(odds(O)),
write("with probability ",P),nl,
write("continue? "),
readln(Q), Q=y,
query(L2).

/* screen out all objects that don't have
   the proper attributes as already
   determined */
trailyes(A):-
  yes(T),!,
  xtrailyes(T,A,[]),!.

xtrailyes(attr(end,_),_,_):-!.
xtrailyes(T,A,L):-
  amember(T,A),!,
  add(T,L,L2),
  yes(X),not(amember(X,L2)),!,
  xtrailyes(X,A,L2).


/* screen out all objects that have
   attributes already determined as
   not belonging to the object */
trailno(A):-
  no(T),!,
  xtrailno(T,A,[]),!.

xtrailno(attr(end,_),_,_):-!.
xtrailno(T,A,L):-
  not(amember(T,A)),!,
  add(T,L,L2),
  no(X),not(amember(X,L2)),!,
  xtrailno(X,A,L2).


/* try a hypothesis */
try(_,[]).
try(O,[attr(X,_)|T]):-
  yes(attr(X,_)),!,
  try(O,T).
try(O,[attr(X,P)|T]):-
  write("is/has/does it ",X," "),
  readln(Q),
  process(O,attr(X,P),Q),!,
  try(O,T).

/* process various responses */
process(_,X,y):-
  asserta(yes(X)),!.
```

```
process(_,attr(X,P),n):-
  P<0.5,
  asserta(no(attr(X,P))),!.
  /* but don't fail - continue */
process(_,X,n):-
  asserta(no(X)),!,fail.
process(0,attr(X,P),why):-
  write("I think it may be"), nl,
  write(O," because it has: "),nl,
  yes(attr(Z,P)),xwrite(attr(Z,P)),nl,
  Z=end,!,
  write("is/has/does it ",X,"? "),
  readln(Q),
  process(O,attr(X,P),Q),!.

xwrite(attr(end,_)).
xwrite(attr(Z,P)):-
  write(Z," with probability ",P).

purge:-
  retract(yes(attr(X,_))),
  X=end,fail.
purge:-
  retract(no(attr(X,_))),
  X=end, fail.
purge:-
  retract(odds(_)), fail.
purge.

append([],List,List).
append([X|L1], List2, [X|L3]) if
  append(L1,List2,L3).

writelist([],_).
writelist([Head|Tail],3):-
  write(Head),nl,writelist(Tail,1).
writelist([Head|Tail],I):-
  N=I+1,
  write(Head," "),writelist(Tail,N).

 amember(attr(N,_),[attr(N,_)|_]).
 amember(N,[_|T]):- amember(N,T).

 member(N,[N|_]).
 member(N,[_|T]):- member(N,T).

/* find greatest probability */
compute_odds([]).
compute_odds([attr(_,P)|T]):-
  odds(N),
  N<P,
  retract(odds(_)),
  asserta(odds(P)),
  compute_odds(T).
compute_odds([_|T]):-
  compute_odds(T).
```

When you run this version, the certainty factor for **apple** and **plum** becomes 1. The certainty factor for **grape** is 0.8.

Choosing a Method

The classical probability method is applicable only in unusual situations, such as an expert system that will predict the probability of certain events that are based upon hypothetical information. For example, you might design an expert system that would give the odds of various outcomes of historical situations if events had been different. However, beyond this sort of use, the classical probability model does not work well with knowledge-based systems.

You should use the weakest-link version when it is a combination of all attributes that must be considered. In this case, you should inform the user of the worst case. If you define the knowledge base properly, the worst case probabilities will still be quite high.

You should use the strongest-link approach when any one attribute can be used to identify an object. In this case, the certainty factor reflects the likelihood of the most compelling argument.

Appearing Human

This chapter deals with writing programs that act like people. The classic example of this is the ELIZA program, mentioned in Chapter 1, which acts like a Rogerian psychiatrist. This chapter will look into how to give a computer program the appearance of personality and emotion, and will develop three simple versions of an ELIZA-type program for illustration.

Because you probably only have a screen and keyboard, the operating scenario is as follows. Imagine that there are two computer terminals, side by side. One is connected to another terminal that is in the next room and that has a human operator, while the second terminal is connected to a computer. Both the computer and the human will respond to whatever you type. If you cannot tell which terminal is connected to the computer and which terminal is connected to the human operator, then the program running on the computer will have succeeded in appearing human.

Trickery?

Many people say that the way that the original ELIZA program functions has little to do with serious AI research, and that what seems to be its intelligence is based upon tricks and not upon solid generalizable principles. However, these critics are missing what is perhaps the most important point about the program: ELIZA is virtually indistinguishable from a person.

As you will soon see, ELIZA-type programs do not need (but may use, if desired) any of the formal natural-language processing techniques. In fact, the average program of this sort is rather mindless: it has very little idea what is going on. Its responses are simply canned replies. However, the point about ELIZA-type programs that is interesting is that they can so successfully mimic a person. It is this aspect that will receive the main emphasis in this chapter.

What Good Is It?

There are a few people who question the value of studying how to make a computer seem like a person. However, these few individuals are forgetting an important point: as an increasing number of achievements are realized through AI research and placed into practical use, there will be a growing need to produce good computer-user interfaces. If people are going to use truly smart machines, then these machines must act somewhat like people because people are most accustomed to this type of interface.

To understand this point, think back to the expert system developed in Chapter 3. As you know, expert systems are AI's first and foremost commercially viable product. However, as of this writing, no expert system actually interacts with the user in the same way that a human expert would. In even the best systems, the prompting is still stilted.

A final point in favor of making a computer appear human is that, at some point, computers will be working autonomously alongside human coworkers. Integrating these machines into a human environment will be much easier if you find their behavior familiar.

Man Versus Machine

Chapter 1 determined that a program was intelligent if it acted in a way that was similar to a human who is confronted with the same problem. However, you should understand that there is a subtle difference between a program that acts intelligently and a program that acts like a person. This difference is based on emotions and personality: generally, appearing human requires more than simple problem-solving intelligence. It implies that the computer must have some sort of total identity as a person does. This raises the following two interesting questions:

- Can a computer have emotions?

- Can a computer have a personality?

It is beyond the scope of this book to discuss fully all proposed answers to these questions, but this chapter will offer a few comments.

Machine Emotions

One of the most frequent arguments against a computer being able to mimic human behavior completely is that humans can feel emotions but computers cannot. Actually, this argument is pointless. Humans have no way of knowing whether a computer has emotions or not. In fact, people do not know what their own emotions really are. Therefore, to say that a computer does not have them is assuming the conclusion!

One view of emotions states that they are not connected with a person's cognitive thought processes, but rather are founded in instinct. In essence, the view is that emotions stem from forces that a person has little or no control over. (It may be possible to avoid acting upon an emotion, but it is impossible not to feel it.) More important, no one knows what causes emotions to occur. If this line of reasoning is true, then it would seem that a parallel situation exists in a computer. A computer also has "instincts" in the form of ROM routines and operating system procedures. When a high-level program —such as a smart program —is executing in the computer it may cause one or more of the low-level routines to execute. The high-level program does not directly know the actions of these routines; in fact, in the case of real-time interrupts, it cannot even stop them from occurring. Hence, a computer's emotions would be those traits that are found in its ROM, its operating system, or a procedural fragment of an intelligent program. The point is that just as one does not have clear knowledge of his or her own emotions, an intelligent computer may not have clear knowledge of some low-level routines that influence its behavior.

However, whether or not a computer can have emotions is not the question because clearly a computer's emotions would be quite different than a human's. The true question is, if you are going to make a computer act like a person, how can you allow the computer to display the semblance of human emotions? All that the computer must do is act as if it had human-type emotions —it does not actually need to "feel" them. This is roughly a behaviorist's approach to the problem. It does not matter what the computer feels —it only matters what the computer acts like.

For the purposes of this chapter, it will be sufficient if a program simply displays behavior that suggests emotions. The program does not need to feel them in the same way that a person would.

Personality

If you are an avid fan of science-fiction movies, then you probably know that computers are supposed to be without personality. However, if a computer is to act like a person, then it seems that it must have some sort of personality.

It is not obvious how a personality develops in a person. Certainly, some of a personality is founded in one's genetic makeup, and some is influenced by experience. Since part of a person's personality is beyond control, it seems justified that one acceptable solution to giving a personality to a computer is simply to let it be programmed that way; that is, programmed to exhibit personality traits through its responses. If you think back to a behaviorist view, you can see that the computer does not actually have to "be" a certain personality, rather that it has to display behavior that suggests personality. (Even people sometimes display actions contrary to their personality, or "act out of character.")

For this chapter, a computer personality will be generated solely upon the way that the computer responds to various inputs. As you will see, it is actually quite easy to give the computer various personalities.

Going to the Doctor

One of the first programs of its kind —and still the most famous program to have the appearance of being a person —is ELIZA, created by Joseph

Weisenbaum. As mentioned earlier, ELIZA acts like a Rogerian psychiatrist. (Rogerian psychiatrists work by simply echoing the patient's response — which theoretically allows the patient to self-analyze.) Although programs of this type seem pretty tame to a present-day computer programmer, they can still impress someone not familiar with the "tricks of the trade." It is in this spirit that this section develops **Doctor**, a simple version of an ELIZA-like program.

How the Original ELIZA Program Worked

The original ELIZA program simply echoed the patient's remarks by using keyword recognition. When the program encountered certain words in the patient's sentence, such as "love," "hate," or "want," the program would respond with a response that related to the keyword. Secondarily, the program would remember selected topics that it could use to keep a conversation going. Finally, the program could recognize a few key phrases like "I hate you" and would display a specific response. The following dialog shows the general idea:

Doctor	How are you today?
Patient	Fine.
Doctor	Are you happy?
Patient	No, I hate my life.
Doctor	Why do you hate your life?
Patient	Because no one likes me.
Doctor	I like you.
Patient	Well, you would!
Doctor	But we were talking about you; go on.
Patient	I don't want to.
Doctor	You said that no one likes you; tell me more.

This type of dialog would continue until the patient, or user, got tired. Several versions of ELIZA-type programs have been developed over the years. Some are extremely well-developed and cannot be distinguished from a human psychiatrist.

A Simple First Version

The first version that this chapter will develop does very little and is easily confused, but it sets the stage for improvements. This version does not remember any topics and simply repeats the patient's responses unless the patient enters a key phrase. This version is completely without personality or emotion. Here is the entire program:

```
/*
  A very simple version of Doctor
*/
database
  responses(string)
  temp(string)
  translate(symbol,symbol)

predicates
  converse
  patient
  doctor(string)
  respond(string)
  purge
goal
  assert(responses("How are you?")),
  assert(responses("Did you have a happy childhood?")),
  assert(responses("Did you hate your father?")),
  assert(responses("Do you have friends?")),
  assert(temp("")),
  assert(translate("I","You")),
  assert(translate("You","I")),
  assert(translate(you,me)),
  assert(translate(your,my)),
  assert(translate(me,you)),
  assert(translate(my,your)),
  assert(translate(am,are)),
  converse.

clauses
  converse:-
    temp(S),
    S=quit,
    purge.
  converse:-
    retract(temp(S)),
    doctor(S),
    patient,
    converse.

  doctor(""):-
    /* no response from patient */
```

```
        retract(responses(R)),
        assertz(responses(R)),
        write(R),nl.
doctor("No"):-
        write("tell me more"),nl.
doctor("Yes"):-
        write("ah...tell me more"),nl.
doctor("I hate you"):-
        write("Why do you hate me?"),nl.
doctor(S):-
        respond(S),
        write("?"),nl.

respond(".").
respond(S):-
        fronttoken(S,T,S2),
        translate(T,T2),
        write(T2," "),
        respond(S2).
respond(S):-
        fronttoken(S,T,S2),
        write(T," "),
        respond(S2).

patient:-
        write(": "),
        readln(S),
        assert(temp(S)).

purge:-
        retract(translate(_,_)),
        fail.
purge:-
        retract(temp(_)), fail.
purge:-
        retract(responses(_)), fail.
purge.
```

This version of **Doctor** works by simply repeating the patient's last statement as a question. To do this, the predicate **respond** uses the **translate** database to reverse the context of a few words, such as "my" to "your." If **respond** does not find a word in the **translate** database, then the word is simply reprinted as is. However, if the patient enters only a "yes" or a "no," or the key phrase "I hate you," the **doctor** predicate handles these responses directly. You could easily expand the phrases and words that the program knows to let it process a greater variety of responses. If the patient enters only a carriage return, then the **doctor** clause will use a stock response from the **responses** database. The program uses the **temp** database to hold the patient's responses until **doctor** can process them.

The following is a sample of the type of dialog that this version will produce. The **Doctor** always begins each dialog and the program prompts the patient with a semicolon.

```
How are you?
: I am fine
You are fine?
: Yes, but my friend isn't
Yes, but your friend isn't?
: He has a problem
He has a problem?
: I hate you
Why do you hate me?
:
Did you have a happy childhood?
: No
Tell me more.
```

Therapy with this doctor would be quite boring! Next, you will see how to add some improvements.

Improving the Doctor Program

One of the most important features of the original ELIZA program is that it would keep a trail of topics that the patient mentioned. When the conversation began to falter, the doctor could prompt the patient to take up one of the topics again. Adding this capability requires another database to store the patient's responses. Also, simply repeating the patient's responses is both boring and not "human" enough. To remedy this, the **translate** database will hold keywords and responses. Each time that the program recognizes a keyword, the screen will display an appropriate response.

The biggest changes to the program are in the **doctor** and **respond** predicates, as shown here.

```
doctor(""):-
  /* no response from patient
     check patient response file */
  retract(topics(R)),
  R<>"",
  write("You just said ",'"'),
  write(R,'"'),nl,
  write("Tell me more..."),nl.
doctor(S):-
  respond(S),
  assert(topics(S)),
  nl.
doctor(_):-
  /* no response from patient
     check patient response file */
  retract(topics(R)),
  R<>"",
  write("You just said ",'"'),
  write(R,'"'),nl,
  write("Tell me more..."),nl.
doctor(_):-
  /* unknown response from patient */
  retract(responses(R)),
  assertz(responses(R)),
  write(R),nl.

respond(""):-fail.
respond(S):-
  fronttoken(S,T,_),
  translate(T,T2),
  write(T2," ").
respond(S):-
  fronttoken(S,_,S2),
  respond(S2).
```

These predicates work like this. If the patient simply enters a carriage return, then the first clause of **doctor** tries to return to a previous topic. If no previous topics are in the **topics** database, then the program selects a stock response from the **responses** database. If the patient does enter a sentence, then **respond** is called. To succeed, **respond** must find a keyword in the sentence. If it does, it prints the response that is linked to that keyword and terminates. If it does not, it tries the next word in the sentence recursively by using the third clause of **doctor**. If it reaches the end of the sentence —which means that a zero-length string is used as an argument —then the entire predicate fails. If this happens, it forces the execution of the final clause of **doctor**. This final clause of **doctor** is the same as the first clause. The entire program is shown here.

```
/*
   An Improved Doctor program that remembers
   topics and uses key words to generate
   responses.
*/

database
   responses(string)
   temp(string)
   translate(symbol,symbol)
   topics(string)

predicates
   converse
   patient
   doctor(string)
   respond(string)
   purge
goal
   assert(responses("How are you?")),
   assert(responses("Did you have a happy childhood?")),
   assert(responses("Do you hate your father?")),
   assert(responses("I'm not sure I understand")),
   assert(responses("Go on")),
   assert(responses("Do you have friends?")),
   assert(temp("")),
   assert(translate("think","Why do you think that?")),
   assert(translate("you","Let's not talk about me.")),
   assert(translate("hate","So you hate tell me more.")),
   assert(translate("what","Why do you ask?")),
   assert(translate("want","What would you do with it?")),
   assert(translate("need","We all need many things.")),
   assert(translate("why","Remember, therapy is good for you.")),
   assert(translate("know","How do you know that?")),
   converse.

clauses
   converse:-
     temp(S),
     S=quit,
     purge.
   converse:-
     retract(temp(S)),
     doctor(S),
     patient,
     converse.

   doctor(""):-
     /* no response from patient
        check patient response file */
     retract(topics(R)),
     R<>"",
     write("You just said ",'"'),
```

```
      write(R,'"'),nl,
      write("Tell me more..."),nl.
   doctor(S):-
      respond(S),
      assert(topics(S)),
      nl.
   doctor(_):-
      /* no response from patient
          check patient response file */
      retract(topics(R)),
      R<>"",
      write("You just said ",'"'),
      write(R,'"'),nl,
      write("Tell me more..."),nl.
   doctor(_):-
      /* unknown response from patient */
      retract(responses(R)),
      assertz(responses(R)),
      write(R),nl.

   respond(""):-fail.
   respond(S):-
      fronttoken(S,T,_),
      translate(T,T2),
      write(T2," ").
   respond(S):-
      fronttoken(S,_,S2),
      respond(S2).

   patient:-
      write(": "),
      readln(S),
      assert(temp(S)).

   purge:-
      retract(translate(_,_)),
      fail.
   purge:-
      retract(temp(_)), fail.
   purge:-
      retract(responses(_)), fail.
   purge:-
      retract(topics(_)), fail.
   purge.
```

This version of the program produces the following dialog:

```
How are you?
: fine
Did you have a happy childhood?
: Yes, but I hated my neighbor's dog
Do you hate your father?
: no
```

```
I'm not sure I understand.
: why
Remember, therapy is good for you.
: I think that everyone is out to get me
Why do you think that?
: because it is true
You just said "I think that everyone is out to get me"
Tell me more...
: I want to find a friend
What would you do with it?
: I need someone to talk to
We all need something
: I know that, but I am lonely
How do you know that?
: I feel lonely
```

As you can see, this version of the program is a substantial improvement over the original version.

Adding Some Personality And Emotion

You can make the program appear to have emotions by altering the response to certain keywords. For example, the keyword "murder" might have the response "I don't like people who murder." Also, you might choose a personality for the doctor and tailor the responses to it. For example, if you want the doctor to be an optimist, you might change a response to the keyword "never" to "Don't be negative; think positive." Finally, it might be fun if the doctor would become annoyed when the patient repeats a statement. To do this requires you to add another database to hold the patient's responses, and to change the predicate **patient** as shown here. The **patresponses** is a database that holds the patient's responses.

```
patient(S):-
  patresponses(S),
  write("You are repeating yourself."),
  nl,
  write(": "),
  readln(S2),
  patient(S2).
patient(S):-
  assert(patresponses(S)),
  assert(temp(S)).
```

With this change, when the patient enters a response that is identical to one that was entered previously, the doctor responds with a reprimand and the program prompts the patient for a new sentence.

The entire expanded version is shown here.

```
/*
  An expanded Doctor program that
  shows some emotions and displays
  a little personality.
*/

database
  responses(string)
  temp(string)
  translate(symbol,symbol)
  topics(string)
  patresponses(string)

predicates
  converse
  patient(string)
  doctor(string)
  respond(string)
  purge
goal
  assert(responses("How are you this beautiful day?")),
  assert(responses("Did you have a happy childhood?")),
  assert(responses("Do you hate your father?")),
  assert(responses("I'm not sure I understand")),
  assert(responses("Go on")),
  assert(responses("Do you have friends?")),
  assert(temp("")),
  assert(translate("unhappy","Why are you unhappy?")),
  assert(translate("think","Why do you think that?")),
  assert(translate("you","Let's not talk about me.")),
  assert(translate("hate","So you hate tell me more.")),
  assert(translate("what","Why do you ask?")),
  assert(translate("want","What would you do with it?")),
  assert(translate("need","We all need many things.")),
  assert(translate("why","Remember, therapy is good for you.")),
  assert(translate("know","How do you know that?")),
  assert(translate("murder","I don't like killing.")),
  assert(translate("kill","It is wrong to kill")),
  assert(translate("jerk","Don't you ever call me a jerk!")),
  assert(translate("never","Don't be negative; think positive!")),
  assert(translate("failure","Make it a success")),
  converse.

clauses
  converse:-
    temp(S),
    S=quit,
    purge.
  converse:-
    retract(temp(S)),
    doctor(S),
    write(": "),
    readln(P),
    patient(P),
    converse.

  doctor(""):-
    /* no response from patient
```

```
    check patient response file */
  retract(topics(R)),
  R<>"",
  write("You just said ",'"'),
  write(R,'"'),nl,
  write("Tell me more..."),nl.
doctor(""):-
  /* no response from patient */
  retract(responses(R)),
  assertz(responses(R)),
  write(R),nl.
doctor(S):-
  respond(S),
  assert(topics(S)),
  nl.
doctor(_):-
  /* no response from patient

     check patient response file */
  retract(topics(R)),
  R<>"",
  write("You just said ",'"'),
  write(R,'"'),nl,
  write("Tell me more..."),nl.

respond(""):-fail.
respond(S):-
  fronttoken(S,T,_),
  translate(T,T2),
  write(T2," ").
respond(S):-
  fronttoken(S,_,S2),
  respond(S2).

patient(S):-
  patresponses(S),
  write("You are repeating yourself."),
  nl,
  write(": "),
  readln(S2),
  patient(S2).
patient(S):-
  assert(patresponses(S)),
  assert(temp(S)).

purge:-
  retract(translate(_,_)),
  fail.
purge:-
  retract(temp(_)), fail.
purge:-
  retract(responses(_)), fail.
purge:-
  retract(topics(_)), fail.
purge:-
  retract(patresponses(_)),fail.
purge.
```

This version of the program produced the following dialog:

```
How are you this beautiful day?
: I don't know, I feel bad
How do you know that?
: I feel like I could kill
It is wrong to kill
: I never seem to win
Don't be negative; think positive!
: why
Remember, therapy is good for you.
: why
You are repeating yourself.
: Hey, who cares jerk
Don't you ever call me a jerk!
: I'll call you a jerk any time I want to
Let's not talk about me.
: I am unhappy
Why are you unhappy?
```

The doctor definitely seems to have both personality and a touch of emotions. In the earlier versions, the doctor was completely passive and seemed to be contented merely to monitor the patient's conversation. However, as shown in this dialog, the doctor acts more aggressively by giving advice and becoming annoyed with a repetitious patient. It is surprising how a small amount of additional code can create the impression of emotions and personality. You should experiment with other personality types and emotions.

Expanding the Doctor Program

There are several approaches to expanding the program. You could add more keywords and response phrases to the **translate** database. This approach is quite straightforward; you should have no trouble thinking up interesting additions. You might also try to give the doctor some emotions.

Another enhancement is much more difficult: you could integrate the recursive-descent natural-language parser from Chapter 4 into the program so that it can respond more specifically to each phrase of the patient's remarks, instead of just looking for keywords.

Finally, you might want to try to have the doctor's emotions change as the discussion progresses; these changes should be based upon the patient's responses. In essence, you will be adding mood changes. Whether you succeed or not is not so important as the insight that you will gain into the simulation of human behavior.

Implications of Humanlike Computers

As a closing section to a chapter on simulating human behavior, it is interesting to consider the sociological implications of artificial people (humanoid robots). If an autonomous robot is sufficiently successful in displaying humanlike actions, will people begin to recognize it as something more than a machine?

For the moment, ignore what the robot may or may not want. The question is, What will society want from a robot of this type? People commonly become emotionally attached to pet dogs and cats. It seems certain that people will come to feel the same affection and loyalty to humanoid robots. The potential for this type of emotional bonding places an unusual responsibility on the programmers of these types of machines —the importance of which is not fully understood.

Another interesting point to consider is that of liability. If a humanoid autonomous robot goes berserk and kills a person, who is to blame? The robot? The programmer who did not safeguard against this contingency? Perhaps the hardware manufacturer for not supplying failsafe systems? These questions are troubling because they have no precedents. Most product-liability cases are decided upon willful neglect. However, in the case of a robot of this sophistication —with literally millions (or billions) of bytes of code forming its mind, and which has the ability to learn and interface with a human environment —it is not clear that there can be a determination of fault.

Finally, will machines that are as smart or smarter than humans, and that act like humans, be granted certain legal rights? This question may seem a bit humorous now, but animal rights seemed ridiculous to many people when they were first proposed in the 1800s. Yet today, there are very few people that would approve of wanton mistreatment of pets.

These, and more, implications affect all programmers who are concerned with creating machines of this type because they are the ones who are ushering in a new world —a world very different from the one in which we now live.

Appendix A

Interfacing With Other Languages

No computer language can be perfect for all tasks. Turbo Prolog is no exception. While Turbo Prolog is excellent for AI applications and database managers, it is not well suited for some of the more common-place procedural jobs, which are commonly associated with real-world applications. Fortunately, you can link Turbo Prolog to code written in other languages. For example, an accounting system could use a natural-language processor "front-end" that is written in Turbo Prolog, but still use C to perform the procedural manipulations.

Aside from expert systems and certain types of database managers, AI-related subsystems usually will be combined with existing applications to create an enhanced or smarter application. Since most AI languages are somewhat cumbersome to use for procedural tasks, it is quite common to find applications that use two or more languages to take advantage of each language's specialty.

You should try to use the code presented in this appendix only if you have a fairly strong knowledge of the architecture and operation of the 8086/8088 family of processors. Linking Turbo Prolog to other languages requires that you understand how memory is accessed, the concepts of segments and offsets, and the difference between 16-bit and 32-bit pointers.

Language Requirements

Turbo Prolog can interface directly with procedures that are written in C, Pascal, FORTRAN, and assembler. However, you should recognize that not every specific implementation of each of these languages will work. There are three requirements that code that is written in another language must meet before you can combine it with Turbo Prolog. The three requirements are as follows:

1. The code must compile (or assemble) to standard .OBJ files.

2. The code must use 32-bit pointers: that is, it must completely support the large memory model for the 8086/8088 family.

3.   If parameters are going to be passed, then the passing conventions of the code must be the same as those that Turbo Prolog supports.

In addition to these requirements, Turbo Prolog uses IEEE floating-point format for reals. Not all compilers support this — so if you intend to write an external routine that uses floating point, you will have to make sure that it conforms to the IEEE format.

Declaring External Predicates

When you want to use a procedure that is written in one of the languages that can be linked to Turbo Prolog, you must declare that procedure to be an external predicate in the **global predicates** section of the Turbo Prolog program. The general format of an external predicate is similar to any other global predicate declaration except that you must tell Turbo Prolog explicitly what language the external procedure is written in. For example, the following declares **mul** to be an external predicate that is written in C.

```
global predicates
  mul(integer, integer, integer)-(i,i,o),(i,i,i) language C
```

Here is a brief explanation of this declaration to help you if you are not familiar with the declaration of global predicates. The **(i,i,o)** and **(i,i,i)** are used to indicate the legal flow patterns. The **i** stands for input (bound at time of call) and the **o** stands for output (free at time of call).

When you create an external procedure, you must remember that the name that Turbo Prolog will use when it calls the procedure will be a combination of the procedure name and the number of the specific flow pattern. For example, the name used for the first flow pattern of **mul** is **mul_0**; the second flow pattern is **mul_1**. Therefore, your external routines must use these names. The name will always be the predicate name, followed by an underscore, and then the number of the flow pattern.

It is important to understand that all external predicates are assumed to succeed: as far as Turbo Prolog is concerned, an external routine cannot fail and cause backtracking. (In the future, Turbo Prolog may be changed to allow this.)

Parameter Passing

Most external procedures that you write will use parameters either to receive information or to pass information back. When working with parameters, you must keep in mind several considerations.

The 8086 family of processors supports a variety of memory models from which the programmer can choose. However, Turbo Prolog requires you to use the large model. This means that all calls and returns from external procedures must be **FAR**. Also, you must only use 32-bit pointers. Turbo Prolog will not work with 16-bit pointers.

Turbo Prolog uses the stack to pass parameters to external procedures. For assembler, Pascal, and FORTRAN, these arguments are placed on the stack in the order in which they appear. However, for C, they are pushed in reverse order because most C compilers create procedures that expect to find their arguments in reverse order. (If you will be using C, you should make sure that the compiler does, indeed, pass parameters in reverse order because there are a few C compilers that pass parameters the other way.)

Table A-1.   Turbo Prolog's Built-In Data Types

Type	Representation
character	1 byte
integer	2 bytes
real	8 bytes (IEEE format)
symbol	4-byte pointer to a null string of characters
string	4-byte pointer to a null string of characters
compound	4-byte pointer to a record

Each data type in Turbo Prolog is represented in memory a particular way. Table A-1 shows each data type and the way that it is stored. When input parameters of type character, integer, or real are passed to a procedure, the value is actually pushed on the stack. For input parameters of type symbol, string, or compound, the address is pushed on the stack. All output parameters, regardless of type, will have their 4-byte address placed on the stack; therefore, for your external procedure to return a value in an output parameter, you must load that value at the address that the output parameter points to. You will find examples of this later in the appendix.

The Activation Record

Each time that Turbo Prolog calls an external procedure, three things must be done. First, any arguments are pushed on the stack. Next, the current BP register value and then the return address are pushed on the stack. Figure A-1 shows what the stack looks like. This arrangement of information is often called an activation record. You should know where each piece of information is located so that you can correctly access the arguments. The return address will always require 4 bytes of storage on the stack. The current BP register state requires 2 bytes, and any arguments will take up the sizes that were listed in Table A-1 for input parameters and 4 bytes for output parameters.

Top of stack	Return address — 4 bytes
	Value of BP — 2 bytes
Bottom of stack	Arguments — varies

Figure A-1. The stack upon entry into an external routine

Calling an Assembler Routine

There are many reasons that you may need to use an assembly language routine. One common reason is that it will support some unusual hardware device, such as a speech synthesizer. Another reason is that an assembly language routine increases the speed of some critical section of code. Whatever the reason, you must follow the same format as you used earlier when the routine is to be called from Turbo Prolog. This section assumes that you are completely familiar with 8086/8088 assembly language programming, have an IBM-compatible assembler (such as MASM), and know how to generate an object file that uses the assembler.

The first version of the *Turbo Prolog Owner's Handbook* contains several errors in its discussion of creating and linking an assembly language routine. Therefore, you should read this section carefully.

The general skeleton that you will use for each assembly code procedure is shown here.

```
segname  SEGMENT BYTE
         ASSUME  CS:segname
PUBLIC   p_name              ; the name of the procedure
p_name   PROC    FAR         ; must be a FAR procedure
         PUSH    BP          ; save BP
         MOV     BP,SP       ; use BP to index the stack
;
;        put your procedure code here
;
         POP     BP          ; restore BP
         RET     Numbytes ;  Numbytes must be the number of
                            ; bytes used by the parameters
                            ; on the stack
p_name   ENDP
segname  ENDS
END
```

As long as you preserve the stack register (SP), you may freely use all other registers because Turbo Prolog saves them prior to the call.

Because the parameters, if any, will be on the stack, you can use BP to access them. For example, the following program will multiply two integers together and place the result in the third parameter. For assembly language procedures, remember that the arguments will be pushed on the stack in the order in which they occur.

```
cseg      SEGMENT BYTE
          ASSUME CS:cseg
PUBLIC    mul_0     ; the name of the procedure
mul_0     PROC      FAR       ; must be a FAR procedure
          PUSH      BP        ; save BP
          MOV       BP,SP     ; use BP to index the stack
;
          MOV       AX,[BP]+12        ; first arg
          MUL       [BP]+10           ; second arg
          LDS       SI, DWORD PTR [BP]+6 ; output arg
          MOV       [SI],AX
;
          POP       BP        ; restore BP
          RET       8
mul_0     ENDP
cseg      ENDS
END
```

This example points out three important features. First, the three arguments to **mul_0** are in the stack at 12, 10, and 6 bytes from the current stack pointer, which has been placed in BP. The BP register is used to index into the stack. Second, the name of the procedure reflects the first flow pattern and function. Hence, it must be called **mul_0**. Third, the **RET 8** instruction clears the parameters from the stack. It is the responsibility of the external assembly language routine to remove the parameters from the stack.

You must use the linker to combine external routines with your Turbo Prolog programs. You cannot use external predicates while you use the interpretive mode of Turbo Prolog. You must use version 2.2 or greater of the standard DOS linker called LINK.EXE; if you do not, errors will result and the link process will be aborted. To see how the process works, enter the following Turbo Prolog program at this time and name it **P**.

```
global predicates
  mul(integer,integer,integer)-(i,i,o) language asm

predicates
  start
goal
  start.

clauses
  start:-
```

```
write("enter two integers: "),
readint(A),
readint(B),
mul(A,B,C),
write("answer is ",C).
```

Next, activate the Options menu and select **compile to .OBJ**. Next, compile the program. After you do this, assemble the assembly language procedure **mul_0**. Finally, link the Turbo Prolog program with the assembler module: if the assembly code module is called MUL, then you can link them by using the following link command.

```
LINK INIT+P+MUL+P.SYM,PROGNAME,,PROLOG
```

When the link is completed, the executable form of the program will be called **Progname**. You will be able to run it like any other program. You should try this process at this time.

External C Routines

Because many computer applications are written in C, it is fortunate that Turbo Prolog can call C routines. It is actually quite easy to call C routines from Turbo Prolog if you follow a few rules. This section assumes that you are an experienced C programmer and understand C's use of pointers.

If you refer to Table A-1, you can see that the values of input parameters of types character, integer, and real are passed directly on the stack. However, the addresses of string, symbol, and compound are pushed on the stack. This means that input parameters of characters, integers, or reals will be treated as the normal C data types of **int**, **char**, and **float**. However, for strings, symbols, and compounds, you will need to use the type **char** * (or perhaps a pointer to a structure for compounds) because only the address (pointer) is passed to the C routine. All output variables must be of the corresponding pointer type. For example, the following function multiplies two real numbers together and returns the result in the third parameter.

```
mul(a,b,c)
float a,b;
float *c;
{
        *c=a*b;
}
```

The following example prints a string to the current output device by using the standard C function **printf**. The example assumes that the second parameter is the format control string.

```
display_string(string,control)
char *string,*control;
{
        printf(control,s);
}
```

Your C compiler must use 32-bit pointers. (Some compilers may refer to this as a "large-memory model option.") Many compilers allow you to select between 16-bit and 32-bit pointers, so make sure that you are using the right one. If your compiler cannot work with 32-bit pointers, it will be impossible for you to link it with Turbo Prolog.

The following command line will link your C modules with Turbo Prolog modules.

```
LINK INIT+P+C+P.SYM,PROGNAME,,PROLOG+CLIB
```

Here, **P** indicates Turbo Prolog code, and **C** indicates the C code. Normally the C library must be included in the library list. Most C compilers call their library **CLIB**, as just shown, but you should check your C user manual.

Linking With Pascal

Generally, as long as your Pascal compiler uses, or can be directed to use, 32-bit pointers, you should have little trouble linking its code to Turbo Prolog's. However, if it cannot handle 32-bit pointers, you will not be able to use it. This section assumes that you are an experienced Pascal programmer. (Note that, until Version 4 of Turbo Pascal is released, you will not be able to link Turbo Prolog to Turbo Pascal.)

You can pass parameters to Pascal in two ways: either as values or as addresses. When you pass parameters as addresses, you specify them as **VAR** parameters. Hence, you must declare input parameters of types string, symbol, or compound to be **VAR** parameters in the Pascal procedure. All output parameters also must be declared to be **VAR**. For example, the following procedure computes the sum of two numbers and returns the result.

```
PROCEDURE mul(A,B:INTEGER; VAR C:INTEGER);
BEGIN
  C:=A+B;
END;
```

The following example displays a string on the screen.

```
PROCEDURE DISPLAY(VAR S: ARRAY[0..100] OF CHAR);
BEGIN
  WRITE(S);
END;
```

As this example shows, even though an input parameter is not to be modified, it must be declared as a **VAR** parameter so that Pascal knows that it is being passed a pointer.

The following command line will link your Pascal modules to Turbo Prolog modules.

```
LINK INIT+P+PASCAL+P.SYM,PROGNAME,,PROLOG+PLIB
```

Here, **P** indicates Turbo Prolog code, and **PASCAL** indicates the Pascal code. Normally, the Pascal library must be included in the library list. Even though many Pascal compilers call their libraries **PLIB**, as shown here, you should check your Pascal user manual.

Linking to FORTRAN

Linking to FORTRAN is straightforward except that standard FORTRAN only allows call-by-reference parameter passing. "Call-by-reference" means that only addresses, or pointers, are passed into and out of routines. This is fine for all output parameters and for input parameters of type string, symbol, or compound; however, Turbo Prolog will pass input parameters of type character, integer, and real as values —not pointers. Some FORTRANs may have provisions that enable you to handle this type of parameter passing, but others may not. Thus, you must refer to your user manual. If you cannot find any way to handle value parameters, then you have to pass all information into FORTRAN functions as strings or symbols, and convert them to the proper type inside the procedure.

The following command line will link your FORTRAN modules to Turbo Prolog modules.

```
LINK INIT+P+F+P.SYM,PROGNAME,,PROLOG+FLIB
```

Here, **P** indicates Turbo Prolog code, and **F** indicates FORTRAN code. Normally, the FORTRAN library must be included in the library list. Many FORTRAN compilers call their libraries **FLIB**, as shown here, but you should check your FORTRAN user manual.

Strings and Symbols: Special Considerations

There are two special and important restrictions that you must be aware of when you use strings or symbols as output parameters.

First, Turbo Prolog only allocates storage for string variables after they are bound. Hence, the following code fragment will fail to operate correctly and will probably crash your computer.

```
global predicates
  strcpy(string,string)-(i,o) language C
  .
  .
  .
clauses
  start:-
    A="this is a test".
    strcpy(A,B),
    write(B).
```

Assume that **strcpy** is C's standard string copy function. (The **strcpy** function simply copies the contents of **A** into **B**.) The reason that this code will fail is that **B** is not bound to any value at the time of the call and, therefore, does not have any storage allocated for it. Hence, when **strcpy** tries to copy the contents of **A** into **B**, **strcpy** will place them at some random point in memory —probably crashing your program. The only way around this problem is to first bind a dummy value to **B** prior to the call. This allocates storage so that the string copy function performs normally. Of course, binding a value of **B** implies that the declaration of **strcpy** will have to be changed to show two input parameters. This may seem a strange method, but it is the only way to do this type of operation. The corrected code is shown here:

```
global predicates
  strcpy(string,string)-(i,i) language C
.
.
.
clauses
  start:-
    A="this is a test".
    B="this is a nonsense string",
    strcpy(A,B),
    write(B).
```

Make certain that the dummy string is long enough to hold whatever your external routine will place in it. This problem is the same no matter what language is used to implement an external routine. (Keep in mind that, in the future, Borland may alter the way that Turbo Prolog works so that you may not need this "inelegant" approach.)

A second restriction comes up when you try to use output parameters that are symbols. The general rule is that you should not use them. The reason for this restriction is that all symbols are stored in a symbol table. If you alter the length of a symbol, then you may be overwriting another symbol and could accidentally corrupt the symbol table.

Appendix B

The Turbo Prolog Toolbox

The Turbo Prolog Toolbox, available as an option to Turbo Prolog, contains many useful and powerful predicates that can be included in your programs. The predicates in the toolbox are grouped into these six categories:

- User interfacing
- Screen layout
- Presentation graphics
- Serial port communications
- Importing data from other programs
- Parser generation.

Although it is beyond the scope of this appendix to closely examine each predicate (doing so could easily fill an entire book), a brief overview of each area is presented. Also, a few specific examples are developed to show some of the possibilities. (Full descriptions of each predicate are found in Borland's excellent *Turbo Prolog Toolbox User Manual.*)

Including the Necessary Domains and Predicates

Many of the predicates found in the Turbo Prolog Toolbox require the use of certain domains and additional predicates. The domains include **STRINGLIST**, **INTEGERLIST**, **KEY**, **ROW**, **COL**, and **LEN**. To ensure that your program will contain these domains and any predicates required by the toolbox routine that you are using, you must include the files **tdoms.pro** and **tpreds.pro** in your file. You must also include the files that correspond to the toolbox predicates that you want to use. To accomplish this you must use the **include** command. For example, the following fragment includes the files required for the use of the **status** and **longmenu** predicates.

```
include "tdoms.pro"
include "tpreds.pro"
include "status.pro"
include "longmenu.pro"
```

Remember, you must always include **tdoms.pro** before **tpreds.pro** because the domains must always precede the predicates.

Some of the predicates, especially those that create presentation graphics, are contained in .OBJ files. To use these predicates, you must first create a **project** file that contains the names of all the files required by your program and then compile the entire project. (Detailed instructions for creating and compiling **project**s are found in the Turbo Prolog user manual.)

Reserved Windows

Some Turbo Prolog Toolbox predicates use windows 80 through 85. Hence, you should consider these windows reserved and not use them.

User Interfacing

The user interface tools consist of predicates that are used to provide an interface between your program and the user. They provide for a status line, menu support, line input, context-sensitive help, and other functions. Table B-1 lists these predicates.

Table B-1.   The User-Interfacing Predicates

Name	Function	Include File
makestatus	Creates a status line	status.pro
removestatus	Removes a status line	status.pro
refreshstatus	Redisplays a status line	status.pro
menu	Displays a popup menu	menu.pro
menu __leave	Variation of menu	menu.pro
menu __mult	Variation of menu	menu.pro
longmenu	Displays a longmenu	longmenu.pro
longmenu __leave	Variation of longmenu	longmenu.pro
longmenu __mult	Variation of longmenu	longmenu.pro
boxmenu	Displays a box menu	boxmenu.pro
boxmenu __leave	Variation of boxmenu	boxmenu.pro
boxmenu __mult	Variation of boxmenu	boxmenu.pro
linemenu	Displays a single-line menu	linemenu.pro
pulldown	Displays a pulldown menu	pulldown.pro
treemenu	Displays a tree menu	tree.pro
lineinput	Reads a line of input	lineinp.pro
lineinput __leave	Variation of lineinput	lineinp.pro
lineinput __repeat	Variation of lineinput	lineinp.pro
readfilename	Reads a filename	filename.pro + lineinp.pro
help	Provides help information	helpdef.pro
push __helpcontext	Support for help	helpdef.pro
pop __helpcontext	Support for help	helpdef.pro
resizewindow	Changes window size	resize.pro
getverify	Gets the state of the disk verify switch	bios.pro
setverify	Sets the state of the disk verify switch	bios.pro
border	Sets the screen border to the specified color	bios.pro
findmatch	Search disk directory for a specified file	bios.pro

Creating Menus

You can create five different types of menus using the predicates in the toolbox. They are

- Single-column popup box
- Multiple-column popup box

- Popup line

- Pulldown box

- Tree.

A simple popup line menu created with the menu predicate has this general form:

menu (Row, Col, Wattr, Fattr, ItemList, Title, InitItem, Choice)

Row and *Col* are the coordinates that determine where the upper left-hand corner of the menu will be placed. *Wattr* and *Fattr* specify the screen attributes of the window and frame, respectively, that hold the menu. (The values these attributes may take and their effect are described in Chapter 7 of the Turbo Prolog user manual.) *ItemList* is a list of strings or symbols that will be displayed as the menu selections. There must be no more than 23 items in the list. (If there are more you must use either **longmenu** or **boxmenu** to accommodate more menu entries.) *Title* is the name of the menu and *InitItem* is an integer that represents the menu item that will be highlighted first. Finally, *Choice* is an integer variable that will be bound to the number of the menu item selected. The first menu item is coded as 1, the second as 2, and so on.

The following program shows how you can use **menu** to let a "contestant" choose among three doors, behind which there are prizes, in the "Door of Fortune" game. Notice the **include** files in this example.

```
/* A simple menu example */

include "tdoms.pro"
include "tpreds.pro"
include "menu.pro"

predicates
  prize
  select(integer)

goal
  prize.

clauses
  prize:-
    makewindow(1,6,10,"Door of Fortune",0,0,25,80),
    Door=[one, two, three],
```

```
    menu(10,10,7,7,Door,"Choose a Door",1,C),
    select(C),
    readln(_).
select(1):-
  write("bag of coal"),
  nl.
select(2):-
  write("bag of gold"),
  nl.
select(3):-
  write("bag of diamonds"),
  nl.
```

When this program is run, the initial screen looks like the one in Figure B-1. The menu options are selected by using the cursor keys to move to the menu choice and then pressing RETURN. The active menu entry is highlighted.

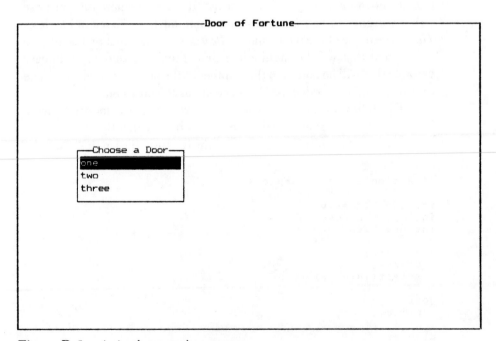

Figure B-1.   A simple popup box menu

Another type of menu support offered by the toolbox is called **linemenu**. It is useful when there are very few choices because all the entries are placed on one line. The general form of this menu predicate is

linemenu(Row, Wattr, Fattr, ItemList, Choice)

Thus, the "Door of Fortune" game can be rewritten as shown here to take advantage of **linemenu**.

```
/* A simple line menu example */
include "tdoms.pro"
include "tpreds.pro"
include "linemenu.pro"

predicates
  prize
  select(integer)

goal
  prize.

clauses
  prize:-
    makewindow(1,7,10,"Door of Fortune",0,0,25,80),
    Door=[one, two, three],
    linemenu(22,7,1,Door,C),
    select(C),
    readln(_).
  select(1):-
    write("bag of coal"),
    nl.
  select(2):-
    write("bag of gold"),
    nl.
  select(3):-
    write("bag of diamonds"),
    nl.
```

When this program is used, the initial screen looks like that shown in Figure B-2.

The **longmenu** predicate is similar to **menu** except that it allows more than 23 menu entries.

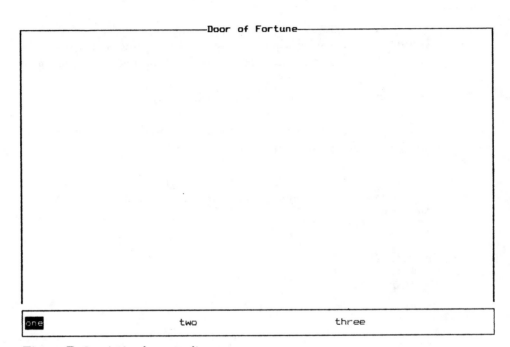

Figure B-2.   A simple popup line menu

The **boxmenu** predicate allows you to create a menu with multiple columns. This is similar to those menus in Turbo Prolog that allow you to select a filename from a directory listing.

You can create pulldown windows using the **pulldown** menu predicate. Pulldown windows are used extensively by the Turbo Prolog user interface. They allow related groups of choices to be grouped together. Each group of choices is given a name and when that name is selected, the appropriate subgroup of choices is displayed in a pulldown window.

Perhaps the most fascinating menu option available in the toolbox is called **treemenu**; it is used to create a tree-structured menu. A tree menu generally is used to represent hierarchical options. The **treemenu** predicate takes this general form:

    treemenu(Direction, Tree, Selector)

Here, *Direction* is a symbol (which must be either *up*, *down*, *left*, or *right*) that specifies which way the tree is to be drawn. **Tree** is a functor of type **TREE**, which must be defined in your program as

```
SELECTOR = integer
TREE = tree(string, SELECTOR, TREELIST)
TREELIST = TREE*
```

As you can see, **TREE** is a recursive data structure. This is necessary because tree menus are essentially a root node plus a tree menu —a recursive definition.

Before treemenu can be used, you must define the following databases:

```
DATABASE
  treewindow(ROW,COL)
  treechoice(SELECTOR)
```

Finally, you need to define clauses for the predicate **treeaction**, which is declared and called by **treemenu** each time a selection is made.

As an example of how tree menus can be used, this simple program gives the user advice on eating out. The program uses **treeaction** to beep when a selection is made.

```
/* a simple tree menu example */

include "tdoms.pro"

DOMAINS
  SELECTOR=integer
  TREE = tree(string,SELECTOR,TREELIST)
  TREELIST = TREE*

DATABASE
  treewindow(ROW,COL)
  treechoice(SELECTOR)

include "tpreds.pro"
include "status.pro"
include "tree.pro"


PREDICATES
  food
  displayfood(symbol,integer)
  comment(integer)
```

```
GOAL
  food.

CLAUSES
  treeaction(_):-beep.  /* called when an item is selected */

  displayfood(Direction, Foodtype):-
    treemenu(Direction,tree("Eat Out",1,
      [tree("fast food",2,
        [tree("burgers",3,[]),
          tree("fish",4,[]),
          tree("hot dogs",5,[])]),
        tree("gourmet delight",6,
          [tree("French",7,[]),
          tree("Chinese",8,[]),
          tree("Cajun",9,[]),
          tree("Seafood",10,[])])]),
    Type),
  clearwindow,
  Foodtype=Type,nl.

  food:- makewindow(5,66,23,"What to Eat?",0,0,25,80),
    displayfood(right,Foodtype),
    comment(Foodtype).

  comment(1):- write("Choose what kind of food"),
    fail.
  comment(2):- write("All right, cheapskate, choose the food."),
    fail.
  comment(6):- write("Hey, big spender, choose what kind of food."),
    fail.
  comment(3):-write("Ugh! Not burgers again!").
  comment(4):-write("Fish is good for your heart!").
  comment(5):-write("Do you KNOW what goes into hot dogs?").
  comment(7):-write("All that rich food is bad for you!").
  comment(8):-write("Good choice.").
  comment(9):-write("All right by me if it's all right by you!").
  comment(10):-write("Get the crab legs.").
```

As the program is coded, the tree menu will be drawn from right to left, as shown in Figure B-3. However, by changing the predicate **food**, as shown here, the tree menu will be drawn from left to right. This tree menu is shown in Figure B-4.

```
food:- makewindow(5,66,23,"What to Eat?",0,0,25,80),
  displayfood(left,Foodtype),  /* <-- change direction */
  comment(Foodtype).
```

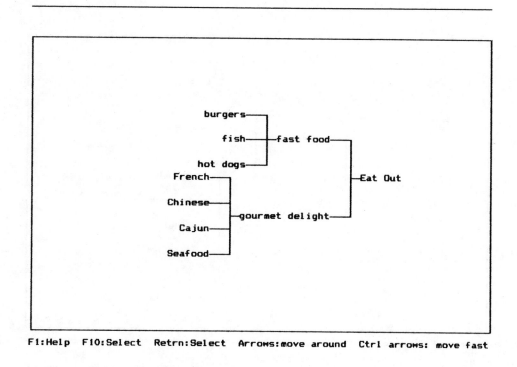

F1:Help F10:Select Retrn:Select Arrows:move around Ctrl arrows: move fast

Figure B-3.   A tree menu drawn right to left

Finally, Figures B-5 and B-6 show the tree menu drawn top to bottom and bottom to top.

Listing the Directory

As a final example of some of the user interface predicates, a short program follows that lists the contents of the current disk directory. The

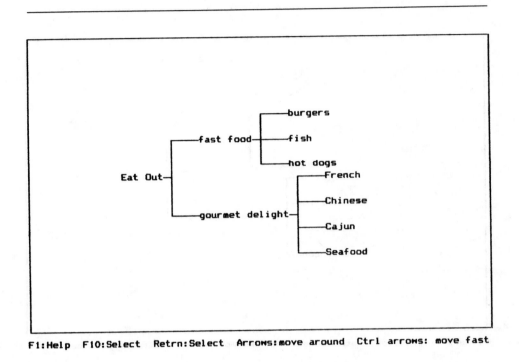

Figure B-4. A tree menu drawn left to right

program was developed using the **findmatch** predicate, which takes this general form:

findmatch (SearchName, Fattr, MatchedName, Mask, Hour, Min, Year, Month, Day, Size)

Here, *SearchName* contains the file specifier that is being searched for. This can be as specific as an actual filename or as general as "*.*". *Fattr* specifies the file attribute according to this table.

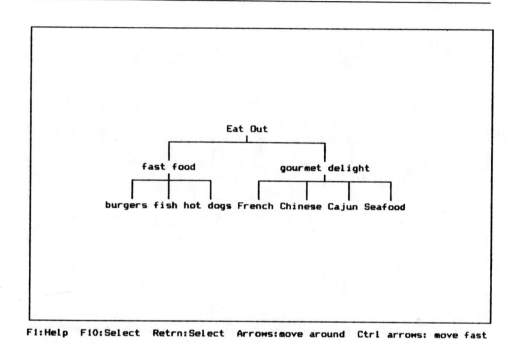

Figure B-5.   The tree menu drawn top to bottom

Fattr	Meaning
0	ordinary files
1	read only files
2	hidden files
4	system files
8	volume label
16	subdirectory
32	archive files

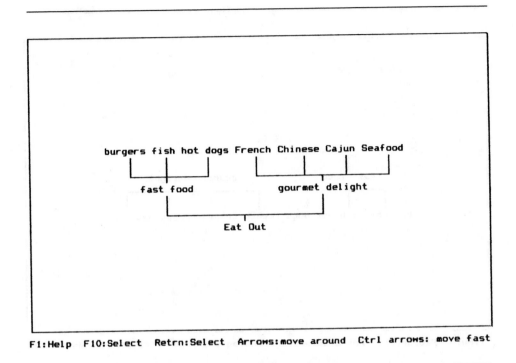

Figure B-6.   The tree menu drawn bottom to top

MatchedName is bound to the first filename that satisfies the attribute and file specifications. *Mask* is bound to the actual attribute mask of the file. The integer variables *Hour* through *Day* are bound to the matched file's creation date, and *Size* is the file's size in bytes.

The following short program uses **findmatch** to list the contents of the directory.

```
/* List the current directory */

include "tdoms.pro"
include "tpreds.pro"
include "bios.pro"

predicates
  dirlist
```

```
clauses
  dirlist:-
    findmatch("*.*", 0, Name, _, _, _, Year, Month, Day, Size),
    write(Name), write(" "),
    write(Month), write(" "),
    write(Day), write(" "),
    write(Year), write(" "),
    write(Size),nl,
    fail.
  dirlist.
```

Screen Layout

The Turbo Prolog Toolbox contains predicates and programs that allow you to easily define screens that will be used by your programs. To do this you first create a screen using the program **scrdef.pro**. Once this has been done, you use the predicate **scrhnd** to activate the screen. The advantage of this approach rather than ''hit and miss'' with **write** statements is that it saves both time and frustration.

Presentation Graphics

The Turbo Prolog Toolbox contains several graphics predicates that let you draw circles, boxes, pie charts, and bar graphs. The predicates that form this group require that the files **gdoms.pro** and **gpreds.pro** be included in any program that uses them. Table B-2 shows a list of the graphics predicates provided by the Turbo Prolog Toolbox. Many of the graphics predicates are actually coded in C and are found in the file **graphics.obj**.

Virtual and Absolute Screen Coordinates

Turbo Prolog, including the Turbo Prolog Toolbox predicates, uses two coordinate systems to implement its graphics routines. The first is called the virtual coordinate system, and the second is called the absolute coordinate system.

Table B-2.   The Graphics Predicates

Name	Function	Include File
AxisLabels	Sets the axes labels	ggraph.pro
bargraph	Displays a bargraph	gbar.pro
bargraph 3d	Displays a 3-d bargraph	gbar.pro
box	Draws a box	
DefineScale	Defines the scaling between the virtual and absolute screens	ggraph.pro
draw	Draws a specified polygon	ggraph.pro
ellipse	Draws an ellipse	
gwrite	Writes a string to a graphics window	
LineShade	Draws a line of specified color and shade	
LoadPic	Loads a screen full of graphics information	
MakeAxes	Draws a pair of axes	ggraph.pro
ModifyAxes	Changes the scaling of the axes	ggraph.pro
PieChart	Draws a pie chart	gpie.pro
plot	Plots a point	
SavePic	Saves a graphics screen	
ScaleCursor	Positions the cursor in a scaled graphics window	ggraph.pro
ScaleLine	Draws a line in a scaled graphics window	ggraph.pro
ScalePlot	Plots a point in a scaled graphics window	ggraph.pro
ScalePolygon	Draws a polygon in a scaled graphics window	ggraph.pro
ScaleText	Converts between text and scaled coordinates in a graphics window	ggraph.pro
ScaleVirtual	Converts between scaled and virtual coordinates	ggraph.pro
sector	Draws a sector of a circle	
SetScale	Determines the scale for a specified image	ggraph.pro
ShiftScale	Moves between scales	ggraph.pro
Virtual __ Text	Converts between text and virtual coordinates	ggraph.pro

The virtual coordinate system is used by all the graphics predicates. In it, the coordinates of the upper left-hand corner of the screen are 0,0 and coordinates of the lower right-hand corner are 31999,31999. This means that the center of the screen is at location 16000,16000. As you probably know, the actual resolution of most video display adapters is significantly less than that supported by the virtual screen. For example, using the Color Graphics Adapter (CGA), the screen is 320 pixels wide and 200 long. The actual resolution of the screen corresponds to the absolute coordinates of the screen. The graphics predicates automatically convert between the virtual coordinates and the absolute coordinates and take advantage of the type of video adapter that is in the system and the graphics mode used.

The graphics predicates use the virtual-absolute approach to the screen coordinates because it allows you, the programmer, to create graphics programs without worrying about the actual graphics hardware that will be used. That is, it allows a great degree of hardware independence. This means that a program can run with both a CGA card with 320×200-pixel resolution and with the Enhanced Graphics Adapter (EGA) in 640×350-pixel mode.

Bar Graphs

The toolbox contains predicates that help you create several different types of graphs. This section will focus on only two types: two-dimensional and three-dimensional bar graphs.

Creating a two-dimensional bar graph requires the use of the **bargraph** predicate. It has the general form

bargraph (Left, Bot, Right, Top, Ratio, Barlist, Scalefactor)

where *Left, Bot, Right,* and *Top* determine how much space to leave around the graph. The *Ratio* parameter is a **real** that specifies the ratio of the bars relative to the space between each bar. *Barlist* is a list of type **BAR** which is defined as

BAR = bar (Height, Title, Framecolor, Fillcolor)

Finally, *Scalefactor* is bound to the scale factor actually used by **bargraph** when it displays the data.

To see how bar graphs can be used, imagine that you are an executive of Widget Incorporated and you are assigned the task of preparing a report on the stock price of Widget over the past ten days. To prepare the report, you use this simple program to create a bar graph that shows the stock prices. Notice that **gwrite** is used to display text on the screen. Also, because the graphics predicates require **graphics.obj** to be linked into the program, these examples must be compiled as a project.

```
/* A simple 2-d bar graph example */
project "simpbar"

include "tdoms.pro"
include "gdoms.pro"
include "gglobs.pro"
include "tpreds.pro"
include "gpreds.pro"
include "gbar.pro"

goal
  write("enter bar ratio "),
  readreal(Ratio),
  graphics(1,0,0),
  gwrite(0,0,"Widget Stock Prices Past 10 Days",1,0),
  BarGraph(3,4,4,4,Ratio,
    [bar(20,"",1,2),
     bar(53,"",1,2),
     bar(95,"",1,2),
     bar(80,"",1,2),
     bar(87,"Widget Incorporated",1,2),
     bar(79,"",1,2),
     bar(94,"",1,2),
     bar(123,"",1,2),
     bar(117,"",1,2),
     bar(120,"",1,2)],_),
  readchar(_).
```

The display created by this program is shown in Figure B-7.

Although two-dimensional bar graphs are useful, the Turbo Prolog Toolbox goes one step further and allows you to create three-dimensional bar graphs. This is done using the **bargraph3d** predicate that has this general form:

bargraph3d (Left, Bot, Right, Top, Angle, Ratio, Barlist, Scalefactor)

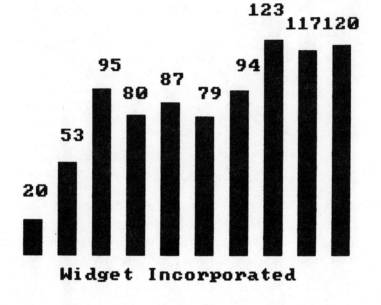

Widget Stock Prices Past 10 Days

Figure B-7. A two-dimensional bar graph with ratio of 0.5

Here, the *Angle* parameter is a **real** that specifies the viewing angle in radians. (In other words, how "thick" the bars will appear.)

The previous example program using **bargraph3d** is shown here.

```
/* A simple 3-d bar graph example */
project "simpbar"

include "tdoms.pro"
include "gdoms.pro"
include "gglobs.pro"
```

```
include "tpreds.pro"
include "gpreds.pro"
include "gbar.pro"

goal
  write("Enter angle of view in radians "),
  readreal(Theta),
  write("enter bar ratio "),
  readreal(Ratio),
  graphics(1,0,0),
  gwrite(0,0,"Widget Stock Prices Past 10 Days",1,0),
  BarGraph3D(3,4,4,4,Theta,Ratio,
        [bar(20,"",1,2),
         bar(53,"",1,2),
         bar(95,"",1,2),
         bar(80,"",1,2),
         bar(87,"Widget Incorporated",1,2),
         bar(79,"",1,2),
         bar(94,"",1,2),
         bar(123,"",1,2),
         bar(117,"",1,2),
         bar(120,"",1,2)],_),
  readchar(_).
```

Figure B-8 shows the display produced by this program with a viewing angle of 0.5 and a bar ratio of 0.7. Figure B-9 shows the same data with a viewing angle of 0.1 and a bar ratio of 0.5.

Serial Port Communications

The Turbo Prolog Toolbox serial port communications predicates allow you to write programs that can check the status and can read and write data to a serial port. The main reasons for doing this are to transfer files between systems, to use a modem, to write data to a serial printer, and to use your PC as a remote terminal on a time sharing system.

The communications predicates are coded in C. Predicates not related to modem communications are found in the file **serial.obj**; those that are are found in **modem.obj**. The file **comglobs.pro** must be included in all programs that use the serial port communications predicates. Table B-3 lists these predicates.

The Turbo Prolog Toolbox comes with several valuable programs that illustrate the use of the serial port communications predicates, including a complete modem program.

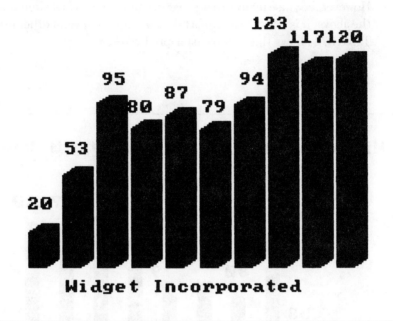

Figure B-8.   A simple three-dimensional bar graph with a viewing angle of 0.5 and a bar ratio of 0.7

Importing Data from Other Programs

The Turbo Prolog Toolbox contains several predicates that let you transfer data created by another program into a Turbo Prolog program. The toolbox supplies predicates that can import data from these programs:

- dBASE III
- Reflex

- 1-2-3
- Symphony.

However, because many other programs use a file format similar to one of the above, it is possible to import data written by several other programs. Table B-4 shows the data transfer predicates.

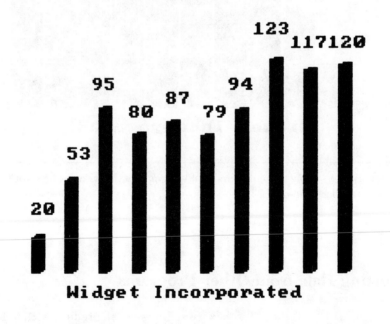

Figure B-9. A simple three-dimensional bar graph with a viewing angle of 0.1 and a bar ratio of 0.5

Table B-3.   The serial communication predicates

Name	Function	Include File
CloseRS232	Closes an open serial port	spreds.pro
DelInBuf__RS232	Deletes input queue associated with the specified port	spreds.pro
DelOutBuf__RS232	Deletes output queue associated with the specified port	spreds.pro
OpenRS232	Initializes a port for communication	spreds.pro
QueueSize	Returns the queue size of the specified port	spreds.pro
Rxch__RS232	Reads a character from the specified port	spreds.pro
RxStr__Modem	Reads a string from the specified port	mpreds.pro
SendBreak__RS232	Sends a break signal	mpreds.pro
SetModemMode	Sets the mode of a Hayes-compatible modem	mpreds.pro
Status__RS232	Returns the status of the specified port	spreds.pro
TxCh__RS232	Sends a character out the specified port	spreds.pro
TxStr__Modem	Sends a string out the specified port	mpreds.pro

Table B-4.   The data transfer predicates

Name	Function	Include File
Init__Dbase3	Initializes a dBASE III-style data structure	dbase3.pro
Init__Reflex	Initializes a Reflex-style data structure	reflex.pro
Rd__Dbase3File	Reads a dBASE III file	dbase3.pro
Rd__Dbase3Rec	Reads a dBASE III record	dbase3.pro
Rd__LotusCell	Reads a 1-2-3 cell	lotus.pro
Rd__LotusFile	Reads a 1-2-3 file	lotus.pro
Rd__ReflexFile	Reads a Reflex file	dbase3.pro
Rd__ReflexRec	Reads a Reflex record	dbase3.pro

The Parser Generator

The Turbo Prolog Toolbox contains the source code to a complete top-down parser generator. A parser is a piece of code that can recognize valid and invalid source code given a set of rules. For example, all high-level computer languages use a parser to help transform source code into executable code. Parsers are also used in natural language processing. There are several ways to construct a parser, including bottom-up, top-down, and ad hoc methods. The parser in the toolbox uses a top-down approach because it is more compatible with Turbo Prolog's backtracking mechanism.

Even with the use of a parser generator, the creation of a parser is a complex operation that normally requires considerable knowledge and experience. However, to help you get started, the Turbo Prolog Toolbox includes a very sophisticated example that creates a parser for a subset of the ALGOL language.

Trademarks

dBASE® III	Ashton-Tate
IBM®	International Business Machines Corporation
1-2-3®	Lotus Development Corporation
Reflex®: The Database Manager	Borland International, Inc.
Symphony®	Lotus Development Corporation
Turbo Prolog®	Borland International, Inc.
Turbo Prolog Toolbox™	Borland International, Inc.
VAL™	Unimation, Inc.

Index

The manuscript for this book was prepared and submitted to Osborne/McGraw-Hill in electronic form. The acquisitions editor for this project was Nancy Carlston. The technical reviewer was Dan Kernan. The copy editor was Cheryl Holzaepfel. Lyn Cordell was the project editor.

Text and display are set in Bodoni. Cover art is by Bay Graphics Design Associates; cover supplier is Phoenix Color Corporation. This book was printed and bound by R. R. Donnelley & Sons Company, Crawfordsville, Indiana.

Other related Osborne/McGraw-Hill titles include:

Using Turbo Prolog™
by Phillip R. Robinson

Using Turbo Prolog™ enables you to maximize your programming skills with Borland's new Prolog compiler. Robinson, a West Coast editor for *BYTE* magazine, gives you "insider" information on this new version of Prolog, one of the most popular "fifth-generation" programming languages in artificial intelligence. *Using Turbo Prolog™* offers detailed coverage of Prolog syntax and design, and discusses all of Turbo Prolog's statements, functions, and operations. You'll use multiple windows to view and modify programs while watching them run, and you'll learn programming techniques using color graphics, turtle graphics, and sound. If you're already familiar with Prolog or other high-level languages, or even if you're a beginning programmer, *Using Turbo Prolog* supplies you with programming techniques that you can use to build expert systems and decision-support systems.

$19.95p
0-07-881253-4 300 pp., 7³⁄₈ x 9¹⁄₄

Using Turbo C®
by Herbert Schildt

Here's the official book on Borland's tremendous new C compiler. *Using Turbo C®* is for all C programmers, from beginners to seasoned pros. Master programmer Herb Schildt devotes the first part of the book to helping you get started in Turbo C. If you've been programming in Turbo Pascal® or another language, this orientation will lead you right into Turbo C fundamentals. Schildt's emphasis on good programming structure will start you out designing programs for greater efficiency. With these basics, you'll move on to more advanced concepts such as pointers and dynamic allocation, compiler directives, unions, bitfields, and enumerations, and you'll learn about Turbo C graphics. When you've finished *Using Turbo C®*, you'll be writing full-fledged programs that get professional results.

$19.95p
0-07-881279-8, 350 pp., 7³⁄₈ x 9¹⁄₄

The Borland-Osborne/McGraw-Hill Programming Series

Advanced Turbo C®
by Herbert Schildt

Ready for power programming with Turbo C®? You'll find the expertise you need in *Advanced Turbo C®*, the Borland/Osborne book with the inside edge. In this instruction guide and lasting reference, Herb Schildt,

the author of five acclaimed books on C, takes you the final step on the way to Turbo C mastery. Each stand-alone chapter presents a complete discussion of a Turbo C programming topic so you can pinpoint the information you need immediately. *Advanced Turbo C®* thoroughly covers sorting and searching; stacks, queues, linked lists, and binary trees; operating system interfacing; statistics; encryption and compressed data formats; random numbers and simulations; and expression parsers. In addition, you'll learn about converting Turbo Pascal® to Turbo C and using Turbo C graphics. *Advanced Turbo C®* shows you how to put the amazing compilation speed of Turbo C into action on your programs.

$22.95p
0-07-881280-1, 325 pp., 7³⁄₈ x 9¹⁄₄

The Borland-Osborne/McGraw-Hill Programming Series

Using Turbo Pascal®
by Steve Wood

Using Turbo Pascal® gives you a head start with Borland's acclaimed compiler, which has become a worldwide standard. Programmer Steve Wood has completely rewritten the text and now provides programming examples that run under MS-DOS®, as well as new information on memory resident applications, in-line code, interrupts, and DOS functions. If you're already programming in Pascal or any other high-level language, you'll be able to write programs that are more efficient than ever. *Using Turbo Pascal®* discusses program design and Pascal's syntax requirements, and thoroughly explores Turbo Pascal's features. Then Wood develops useful applications and gives you an overview of some of the advanced utilities and features available with Turbo Pascal. *Using Turbo Pascal®* gives you the skills to become a productive programmer—and when you're ready for more, you're ready for *Advanced Turbo Pascal®*.

$19.95p
0-07-881284-4, 350 pp., 7³⁄₈ x 9¹⁄₄

The Borland-Osborne/McGraw-Hill Programming Series

Advanced Turbo Pascal®
by Herbert Schildt

Advanced Turbo Pascal® is the book you need to learn superior programming skills for the leading Pascal language development system. Revised and expanded, *Advanced Turbo Pascal®* now covers Borland's newly released Turbo Database Toolbox®, which speeds up database searching and sorting, and the Turbo Graphix Toolbox®, which lets you easily create high-resolution graphics. And, *Advanced Turbo Pascal®* includes techniques for converting Turbo Pascal for use with Borland's hot new compiler, Turbo C®. Schildt provides many programming tips to take you on your way to high performance with Turbo Pascal. You'll refine your skills with techniques for sorting and searching; stacks, queues, linked lists and binary trees; dynamic allocations; expression parsing; simulation; interfacing to assembly language routines; and efficiency, porting, and debugging. For instruction and reference, *Advanced Turbo Pascal®* is the best single resource for serious programmers.

$21.95 p
0-07-881283-6, 350 pp., 7³/₈ x 9¹/₄

The Borland-Osborne/McGraw-Hill Programming Series

Turbo Pascal® Programmer's Library
by Kris Jamsa and Steven Nameroff

You can take full advantage of Borland's famous Turbo Pascal® with this outstanding collection of programming routines. Now revised to cover Borland's new Turbo Pascal Numerical Methods Toolbox™, the *Turbo Pascal® Programmer's Library* includes a whole new collection of routines for mathematical calculations. You'll also find new date and time routines. Kris Jamsa, author of *DOS: The Complete Reference* and *The C Library*, and Steven Nameroff give experienced Turbo Pascal users a varied library that includes utility routines for Pascal macros as well as routines for string and array manipulation, records, pointers, and pipes. You'll find I/O routines and a discussion of sorting that covers bubble, shell, and quick-sort algorithms. And there's even more … routines for the Turbo Toolbox® and the Turbo Graphix Toolbox® packages. It's all here to help you become the most effective Turbo Pascal programmer you can be.

$21.95 p
0-07-881286-0, 625 pp., 7³/₈ x 9¹/₄

The Borland-Osborne/McGraw-Hill Programming Series

Using REFLEX®: THE DATABASE MANAGER
by Stephen Cobb

Using REFLEX® THE DATABASE MANAGER, the first book in *The Borland-Osborne/McGraw-Hill Business Series,* is a comprehensive guide to Borland's analytical database program for the IBM®PC.REFLEX® offers something for everyone: powerful graphical representation of data for analysis and strong reporting capabilities. If you're a beginner,

this book gives in-depth descriptions of all REFLEX features along with clear, step-by-step examples of their use. If you're an advanced user, you'll find practical and inventive REFLEX applications, as well as power tips and sophisticated techinques. Cobb, an experienced computer instructor and consultant, shows you how to take full advantage of REFLEX by using SuperKey®, the software that lets you build powerful macros to streamline computing tasks. Cobb reviews REFLEX Workshop™, a new series of adaptable business templates and provides applications that you can use right away. You'll also learn about data transfer between REFLEX and Lotus® 1-2-3®, dBASE®, and other database programs. With Cobb's expert techniques, greater REFLEX-ability will be at your command for any task you choose.

$21.95 p
0-07-881287-9, 400 pp. 7³/₈ x 9¹/₄

The Borland-Osborne/McGraw-Hill Programming Series

Using SPRINT™: The Professional Word Processor
by Kris Jamsa and Gary Boy

Borland's fabulous new word processing system puts you in first place with increased capabilities for users at every level in your office. Now Jamsa and Boy show you how to SPRINT™ with this fast-paced user guide. You'll learn the basics in not time since SPRINT emulates the command sets of WordPerfect® and WordStar®: it also supports file conversion for XyWrite™II and III, MultiMate®, and MultiMate Advantage™, as well as WordStar®, WordStar® 2000, and WordPerfect®. You'll find out how to customize menus with the Soft User Interface and how to use SPRINT's full text editor, desktop publishing capabilities, automatic text recovery, and built-in spelling checker/thesaurus. Jamsa and Boy pay special attention to programming with SPRINT's macros so you can speed-up word processing routines with a simple keystroke. *Using SPRINT™* puts you ahead in the race with the skills you need to take full advantage of Borland's new professional word processor.

$21.95 p
0-07-881291-7, pp., 7³/₈ x 9¹/₄

The Borland-Osborne/McGraw-Hill Programming Series

C: The Complete Reference
by Herbert Schildt

Once again Osborne's master C programmer and author Herb Schildt, shares his insight and expertise with all C programmers in his latest book, *C: The Complete Reference.* Designed for both beginning and advanced C programmers, this is an encyclopedia for C terms, functions, codes, applications, and more. *C: The Complete Reference* is divided into five parts, each covering an important aspect of C. Part one covers review material and discusses key words in C. Part two presents an extensive summary of C libraries by category. Part three concentrates on various algorithms and C applications and includes information on random number generators as well as artificial intelligence and graphics. Part four addresses interfacing efficiency, porting, and debugging. Finally, part five is for serious programmers who are interested in C++, C's latest direction. The book also includes complete information on the proposed ANSI standard.

$24.95p
0-07-881263-1, 740 pp., 7³⁄₈ x 9¹⁄₄
AVAILABLE: 5/87

The C Library
by Kris Jamsa

Design and implement more effective programs with the wealth of programming tools that are offered in *The C Library*. Experienced C programmers will find over 125 carefully structured routines ranging from macros to actual UNIX™ utilities. There are tools for string manipulation, pointers, input/output, array manipulation, recursion, sorting algorithms, and file manipulation. In addition, Jamsa provides several C routines that have previously been available only through expensive software packages. Build your skills by taking routines introduced in early chapters and using them to develop advanced programs covered later in the text.

$18.95p
0-07-881110-4, 220 pp., 7³⁄₈ x 9¹⁄₄

C Made Easy
by Herbert Schildt

With Osborne/McGraw-Hill's popular "Made Easy" format, you can learn C programming in no time. Start with the fundamentals and work through the text at your own speed. Schildt begins with general concepts, then introduces functions, libraries, and disk input/output, and finally advanced concepts affecting the C programming environment and UNIX™ operating system. Each chapter covers commands that you can learn to use immediately in the hands-on exercises that follow. If you already know BASIC, you'll find that Schildt's C equivalents will shorten your learning time. *C Made Easy* is a step-by-step tutorial for all beginning C programmers.

$18.95p
0-07-881178-3, 350 pp., 7³⁄₈ x 9¹⁄₄

Advanced Graphics in C: Programming and Techniques
by Nelson Johnson

Add graphics to your C programs, and you'll add significantly to your programming skills and to the effectiveness of your software. With *Advanced Graphics in C* you'll write graphics program for the IBM® EGA (enhanced graphics adapter). This guide offers a complete toolkit of all the routines you'll need for such graphics operations as drawing a line, an arc, or a circle; plotting; and filling in shapes. A complete sample graphics program with a rotatable and scalable character set is included. All the code is provided so that you can easily create the graphics you need. Johnson also includes instructions for interrupt-driven serial and parallel interfacing to mice, light pens, and digitizers. You'll learn state-of-the-art techniques from Johnson, a software developer, author, and worldwide lecturer.

$22.95p
0-07-881257-7, 430 pp., 7³⁄₈ x 9¹⁄₄

Advanced C
by Herbert Schildt

Herbert Schildt, author of *C Made Easy*, now shows experienced C programmers how to develop advanced skills. You'll find thorough coverage of important C programming topics including operating system interfacing, compressed data formats, dynamic allocation, linked lists, binary trees, and porting. Schildt also discusses sorting and searching, stacks, queues, encryption, simulations, debugging techniques, and converting Pascal and BASIC programs for use with C. A complete handbook, *Advanced C* is both a teaching guide and a lasting resource.

$19.95p
0-07-881208-9, 350 pp., 7³⁄₈ x 9¹⁄₄

Artificial Intelligence Using C
by Jonathan Sachs

With Herb Schildt's newest book, you can add a powerful dimension to your C programs—artificial intelligence. Schildt, a programming expert and author of seven Osborne books, shows C programmers how to use AI techniques that have traditionally been implemented with Prolog and LISP. You'll utilize AI for vision, pattern recognition, robotics, machine learning, logic, problem solving, and natural language processing. Each chapter develops practical examples that can be used in the construction of artificial intelligence applications. If you are building expert systems in C, this book contains a complete expert system that can easily be adapted to your needs. Schildt provides valuable insights that allow even greater command of the systems you create.

$21.95 p
0-07-881255-0, 360 pp., 7⅜ x 9¼

Modula-2 Made Easy
by Herbert Schildt

Herbert Schildt, author of *C Made Easy,* has written a new "Made Easy" tutorial on the Modula-2 programming language. Modula-2's modular structure allows teams of programmers to write segments that can be easily linked together. In many ways, Modula-2 is more suited to today's competitive programming environment than are C and Pascal. With *Modula-2 Made Easy,* beginning programmers can quickly learn Modula-2 techniques through step-by-step, hands-on exercises. Start with the fundamentals — basic structure, variables, constants, and program control statements — and you'll soon be handling more advanced procedures — pointers, arrays, modules, and co-routines. By the time you finish *Modula-2 Made Easy,* you'll be writing and debugging effective, full-scale applications programs.

$18.95 p
0-07-881241-0, 375 pp., 7⅜ x 9¼

Advanced Modula-2
by Herbert Schildt

In the style of *Advanced C* and *Advanced Turbo Pascal®,* Schildt's *Advanced Modula-2* shows experienced users how to refine their programming techniques with this widely used modular language. Written specifically for IBM® PC users, Schildt presents a *complete* discussion of a programming topic in each stand-alone chapter so you can concentrate on areas of particular interest. You'll find thorough coverage of sorting and searching; stacks, queues, linked lists, and binary trees; dynamic allocation using pointers; expression parsing; and operating system interfacing. Encryption and compressed data formats, as well as random numbers and simulations, are also explained. Follows *Modula-2 Made Easy.*

$18.95 p
0-07-881245-3, 300 pp., 7⅜ x 9¼

DOS: The Complete Reference
by Kris Jamsa

Why waste computing time over a baffling PC-DOS™ command or an elusive MS-DOS® function? *DOS:*

The Complete Reference has the answers to all of your questions on DOS through version 3.X. This essential resource is for every PC- and MS-DOS user, whether you need an overview of the disk operating system or a reference for advanced programming and disk management techniques. Each chapter begins with a discussion of specific applications followed by a list of commands used in each. All commands are presented in the same clear, concise format: description, syntax, discussion of arguments or options, and examples. For comprehensive coverage, *DOS: The Complete Reference* discusses Microsoft® Windows and EDLIN, and provides two special appendixes covering the ASCII chart and DOS error messages. A ready resource, *DOS: The Complete Reference* is the only DOS consultant you'll need.

$24.95 p
0-07-881259-3, 840 pp., 7⅜ x 9¼

The Osborne/McGraw-Hill MS-DOS® User's Guide
by Paul Hoffman and Tamara Nicoloff

A comprehensive guide to the MS DOS® operating system, this book is designed to familiarize you with all the versions of this powerful system from Microsoft. Ideal for beginners and experienced users alike, this guide covers each computer running MS DOS®, gives the version it runs and any improvements the manufacturer has made to the system. It also gives complete information on the PC DOS version designed for the IBM® PC. Additional programs and reference material make this guide a tool of lasting value.

$18.95 p
0-07-881131-7, 250 pp., 7½ x 9¼

PC-DOS Tips & Traps
by Dick Andersen, Janice M. Gessin, Fred Warren, and Jack Rodgers

Solve immediate problems and quickly perform specific business tasks on your IBM® PC or PC-compatible with *PC-DOS Tips & Traps.* Written for everyone using PC-DOS 2.1 or MS-DOS 2.11, Andersen provides an array of tips and discusses frequently encountered traps with their solutions. You'll find a broad range of helpful information from initializing your system and formatting disks, to controlling peripherals, and managing the DOS environment. Throughout the book Andersen shows you how to use the DOS Batch files to design your own commands and automate certain tasks. Tips for using DOS utilities including EDLIN for text editing and DEBUG for programming are also discussed. You'll save time and minimize the chance for error with Andersen's insights on the PC- and MS-DOS® operating systems.

$16.95 p
0-07-881194-5, 250 pp., 7⅜ x 9¼

PC Secrets: Tips for Power Performance
by James E. Kelley

Power performance is at your command with these secrets for mastering the PC. This collection of shortcuts and solutions to frustrating and frequently encountered problems gives users of the IBM® PC and PC compatibles the inside edge. James Kelley, author of numerous books on the IBM PC, discloses his secrets for controlling hardware, peripherals, DOS, and applications software. You'll learn tips for keyboard harmonics, display enhancements, controlling fixed disks, managing the printer, and manipulating DOS routines that include batch files, directories and subdirectories, as well as system menus. You'll also find programs that help you use WordStar® and Lotus™ 1-2-3™ to greater advantage. With *PC Secrets*, you don't need to be a technical expert to become a PC power user.

$16.95p
0-07-881210-0, 224 pp., 7⅜ x 9¼

Your IBM® PC: A Guide to the IBM PC (DOS 2.0) and XT
by Lyle Graham and Tim Field

"Excellent reference for the IBM PC with PC-DOS version 1.0, 1.05 and 1.1. Provides a clear overview of IBM PC hardware and software, step-by-step operating instructions, and an introduction to BASIC programming, color graphics, and sound. Also includes a chapter on trouble-shooting and IBM's PDP (Problem Definition Procedure). Rating: A"
(Computer Book Review)

$18.95p
0-07-881120-1, 592 pp., 6⅞ x 9¼

Your IBM® PC Made Easy (Includes IBM PC (DOS 2.0) And PC-XT)
by Jonathan Sachs

"In one word, OUTSTANDING! Perfect for beginning and advanced users, an excellent tutorial/reference. A very thorough guide to most facets of your IBM PC, from PC-DOS, hardware, software, resources supplies, batch files, etc. Rating: A"
(Computer Book Review)

$14.95p
0-07-881112-0, 250 pp., 7½ x 9¼

1-2-3®: The Complete Reference
by Mary Campbell

1-2-3®: The Complete Reference is the authoritative desktop companion for every Lotus® 1-2-3® user. All commands, functions, and procedures are explained in detail and are demonstrated in practical "real-world"

business applications. Conventionally organized according to task, this essential reference makes it easy to locate information on topics such as printing, macros, graphics production, and data mangement. Each chapter thoroughly describes a 1-2-3 task and all the procedures it requires, followed by an alphabetical listing of every command or function applied. Special emphasis is placed on compatible software packages, including Report Writer™, Reflex™ and others, that you can use to extend 1-2-3's capabilities. Campbell, a consultant and writer whose magazine columns appear monthly in *IBM PC UPDATE, Absolute Reference*, and *CPA Journal*, draws on her years of 1-2-3 expertise to provide you with this outstanding, comprehensive resource.

$22.95p
0-07-881005-1, 928 pp., 7⅜ x 9¼

The Osborne/McGraw-Hill Guide to Using Lotus™ 1-2-3,™ Second Edition, Covers Release 2
by Edward M. Baras

Your investment in Lotus™1-2-3™ can yield the most productive returns possible with the tips and practical information in *The Osborne/McGraw-Hill Guide to Using Lotus™ 1-2-3.™* Now the second edition of this acclaimed bestseller helps you take full advantage of Lotus' new 1-2-3 upgrade, Release 2. This comprehensive guide offers a thorough presentation of the worksheet, database, and graphics functions. In addition, the revised text shows you how to create and use macros, string functions, and many other sophisticated 1-2-3 features. Step by step, you'll learn to implement 1-2-3 techniques as you follow application models for financial forecasting, stock portfolio tracking, and forms-oriented database management. For both beginners and experienced users, this tutorial quickly progresses from fundamental procedures to advanced applications.

$18.95p
0-07-881230-5, 432 pp., 7⅜ x 9¼

The Advanced Guide to Lotus™ 1-2-3™
by Edward M. Baras

Edward Baras, Lotus expert and author of *The Symphony™ Book, Symphony™ Master*, and *The Jazz™ Book*, now has a sequel to his best-selling *Osborne/McGraw-Hill Guide to Using Lotus™ 1-2-3.™* For experienced users, *The Advanced Guide to Lotus 1-2-3* delves into more powerful and complex techniques using the newest software upgrade, Release 2. Added enhancements to 1-2-3's macro language, as well as many new functions and commands, are described and thoroughly illustrated in business applications. Baras shows you how to take advantage of Release 2's macro capabilities by programming 1-2-3 to simulate Symphony's keystroke-recording features and by processing ASCII files automatically. You'll also learn to set up your own command menus; use depreciation functions, matric manipulation, and regression analysis; and convert text files to the 1-2-3 worksheet format.

$18.95 p
0-07-881237-2, 325 pp., 7³/₈ x 9¹/₄

Financial Modeling Using Lotus™ 1-2-3,™ Covers Release 2
by Charles W. Kyd

Readers of Kyd's monthly "Accounting" column in *Lotus*™ magazine already know how helpful his 1-2-3™ tips can be. Now his *Financial Modeling Using Lotus*™ *1-2-3*™ shows experienced users how to set up a data bank that can be used by everyone in the office to make more effective use of numerous financial applications. Kyd provides models for managing the balance sheet, controlling growth, handling income statements and management accounting, using Z scores for business forecasts, and more. Each model features a summary of 1-2-3 techniques, including helpful information for using the new Release 2, and explains the financial theories behind the application. You'll also find out how data for many of these financial models can be shared in the office data bank, creating an even greater resource for business productivity.

$16.95 p
0-07-881213-5, 225 pp., 7³/₈ x 9¹/₄

Using HAL™
by Andrew Postman

Using HAL™ helps you tap into the full capabilities of Lotus® 1-2-3®. Whether you're a beginning 1-2-3 user or an experienced one who demands top software performance, you'll be amazed at the increased productivity that HAL adds to 1-2-3. Postman shows you how to use HAL to execute 1-2-3 commands and functions through English phrases that you select. You'll find out about graphing with HAL and how to use the undo command, which lets you experiment with "what-if" questions without losing data. You'll also master cell relations for greater analytical abilities, linking worksheets for data consolidation, macros, and table manipulation. *Using HAL*™ gets you past the introduction so you can become thoroughly acquainted with Lotus' new 1-2-3 companion.

$19.95 p
0-07-881268-2, 380 pp., 7³/₈ x 9¹/₄

dBASE III PLUS™: The Complete Reference
by Joseph-David Carrabis

This indispensable dBASE III PLUS™ reference will undoubtedly be the most frequently used book in your dBASE III® library. *dBASE III PLUS™: The Complete Reference* is a comprehensive resource to every dBASE III and dBASE III PLUS command, function, and feature. Each chapter covers a specific task so you can quickly pinpoint information on installing the program, designing databases, creating files, manipulating data, and many other subjects. Chapters also contain an alphabetical reference section that describes all the commands and functions you need to know and provides clear examples of each. Carrabis, author of several acclaimed dBASE books, discusses the lastest features of dBASE III PLUS, including networking capabilities; the Assistant, a menu-driven interface; and the Applications Generator, a short-cut feature for creating database files and applications without programming. *dBASE III PLUS™: The Complete Reference* also includes a glossary and handy appendixes that cover error messages, converting from dBASE II to dBASE III PLUS, and add-on utilities.

$22.95 p
0-07-881012-4, 600 pp., 7³/₈ x 9¹/₄

Using dBASE III® PLUS™
by Edward Jones

Osborne's top-selling title, *Using dBASE III,*® by Edward Jones, has now been updated to include Ashton-Tate's new upgrade, dBASE III® PLUS.™ With Jones' expertise you'll be in full command of all the new features of this powerful database software. Learn to design, create, and display a dBASE III PLUS database, devise entry forms with the dBASE III PLUS screen painter, generate reports, use Query files, and plug into dBASE III PLUS networking. In addition, you'll find out how to install dBASE III PLUS on a hard disk, conduct data searches, and manipulate assistant pull-down menus. *Using dBASE III® PLUS*™ is a thorough and practical handbook for both beginning and experienced dBASE III users.

$18.95
0-07-881252-6, 350 pp., 7³/₈ x 9¹/₄

Advanced dBASE III PLUS™: Programming and Techniques
by Miriam Liskin

Liskin's enormously successful *Advanced dBASE III*® has been completely revised to offer comprehensive coverage of dBASE III PLUS.™ Expand your dBASE®

skills as you learn programming techniques that let you design and implement more effective dBASE III PLUS business applications. Nationally known columnist and consultant Miriam Liskin addresses the "real world" business environment so you can make the most of dBASE III PLUS modes of operation. Liskin's discussion of new features offers you greater convenience when you work with multiple files at the dot prompt. You'll learn how to write portable, hardware-independent systems and use new error-trapping capabilities so you can work with more flexible on-line help systems. You'll also find out how to benefit from file- and record-locking features that enable you to design a multiuser data base system that can be especially important in networking.

$21.95 p
0-07-881249-6, 816 pp., 7³/₈ x 9¹/₄

dBASE III® Tips & Traps
by Dick Andersen, Cynthia Cooper, and Bill Demsey

Take some tips from Dick Andersen and his co-authors and you'll save computing time and avoid troublesome dBASE traps with this helpful collection of creative shortcuts. *dBASE III® Tips & Traps*, another in Andersen's *Tips & Traps* series, is written for all dBASE III® users, beginning and experienced. You'll find hundreds of tips and trap solutions for planning an application system and establishing a database, entering and updating data, ordering and retrieving data, relating databases, customizing screen displays, generating reports, interfacing with other software, and converting files from dBASE II.® All tip and trap entries are illustrated and follow a concise "how-to" format.

$17.95 p
0-07-881195-3, 300 pp., 7³/₈ x 9¹/₄

The 8086 Book
by Russell Rector and George Alexy

". . .is far superior to any other book about the 8086." (Dr. Dobbs Journal)

Anyone using, designing, or simply interested in an 8086-based system will be delighted by this book's scope and authority. As the 16-bit microprocessor gains wider inclusion in small computers, this book becomes invaluable as a reference tool which covers the timing, architecture and design of the 8086, as well as optimal programming techniques, interfacing, special features and more.

$18.95 p
0-07-931029-X, 624 pp., 6¹/₂ x 9¹/₄

80386/80286 Assembly Language Programming
by William H. Murray and Chris Pappas

This comprehensive guide enables serious programmers to take full advantage of the unique design of the 80386 and 80286 microprocessors found in the IBM® PC AT, COMPAQ® Desk Pro 286, TANDY 6000,® and other major computer systems. Instructions for programming the 8087/80287/80387 coprocessor are also included. The authors carefully detail the use of assembler pseudo-ops; macros, procedures, and libraries; and testing and debugging techniques. You'll also find instructions for interacting with high-level languages such as BASIC, Pascal, and FORTRAN. Many practical programming examples show beginners how to implement assembly language, while experienced programmers have an invaluable reference to the 80386 and 80286 instruction set.

$19.95 p
0-07-881217-8, 400 pp., 6³/₈ x 9¹/₄

Available at fine bookstores and computer stores everywhere.

For a complimentary catalog of all our current publications contact: Osborne/McGraw-Hill, 2600 Tenth Street, Berkeley, CA 94710

Phone inquiries may be made using our toll-free number. Call 800-227-0900 or 800-772-2531 (in California). TWX 910-366-7277.

Prices subject to change without notice.

Announcing
Two Dynamic New Imprints

The Borland-Osborne/McGraw-Hill Business Series

◄ **Using REFLEX®: THE DATABASE MANAGER**
by Stephen Cobb
Features sophisticated SuperKey® macros and REFLEX Workshop™ applications.
$21.95 paperback, *ISBN 0-07-881287-9*

◄ **Using SPRINT™: The Professional Word Processor**
by Kris Jamsa and Gary Boy
Take advantage of this fabulous new word processing system that is powerful, fast, and includes many desktop publishing features.
$21.95 paperback, *ISBN 0-07-881291-7*

The Borland-Osborne/McGraw-Hill Programming Series

◄ **Using Turbo C®**
by Herbert Schildt
Here's the official book on Borland's tremendous new language development system for C programmers.
$19.95 paperback, *ISBN 0-07-881279-8*

◄ **Advanced Turbo C®**
by Herbert Schildt
For power programmers. Puts the amazing compilation speed of Turbo C® into action.
$22.95 paperback, *ISBN 0-07-881280-1*

◄ **Advanced Turbo Prolog® Version 1.1**
by Herbert Schildt
Now Includes the Turbo Prolog Toolbox™ with examples of spreadsheets, databases, and other business applications.
$21.95 paperback, *ISBN 0-07-881285-2*

◄ **Turbo Pascal® Programmer's Library**
by Kris Jamsa and Steven Nameroff
Revised to cover Borland's Turbo Numerical Methods Toolbox™
$21.95 paperback, *ISBN 0-07-881286-0*

◄ **Using Turbo Pascal®**
by Steve Wood
Featuring MS–DOS programs, memory resident applications, in-line code, interrupts, and DOS functions
$19.95 paperback, *ISBN 0-07-881284-4*

◄ **Advanced Turbo Pascal®**
by Herbert Schildt
Expanded to include Borland's Turbo Pascal Database Toolbox® and Turbo Pascal Graphix Toolbox®
$21.95 paperback, *ISBN 0-07-881283-6*

Osborne **McGraw-Hill**
2600 Tenth Street
Berkeley, California 94710

**Available at Book Stores and Computer Stores.
OR CALL TOLL-FREE 800-227-0900**
800-772-2531 (In California)

In Canada, contact McGraw-Hill Ryerson, Ltd. Phone 416-293-1911

BORLAND·OSBORNE

MAXIT™ increases your DOS addressable conventional memory beyond 640K for only $195.

- Add up to 256K above 640K for programs like FOXBASE+ and PC/FOCUS.

- Short card works in the IBM PC, XT, AT, and compatibles.

- Top off a 512 IBM AT's memory to 640K and add another 128K beyond that.

- Run resident programs like Sidekick above 640K.

- Add up to 96K above 640K to all programs, including PARADOX and 1-2-3.

- Compatible with EGA, Network, and other memory cards.

Break through the 640 barrier.
MAXIT increases your PC's available memory by making use of the vacant unused address space between 640K and 1 megabyte. (See illustrations)

Big gain—no pain.
Extend the productive life of your, IBM PC, XT, AT or compatible. Build more complex spreadsheets and databases without upgrading your present software.

Installation is a snap.
The MAXIT 256K memory card and software works automatically. You don't have to learn a single new command.

If you have questions, our customer support people will answer them, fast. MAXIT is backed by a one-year warranty and a 30-day money-back guarantee.

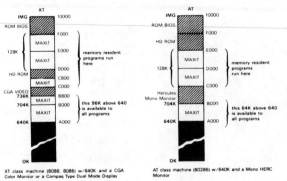

Order toll free 1-800-227-0900. MAXIT is just $195 plus $4 shipping, and applicable state sales tax. Buy MAXIT today and solve your PC's memory crisis. Call Toll free 1-800-227-0900 (In California 800-772-2531). Outside the U.S.A. call 1-415-548-2805. We accept VISA, MC.

MAXIT is a trademark of Osborne **McGraw-Hill**. IBM is a registered trademark of International Business Machines Corporation; 1-2-3 and Symphony are registered trademarks of Lotus Development Corporation; Sidekick is a registered trademark of Borland International, Inc; PARADOX is a trademark of ANSA Software; FOXBASE+ is a trademark of Fox Software; Hercules is a trademark of Hercules Computer Technology, Inc; XT and AT are registered trademarks of International Business Machines Corporation; Compaq is a registered trademark of Compaq Computer Corporation.